Ethno-Architecture and the Politics of Migration

Ethno-Architecture and the Politics of Migration explores the interface between migration and architecture. Cities have been substantially affected by transnational migration but the physical manifestations of migration in architecture – and its effect on streetscape, neighbourhood and city – have so far been under-studied.

This contributed volume examines how migrants interact with, adapt, and construct new architecture. Looking at the physical, urban and cultural impact of these changes on a variety of sites, the authors explore architecture as an identity category and investigate what buildings and places associated with migration tell us about central questions of belonging, culture, community and home in regions such as North America, Australia and the UK.

This book makes an important contribution to debates on place identity and the transformation of places as a result of mobility and globalised economies in the twenty-first century.

Mirjana Lozanovska is a Senior Lecturer and leads the Cultural Ecology Research Group at the School of Architecture and Built Environment at Deakin University, Australia.

THE ARCHI*TEXT* SERIES

Edited by Thomas A. Markus and Anthony D. King

Architectural discourse has traditionally represented buildings as art objects or technical objects. Yet buildings are also social objects in that they are invested with social meaning and shape social relations. Recognizing these assumptions, the Archi*text* series aims to bring together recent debates in social and cultural theory and the study and practice of architecture and urban design. Critical, comparative and inter-disciplinary, the books in the series, by theorizing architecture, bring the space of the built environment centrally into the social sciences and humanities, as well as bringing the theoretical insights of the latter into the discourses of architecture and urban design. Particular attention is paid to issues of gender, race, sexuality and the body, to questions of identity and place, to the cultural politics of representation and language, and to the global and postcolonial contexts in which these are addressed.

Edited by
Mirjana Lozanovska

Ethno-Architecture and the Politics of Migration

Routledge
Taylor & Francis Group

LONDON AND NEW YORK

First published 2016
by Routledge
2 Park Square, Milton Park, Abingdon, Oxon OX14 4RN

and by Routledge
711 Third Avenue, New York, NY 10017

Routledge is an imprint of the Taylor & Francis Group, an informa business

British Library Cataloguing-in-Publication Data
A catalogue record for this book is available from the British Library

Library of Congress Cataloging-in-Publication Data
Ethno-architecture and the politics of migration / [edited by] Mirjana
Lozanovska.
pages cm
Includes bibliographical references and index.
1. Architecture and globalization. 2. Place (Philosophy) in architecture.
3. Cultural geography. 4. Emigration and immigration—Social aspects. I.
Lozanovska, Mirjana, editor.
NA2543.G46E86 2016
720.1'03—dc23
2015019530

ISBN: 978-1-138-82871-1 (hbk)
ISBN: 978-1-315-73813-0 (ebk)

Typeset in Frutiger
by Swales & Willis Ltd, Exeter, Devon, UK

Printed and bound in Great Britain by
TJ International Ltd, Padstow, Cornwall

Contents

Figures

Contributors

David Beynon is a Senior Lecturer at Deakin University. His research involves investigating the social, cultural and compositional dimensions of architecture and urban environments, in particular the adaptation of architectural content and meaning through motifs, rituals and form, and investigation of notions of identity in Australia and Asia. His publications include *Digital Archetypes: Adaptations of Early Temple Architecture in South and Southeast Asia* (with S. Datta, Ashgate, 2014), 'Architecture, Identity and Sustainability in Southeast Asian Cities,' in *Review of Indonesian and Malaysian Affairs* (2011); 'Refusal of Home: Architecture ex-patriota,' in *Interstices* (2008); and 'Melbourne's Third-World-looking Architecture,' in *Suburban Fantasies: Melbourne Unmasked* (Australian Scholarly Publishing, 2005). He is currently a Chief Investigator in the Australian Research Council Linkage Project, 'Sea change' communities: inter-generational perception and sense of place. David Beynon is also a registered architect in Victoria and a partner in alsoCAN Architects.

Ayona Datta is a Senior Lecturer and Research Cluster Leader in Citizenship and Belonging in the School of Geography at the University of Leeds. Her research and writing broadly focus on the gendered processes of citizenship and belonging and the politics of urbanization across the global north and south. Datta uses interdisciplinary approaches from sociology, anthropology, feminist studies and critical geography, combining qualitative and visual research methods to pursue her research interests.

Karen A. Franck teaches in the College of Architecture and Design at the New Jersey Institute of Technology. Her co-authored chapter in this collection merges her interests in the city as kitchen and restaurant (*Food + City*, 2004) and people's appropriation of urban public space (*Loose Space*, 2007; *Memorials as Spaces of Engagement*, 2015).

John W. Frazier is a State University of New York Distinguished Service Professor, Binghamton Campus, and has produced six books and authored numerous articles, including many dealing with the applied aspects of geography and racial/ethnic studies. He has served as a consultant to U.S Department of Housing and Urban Development, both the Planning and Fair Housing and Equal Opportunity Divisions. Awards received include the James R. Anderson Medal of Applied Geography (1996), the highest honor bestowed by the Association of American Geographers for Applied Geography, the Binghamton University Equal Opportunity Outstanding Faculty Service Award (2006), and the AAG's Career Diversity Award (2009), which recognizes career contributions in research, teaching, and service related to diversity.

Mark Gillem is an Associate Professor in the Departments of Architecture and Landscape Architecture at the University of Oregon. He has a Bachelor of Architecture with Highest Distinction from the University of Kansas, a Masters of Architecture from the University of California (UC) at Berkeley and a PhD from UC Berkeley. He is the Director of the International Association for the Study of Traditional Environments and the University of Oregon's Urban Design Lab. He is also a practicing architect and a Fellow of the American Institute of Architects.

Christien Klaufus is Assistant Professor of Human Geography at the Center for Latin American Research and Documentation (CEDLA) in Amsterdam. Her research interests include urbanization processes, housing, mobility, and urban cultural dynamics in Latin America, especially in the Andean countries. She is the author of *Urban Residence: Housing and Social Transformations in Globalizing Ecuador* (Berghahn, 2012), and co-editor of *Housing and Belonging* (Berghahn, 2015). She has published various international articles about the influence of migration and remittances on architecture and the built environment in Latin America. Her current research involves the planning of deathscapes in the region's metropolitan areas.

Iris Levin is currently a Research Fellow at Southgate Institute for Health, Society and Equity, Flinders University, researching housing and social planning issues for diverse groups in the city. She completed her doctoral research at the Faculty of Architecture, Building and Planning in 2010 and was awarded 'The John Grice Prize: The Best PhD Thesis in Architecture for 2010' from the University of Melbourne. She is an architect holding a Bachelor of Architecture (1996) and a Master of Urban and Regional Planning (2004) from the Faculty of Architecture and Town Planning, Technion, Israel. During her architecture and planning studies she has worked as an architect and planner in Tel Aviv, Israel. Her research interests include housing and residential environments; social justice and planning; home/house; and immigrants and the urban outcomes of their presence in the city.

Sarah Lopez is an architectural and urban historian, as well as a migration scholar, with a PhD from the University of California, Berkeley (2011). She is an Assistant Professor in the School of Architecture at the University of Texas, Austin. Her book, entitled *The Remittance Landscape: Spaces of Migration in Rural Mexico and Urban USA*, was published by the University of Chicago Press in 2015. Broadly speaking, Lopez educates about the US and Mexican cultural landscapes, the interface between migration, architecture and cities, and the use of interdisciplinary methods to study space and society. She is a board member of the Vernacular Architecture Forum.

Mirjana Lozanovska is Associate Head of School International, School of Architecture and Built Environment at Deakin University, Australia, where she teaches history/theory and design. This book evolved from her long-term research into the ways architecture mediates human dignity and identity through multidisciplinary theories of space. Recent chapters in *Consuming Architecture* (Routledge 2014) and *The Politics of Subjectivity* (Routledge 2014) develop an archi-textual methodology that challenge mainstream frameworks of the subject and object in architecture. Drawing on psychoanalytic and cultural theories, she has published in *Postcolonial Space(s)* (Princeton Architectural Press 1997) and *Migrancy and Architecture* (Routledge 2004), in addition to essays in *Space and Culture, Interstices* and *Architectural Theory Review*. She leads the Cultural Ecology Research Group and has published *Cultural Ecology: New Approaches to Culture, Architecture and Ecology*.

Yannik Porsché works in the Sociology Department of the Johann Wolfgang Goethe-Universität Frankfurt/Main in an ethnographic project on social, cultural and organizational practices, forms of knowledge generation and circulation in criminal prevention. His previous studies include Philosophy at the University of Stuttgart and the University of Paris 8, Psychology at the University of Edinburgh and a PhD. at the Sociology Department of the Johannes Gutenberg-University, Mainz, and the Université de Bourgogne, Dijon, concerning museum exhibitions as sites of knowledge production. In this, Porsché combines methods of interaction analysis, discourse analysis and ethnography in a Microsociological Contextualisation Analysis in order to investigate how immigrants and national citizens are represented in France and Germany at the intersection of institutional, academic and public discourse. Porsché has also served as an educator in the Social Sciences at the University of Mainz and the University of Magdeburg. His research interests in the Sociology of Knowledge and Discursive Psychology include public representations, migration and museums, cultural identities, methods and methodologies of interaction and discourse analysis.

Lyndsey Pruitt is the Associate Director for the Urban Design Lab in the School of Architecture and Allied Arts at the University of Oregon. She is a practicing licensed Architect and planner with work across four continents. Her design for net zero energy, water, and waste for a site in rural Missouri (USA) received an Honorable Mention in the 2011 North American Holcim Awards for Sustainable Construction and was featured in *Architect Magazine*.

Arijit Sen is an architect and vernacular architecture historian who writes, teaches and studies urban cultural landscapes. His research includes studies of South Asian immigrant landscapes in Northern California, New York, and Chicago. He has worked on post-disaster reconstruction and community-based design in the Lower Ninth Ward, New Orleans and directed public history and cultural landscapes in schools across Milwaukee. Currently an Associate Professor of Architecture at the University of Wisconsin-Milwaukee with an honorary appointment with the Department of Art History at the University of Wisconsin Madison, Sen cofounded the multi-campus based Buildings-Landscapes-Cultures area of doctoral research on cultural landscapes. He has served as a fellow at various humanities centers such as the Center for 21st Century Studies, University of Wisconsin-Milwaukee, and the Center for Advanced Study, University of Minnesota. He has coedited *Landscapes of Mobility: Culture, Politics and Placemaking* (Ashgate, UK 2013) and *Making Place: Space and Embodiment in the City* (Indiana University Press 2013).

Philip Speranza is an Assistant Professor in Architecture at the University of Oregon. He is a practicing architect with urban design projects in Eugene, Oregon and Barcelona, Spain. He holds a Masters of Architecture degree from Columbia University. The survey research for his co-authored chapter in this volume reflects his interest in conducting geo-spatial analysis with parametric methods to measure phenomena in public space.

Marcel Vellinga is Reader in Anthropology of Architecture and Director of the Place, Culture and Identity Research Group in the School of Architecture, Oxford Brookes University. He holds a PhD in Cultural Anthropology from Leiden University and his teaching and research are concerned with the anthropological study of architecture, vernacular architecture and architectural regeneration. His publications include *Consuming Architecture: On the Occupation, Appropriation and Interpretation of Buildings*, with Dan Maudlin (Routledge 2014); *Atlas of Vernacular Architecture of the World*, with Paul Oliver (Routledge 2007); *Vernacular Architecture in the 21st Century: Theory, Education, and Practice*, with Lindsay Asquith (eds.) (Taylor and Francis 2006) and *Constituting Unity and Difference: Vernacular Architecture in a Minangkabau Village* (KITLV Press 2004) and various journal articles. Marcel is a Director of the Paul Oliver Vernacular Architecture Library.

Ian Woodcock is Associate Lecturer within the College of Design and Social Context at RMIT University in Melbourne. His research and teaching focus on issues of place, identity and urban design in relation to sustainable urban transformation. Ian is a UK-registered architect and holds architectural and urban design qualifications from the universities of Bath and Melbourne. He migrated to Australia from the UK as an adult, the offspring of a European and an Asian who met in Hong Kong. The material in his chapter is drawn from his doctoral research.

Preface and acknowledgements

This book has been a long time in the making. In addition to the process of proposing the manuscript to the Routledge editors and team, and collecting the chapters, the initial seeds for such a book were planted in Singapore in 1993. At the *Architecture (post)Modernity and Difference* conference organized by Gülsüm Baydar Nalbantoğlu and Wong Chong Thai, both then at the National University of Singapore, a group of engaged scholars met and founded Other Connections. Members of Other Connections went on to organize three more conferences, and two publications, *Postcolonial Spaces* (1997) and *Migrancy and Architecture* (2004), evolved out of the papers of the first and third conferences.

The theme of migration was explored in my chapter in the first book. It became a discussion point at the second conference with the proposal to hold a conference in Melbourne on that theme. Due to an appointment at the American University of Beirut, my role in this conference was limited, but the publication *Migrancy and Architecture* (2004) focuses on this theme and includes my chapter addressing homeland sites and emigration. These two books collected works from authors outside the usual privileged institutions, and pioneered a critical study of architecture at the intersection of identity, culture and otherness, and remain seminal in this field. Many Other Connections authors were at their initial stages of academic life in 1993, but have gone on to produce work generating cultural questions in architectural discourse. Other Connections had the spark of something new and exciting, and provided an engaged and rigorous forum for theories to take seed and develop.

The role of editor is rarely discussed and, as many of us know in the new neo-liberal regime of the university institution, it is not highly valued. However, I have enjoyed it thoroughly. Once the first drafts of the chapters were submitted, as editor I became involved in shaping the book as a whole and, therefore, the argument of each chapter. This became a productive dialogue between each author and myself, often focusing on the theoretical consolidation of the argument, and also on the active role the visual material would have in the emphasis on architecture. In addition, I called upon a community of scholars to review the chapters. My sincere gratitude goes to colleagues who found the time in their very busy schedules: Peter Kohane, Marwan Ghandour, Anoma Pieris, Hannah Lewi, Flavia Marcello, Louise Johnson, Suzanne Hall. Thank you to Iris Levin, who assisted me in the initial preparation of the manuscript; to Brad Warren, who assisted with the line-editing; to Diana Barnes, who provided the right feedback; to Helen Miekle, who started organizing the administrative tasks; and to Brandon Gardiner, who came in at the last minute and saved the day. Financial support from the School of Architecture and Built Environment and from the Centre for Memory, Imagination and Invention at Deakin University enabled the production.

It has been a privilege to work with the team at Routledge. From the first expression of interest from Francesca Ford that arrived almost immediately after I had sent the email at midnight, through the work with the Series Editors, Anthony King and Thomas Markus, to the arrival of the contract from Jennifer Schmidt (on my birthday), the support and communication has been exceptional. I have appreciated the prompts from Grace Harrison in taking the manuscript towards completion and submission.

Each of us has one or two people that we call upon – either actually or as reflective dialogue – to spur us on and remind us of the value of the work we do. I would like to note the inspiring voice of Professor Sneja Gunew, and encourage the next generation of scholars who will carry the work forward in new and unprecedented ways: Sally Winkler, Leila Mahmoudi Farahani, Alexandra Anda Florea, Nasim Yazdani, Diasana Dewa Gede Agung; as well as a few who are introduced in this book, Iris Levin and Yannik Porsché.

Finally, I would like to thank the family and friends that come and go at Park Street, weaving the migration field into the home environment.

Mirjana Lozanovska.
Editor.
Melbourne, March 2015

Introduction

Ethnically differentiated architecture in a global world

Mirjana Lozanovska

Cities have been substantially affected and many transformed by increasing cultural diversity resulting from waves of migration. The central role and dynamism of cultural diversity evident in retail and commercial streetscapes has dominated the debates on global and contemporary urban culture (Sandercock 2003). Architecture has been implicit as the background to these debates, but restaurants, residential, religious, institutional and community buildings, ethnic clubs and reception centres, constructed and adapted by migrant communities, provide evidence of the material change of the architecture of localities and neighbourhoods. A focus on architecture gives concrete form to the on-going negotiation between identity and locality, extending the argument related to urban culture across the various configurations of public, urban and suburban. Architecture is a term that may be associated linguistically with abstract concepts, but it is also a body of knowledge and part of a much larger debate that oscillates between binary frameworks of architecture and building. The boundary of architecture is persistently contested for example by the field of vernacular or everyday architecture. At the intersection of migration and identity, the focus of this book, architecture as a signifying field frames the ritualistic, associative and public role of buildings associated with ethnic communities and individuals. Migrant architecture as expression, form of settlement and inscription through use interacts with existing architectural conditions; and as such poses challenges, stimulates conflict and creates opportunities in places of departure and resettlement. Conversely, due to its relatively enduring nature, architecture appears to define the identity of places, highlighting that the production of migrant architectural and urban environments is critical in these debates (King 2004; Abbas 1997). Migrant buildings serve peoples' everyday lives and also present alternative cultural references and readings that are seen as contesting the aesthetic traditions of the cities and countries in which they are constructed. Particularized flows and routes of migration, and the physical forms of migrant construction generate new trans-cultural formations of contemporaneous modernities.

Addressing both material and spatial conditions, this study probes the different sites impacted by migration, and develops a complex set of references for the use of the term 'ethno-architecture'. In contrast to the scope of traditional vernacular architecture associated with a particular ethnicity and place, ethno-architecture recognizes ethnicity as a signifying marker in the context of globalizing processes of aesthetic taste, design and construction. Conventional discussions of ethnic traditional architecture locate it geographically, defining the ethnic aesthetic through stylistic characteristics that have become attractive to global and cultural tourism. By contrast, ethno-architecture foregrounds the politics of migration; its critical foundation is on how architecture produces local environments that are networked globally through association, genealogies and travel.

Identity theory has been defined through discourse in culture, ethnicity, race or gender. Informed by poststructuralist and postcolonial theory, many of the key scholars in this field have invested in communities and groups of inhabitants that do not readily represent themselves publicly and who are consequently side-lined by hegemonic productions of knowledge and power. Hall's (1997) work on ethnicity and globalisation, and Spivak's (1988) work on the 'subaltern' have laid the key points of the migrant as human subject and agent. The 'migrant' is a very broad category in contemporary global economies. The focus of this collection is squarely on the pejorative connotations of the term 'ethnic' and the conditions of under-privileged migration. The constructions of this group of migrants within immigrant cities result from 'grass roots' processes. 'Grass roots' is a shifting category, however, because the figure of the migrant is not a static entity but, rather, one aspiring to, and working towards, 'a better life'. Even with upward migrant social mobility, ethnicity sticks across class boundaries, as demonstrated by the fierce battles over the 'monster houses' of wealthy Hong Kong immigrants in Vancouver (Mitchell 1998).

This collection can be seen as a sequel to *Drifting: Architecture and Migrancy* (2004), edited by Stephen Cairns. The focus on the architecture of under-privileged migration is a key point of distinction. Studies of ethnically differentiated migrant architecture have been limited by theoretical frameworks that depend on a host–guest paradigm prioritizing the nation-state, and assuming assimilation or integration within existing contexts. In contrast, and in dialogue with the theories in the essays in *Postcolonial Spaces* (Nalbantoğlu and Wong 1997), and with the objects in *Journeys* (Borasi 2010), this book emphasizes that the global is differentiated by migration. It invests in diverse perspectives that are not absorbed within nation-state paradigms. To that end, examination of the global networks of migration, and the ways in which they disseminate building technologies, spatial orders, materiality and architectural images, become critical factors in the study of the local environments.

The essays have a strong research base in the form of empirical work or case studies of particular sites. This detail of how migration manifests, directs and stages architectural productions gives emphasis to the specific and the local story as the building blocks of theory. The book aims to build on and develop theories on the relation between migration and architecture, and it also aims to illustrate why these theories and knowledge matter, and to whom. Much of this has depended on each author's expertise to develop research methodologies that capture the complexities of the intersection between migration and architecture 'on the ground', reacting to and remaking sites, realities and contexts. And it has depended on the narrative position of each author as authority in the field. Unlike related disciplines such as sociology or ethnography, the methodologies are not at the front of positions or arguments, but provide the infrastructure to the discussions. The sample sizes of interviewed participants and areas are small, relative to sociological studies. These complement and are combined with architectural methodologies, including fine-grain observation methods and an emphasis on spatial and material conditions that is evident in architectural documentation. Studies have given rise to a question of aesthetics, and the production of normative taste. This focus on architecture produces a compelling interdisciplinary discourse whereby architecture is not assumed as the neutral and passive background, but shown as intervening in the continuity or change of social and cultural environments. This basis of architecture's active role in the socio-cultural production of neighbourhoods, environments and place reframes the discourse and its interdisciplinary platform.

Migrants returning to build in their homelands gain access to organizational and symbolic fields that are often foreclosed to the local non-migrants. A diasporic aesthetic emerges in the global phenomenon of remittance architecture, defining the constructions in homelands financed by individual or collective migrant funds. The essays examining particular communities and settings question how to critically discuss the ethno-architectural constructions of migrants. These communities are located in place, but the ideas, processes and affects invested in the constructions result from the on-going global flows of migration. How is 'architecture' defined when it is viewed through the lens of 'migration'? What kind of field is produced by the combination of 'migrant' and 'architecture'? A conceptual 'relocation' attends to the migratory flows of peoples across the globe, one that also raises important questions about the assumed boundaries of the discipline of architecture. The framework of identity and how architecture participates in social and cultural processes shift the emphasis.

Socio-cultural perspectives in architecture have a long tradition (Kostof 1995, Chermayeff et al. 1971), and yet architecture as a body of knowledge is undecided about where and how to locate the socio-cultural. Especially since the 1990s, the importation of critical theory into architecture has subjected the definition of architecture to renewed questions. This book sets out to re-examine the socio-cultural perspective of architecture by bringing discourses of signification towards defining architecture, shifting it from traditional terms as a fixed and autonomous entity embedded within structuralist linguistic frameworks, and from the behavioural emphasis of people–environment studies. The poststructuralist reorientation of language put pressure on the structural organization of knowledge. The discipline of architecture was not immune. The long-standing distinction between architecture and building, the former defined as architect-designed and critically framed, and the latter as mere structure, shelter or construction, is still invoked to frame arguments concerning architecture. Collectively, the essays constituting this volume suggest that this problematic division can be by-passed by conceptualizing 'architecture' and 'building' as significatory entities related to language rather than structured and transparent frameworks. As such, concepts and language are not equivalent to their efficient communicative functions and their operations fluctuate: meanings shift depending on the context, the speaker and his or her interests. While not interrogating this division within the dominant canonical parameters, the chapters in this book develop arguments that reveal that the boundary between architecture and building remains unresolved, and how architecture is further tested against the perception and reception of migrant ethno-architecture. For example, innovative accounts of the problematic place occupied by vernacular architecture outside of the grand narrative of western architecture (Baydar 2004) represent a critical field for the kinds of material and spatial inscriptions discussed in these essays. The case studies within chapters also establish, individually and collectively, the narratives that highlight the significant role of making and producing spaces in the production of identity and belonging whereby the inscription of meaning is reiterated through ritual and use.

By foregrounding the built inscriptions of migrants, each chapter develops a toolkit for collecting data and reading architecture as an identity category, with analysis about how it is critically conditioned by contemporary global flows and economies. In other words, identity is not assumed to have a static relation to belonging, community or place. It would be simple to state that identity is on the move, but significantly, in processes of migration, identity derives from specific practices of departure, arrival, dis-placement, and re-placement, and their corollaries related to the ancestral home and homeland, and resettlement and home-building. Architectural references to movement, transportation, importation and translation are not the boundless terms associated with the privileged flows of capital when associated with migration, identity and ethnicity.

The proposed tripartite structure of the book reflects fields of inquiry developed through the essays: Ethno-landscapes of Migration, Materialities of Home, and Temporality of Migrant Constructions. The aim is to frame and elaborate a critical debate within each section and across the whole volume, while preserving the particularity of each chapter. In order to investigate the intersection between migration and architecture, scholars borrow, adapt, translate critical theories and invent methodologies towards an interdisciplinary approach to understand how migrants build, modify, adapt and inscribe their environments. But issues critical to architecture mediate these. Site-specific studies detail the ways in which architecture mediates and manifests the cultural and political complexities. These provide a platform for dialogue and debate within the tripartite structure, and between chapters, across the migrant-intensive zones and points of geographical difference. Visual methodologies emerging from architectural traditions are creatively combined with critical cultural theories, as in Datta's experiment (Chapter 1, this volume) in the visual narrative of the city produced by Polish construction workers.

The first part, with a focus on 'Ethno-landscapes of Migration' examines the exclusionary effects of a global whiteness and how the global city and place manifest these both physically and through discursive forums. For example, if many traditional and colonial world cities were transformed by late-twentieth and early-twenty-first century migration, why are they still conceived as 'European'? What is the ethos informing historical frameworks, and how is it negotiated in places where many diverse peoples lay claim to traditions of architecture? Frazier's and Gillem and Pruitt's chapters (Chapter 3 and Chapter 4) engage directly with the political debates over migration and the claim to space and territory, examining new manifestations of an age-old tension in modern communities. In contemporary plural society, is the local authority playing the role of the manager of space, and is the situation locked into a power discourse where the 'ethnic' communities are persistently perceived as guests? Gillem's chapter zooms out of the local in order to see the big picture and to examine how migrant communities in more hostile environments seek dispersion and invisibility, in contrast to previously gathering in ethnic enclaves. Rather than confronting politics directly, Beynon (Chapter 2) and Datta (Chapter 1) interpret architectural/suburban landscapes through the lens of the migrant as subject and agent of their environment. In that sense their chapters produce a counter-narrative of migrant landscapes by-passing the nation-state as reference or framework.

Linking these larger-scale questions to how people construct homes and houses, in the second part, 'Materialities of Home', is the work of everyday multiculturalism, and the production of neighbourhoods and locality. Dwellings are the most significant constructions, built for and by migrants, and they give rise to questions about how migrants negotiate their identities within the immediate spaces of existing and being, and how effectively they do so. Migration discourse has been dominated by the problem of housing migrants. This section emphasizes a new global perspective of multiple place attachments. Chapters in this part build on empirical fieldwork, and their consideration of the built forms and adaptations constructed by migrants presents the redefinition of the practices of vernacular architecture. Lopez and Klaufus (Chapters 5 and 6), for example, examine the effect of migrant building and architecture on the places of origin and villages that have traditional architecture. In contrast, Levin and Vellinga (Chapters 7 and 8) focus on elderly citizens and examine how architecture is called upon to define nostalgic migrant identity. Migrant building as a result of continuing migratory travel, whether temporary, permanent or imagined, produces ethno-architecture within a two-way global exchange.

The chapters included in the third part on 'Temporality of Migrant Constructions' undertake socio-spatial explorations of the embodied sensibilities of architectural environments. They extend the spatial discourse through exploring time as a factor in the production of environments, their atmosphere and affects. Woodcock (Chapter 10) and Franck and Speranza (Chapter 11), focussing on particular sites, examine the ways that migrants have made many cities dynamic at the local level, by looking at the piecemeal, fragmented and complex contributions and how they come together at particular times in the making of diverse spatial environments. Sen (Chapter 9) complements and extends this narrative by focussing on the interface between the scale of volume/urban site and interior/affect in an Indian supermarket. The resulting diversity contributes to liveable world cities that combine the sense of communality associated with diaspora with the worldliness associated with the term 'cosmopolitan'. Close reading of the spatial environment as a fine-grained socio-architectural scene is elaborated here as a methodology, and has highlighted the productive capacities of the migrants operating with initiative and agency across the macro and micro scales of the built environment. The last chapter in this section by Yannik Porsché (Chapter 12), looks closely at a different kind of site, a site of an exhibition on migration in two world cities, Paris and Berlin. His critical review of the exhibition addresses the visual representation of migration, and focusses on the different approach of each institution.

With a focus on the architecture of under-privileged migration the concluding chapter (Chapter 13), outlines some of the theories that both underlie and evolve from the particular examinations in each section, highlighting the key role that architecture plays, adding critical content and focus to the recent surge of scholarship that is examining the transformation of places.

REFERENCES

Abbas, A. (1997) *Hong Kong: Culture and the Politics of Disappearance*, Minneapolis: University of Minnesota Press.

Baydar, G. (2004) 'The Cultural Burden of Architecture', *Journal of Architectural Education*, 57:4, 19–27.

Borasi, G. (ed.) (2010) *Journeys: How Travelling Fruit, Ideas and Buildings Rearrange our Environment*, Montreal: Canadian Centre for Architecture.

Cairns, S. (ed.). (2004) *Drifting-Architecture and Migrancy*, London: Routledge.

Chermayeff, S., Tzonis, A. and Chermayeff, I. (1971) *Shape of Community: Realization of Human Potential*, Harmondsworth: Penguin.

Hall, S. (1997) 'Old and New Identities, Old and New Ethnicities', in A. King (ed.) *Culture, Globalization and the World-System: Contemporary Conditions for the Representation of Identity*, Minnesota: University of Minnesota Press.

King, A. (2004) *Spaces of Global Cultures; Architecture, Urbanism, Identity*, London: Routledge.

Kostof, S. (1995) *A History of Architecture: Settings and Rituals*, New York: Oxford University Press.

Mitchell, K. (1998) 'Fast Capital, Race, Modernity, and the Monster House', in R.M. George (ed.) *Burning Down the House: Recycling Domesticity*, pp. 187–211, Boulder, CO: Westview Press.

Nalbantoğlu, G.B. and Wong, C.T. (eds) (1997) *Postcolonial Spaces*, New York: Princeton Architectural Press.

Sandercock, L. (2003) *Cosmopolis II: Mongrel Cities in the 21st Century*, London: Continuum.

Spivak, G.C. (1988) 'Can the Subaltern Speak?' in C. Nelson and L. Grossberb (eds) *Marxism and the Interpretation of Culture*, Chicago: University of Illinois Press, Macmillan Education.

Ethno-landscapes of migration

Chapter 1: 'Where is the global city?'

Visual narratives of London among East European migrants

Ayona Datta

INTRODUCTION

> I don't want to picture you know Big Ben or London Eye. Its common you know
> everyone took it so why should I? Something interesting, something different.
> You don't have to be like everyone else, yeah? We were trying to show our lives
> in London.

Mikolaj, a young Polish migrant from Lublin came to live and work in London just after
the 2004 European Union expansion when eight central and east European countries
were given rights to work in the UK.[1] Coming into London without the relevant skills
or language proficiency, Mikolaj and his brother worked as labourers on building sites
during London's construction boom in 2005–7. His photo of 'life in London' (Figure 1.1)
is significant in this context because he constructs a different kind of city that is set
away from its iconic buildings. For Mikolaj, the iconic city is 'common' and *blasé*.
Instead, he narrates a more affective relationship with a city whose spaces are shared
with family and friends, and which makes the iconic city irrelevant to his everyday life.
Crucially, his narrative is highly visual, articulated through photographs of different
kinds of spaces and buildings, in which he is often present. Mikolaj therefore provides
a visual critique of London that is highly personal and subjective, and in doing so he
retrieves a sense of agency to construct and experience the city on his own terms.

Visual narratives in this paper refer to the simultaneous textual and pictorial narrating of migrant experiences of everyday life in the city. They are provided
by migrants like Mikolaj and suggest a complex picture – that while migrants like
him are relatively more engaged and in control of their own mobility (than those
who are forced or coerced to move across transnational spaces), their decisions to
move nevertheless do not always materialise in terms of expectations and intentions. Yet even in the disjunctions between expectations and experiences, migrants

First published in A. Datta, *Urban Studies* (June 2012) 49: pp. 1725–1740, copyright © 2012.
Reprinted by permission of SAGE.

Figure 1.1
Mikolaj's photo of
his housemate in east
London.

like Mikolaj are able to take affective charge of certain aspects of their everyday mobilities in the global city. In so doing, visual narratives diverge greatly from conventional urban pictorial and documentary approaches to the city that often situate the observer as static and distanced from the migrant subject. In relocating the observer as the mobile migrant in these photographs, visual narratives then indicate the assembling of a migrant self through the multiplicities of everyday urban life.

In this chapter, I take visual narratives as the analytical starting-point for research on migrants' mobilities and experiences of the global city. This has several dimensions. First, in presenting highly subjective participant photographs, visual narratives critique earlier urban pictorial traditions that produce disembodied and aestheticised subjects for the observer gaze. Secondly, through a relationship between pictorial and textual, visual narratives convey ways of inhabiting particular places by migrant bodies, of coming to and moving through/from urban spaces and of the destabilising of categories of near/far, home/abroad through these movements. Thirdly, while migrants' photographs are located in urban spaces, as part of visual narratives they also relate to experiences on a national, political scale (Burrell, 2008) and represent locality dynamics or even materialities of migration, such as stories of significant objects and material culture (Tolia-Kelly, 2004). This multiple positionality is important, since it suggests the competence and desire among migrants to contribute to and be involved in urban life in ways that are not just to do with survival in a new context.

VISUALISING THE CITY

There has always been a strong pictorial tradition of visualising the city – as part of professional knowledge, as an aesthetic product (whether heritage or touristic) and as documentary knowledge. As professional knowledge, the pictorial tradition attempts to map an 'objective' version of social reality, with the explicit purpose of proposing policy or design interventions to the 'problems' of urban spaces. Aesthetic and documentary visualisations of the city, on the other hand, have focused on museumified visions of urban spaces (Crang, 1996) that valorise urban landscapes. Crucially in these urban pictorial traditions, the observer-photographer is removed (both socially and physically) from the frame. This approach tends to produce a view of the city that is voyeuristic, disembodied and distanced.

It is now widely accepted that photographs are highly subjective accounts of space and place as they 'reveal something about the world and the people and places in it, and all the meanings and associations we conjure up' (Haywood, 1990, p. 25). Indeed, as Hirsch (1981) notes, photographs are aesthetic, social and moral products constructed by those who take them. Like text, photos too are ways of constructing social reality, albeit in very visual ways, and they get their meanings from the cultural, social historical and political contexts in which they are made (Becker, 1995). Crang (1996) notes that even photographs that attempt to capture 'reality' and present 'objective' knowledge cannot be seen as naive documents; rather, they require knowledge from the observer to ascribe meanings to them. Different urban pictorial traditions therefore should be seen to set up relations between different ways of seeing in ways that construct different visual discourses of the city (Crang, 1996).

In this chapter, I am particularly mindful of the need to develop more locally and materially grounded understandings of the migrant urban experience that move away from earlier urban pictorial traditions. I draw therefore from Latham (2003), who has argued that a cosmopolitan urban culture made through places such as bars, cafés and restaurants and performed by some of its urban citizens can be studied effectively through the urban photo-diaries and photo-interviews of such actors. Latham's approach attempts to understand the 'cultural turn' in urban geography which, he notes, has to be examined through new methodological insights beyond 'canonical' ethnography. Such methodological concerns are echoed by Farrar, who notes that it is important for photography 'to produce narratives which normalize, rather than racialise; which lower, rather than raise, boundaries between humans' (Farrar, 2005). While Farrar does not use participant photography in the same way as I do in this chapter, his point remains relevant in the context of migrants' visual narratives, which attempt to move away from the fetishisation of a global city and towards a construction of an ordinary city.

Participant-directed photography is not a novel concept. It has been referred to in its various forms as 'autophotography' (Dodman, 2003; Emmison and Smith, 2000; Thomas, 2007) – a visual equivalent to an autobiography; 'photo elicitation' (Harper, 2002); and 'photo documentation' (Markwell, 2000). As part of visual narratives, however, participant photographs look at migrants' everyday lives on their own terms rather than those of the researcher. This allows participants to engage actively with the research process by 'telling their own stories' (Markwell, 2000, p. 92) of the city through their photographs. These stories are of the ordinary city, of ordinary spatial practices and events occurring in the city that are significant to them. This power (albeit partial) in directing the research process allows participants who are often marginalised in other spheres of society, 'to take possession of the spaces in which they are insecure' (Sontag, 1973, p. 9) and in which their location is often overlooked. These are places where everyday lives materialise – the homes, buildings, shops and urban neighbourhoods. These are also connected to other real and imagined spaces of mobility which present multiple ways of seeing, experiencing and negotiating urban landscapes. Produced by the mobile migrant, these visual narratives then give us a highly subjective and embodied optics of understanding and imagining the city as a transnational space.

Thus participant-directed photographs depart from visual documentary traditions of representing the city through a different optics of affect, emplacement and critique in transnational urban spaces. Firstly, researchers do not work with 'found' images (Rose, 2007), nor do they produce their own images (Pink, 2007). Visual narratives of participants displace 'authentic' representations of the global city circulated through 'public' photography (which includes professional, journalistic, touristic or artistic endeavours) and present an ordinary, everyday city negotiated by migrants. In doing so, they destabilise the gaze of the disembodied and distanciated observer and replace it with that of the mobile migrant-subject. Secondly, they bring into 'view' those absent spaces and places of the everyday lives of participants, prompting discussions of more private and affective spaces of the city, where participants take charge of their experiences of home and migration. Finally, visual narratives allow participants to question the 'taken for granted' aspects of everyday urban life and become reflexive about the processes through which embodied experiences of urban mobility are produced. In doing so, they connect the experiences of moving across transnational urban spaces to the practices of moving through, seeing and picturing everyday urban spaces.

MOBILITY AND EMBODIMENT IN VISUAL NARRATIVES

Cities are full of mobile subjects – urban dwellers continuously on the move between different spaces of the city, between public and private, between home, work, leisure and retail. In the case of migrants, these moves are both transnational and translocal (Brickell and Datta, 2011). They are always negotiated through embodied and corporeal relationships with real places separated across geographical distances and through material experiences in particular urban settings. Thus it is not just migrants' social or economic relations with the wider city; rather, the city itself becomes 'a fractured collection of mundane spaces and places that produces connections (both social and material) with other spaces, places and locales within and beyond the city' (Brickell and Datta, 2011, p. 17).

Yet images of everyday life in the city often position the migrant subject as static (Crang, 2002). We see aerial shots of migrants in the city living in shantytowns, made iconic in films like *Slumdog Millionaire*, and voyeuristic and disembodied observations of everyday urban life in films like *Wings of Desire*. Critiques of such representations have been made by a number of feminist researchers (Biemann, 2004; Kindon, 2003). Biemann (2004), for instance, critiques the production of knowledge from visual data that produce distanciated and disembodied understandings of women's lives. She employs particular aesthetic strategies in her own videos to map women's multiple subject positionalities by juxtaposing satellite images of distant places with those of women on ground. While these 'reorganise and visually recode the space in which we write femininity' (Biemann, 2004, p. 71), Biemann nevertheless remains the cultural and artistic producer of these images, her primary strategy being aesthetic rather than collaborative.

How, then, can images of everyday urban life relate to the mobile observer and how can they depict mobile subjectivity? Crang (2002) suggests a process of 'proprioception', in which observation occurs on the same ontological plane as images, as a normal run of things, which makes a clearer way of looking at the mobile and involved observer. This can be observed to a certain extent in Kindon's (2003) use of participatory videos, which pay greater attention to the practices of 'looking alongside' rather than 'looking at' participants' lives. Her videos make participants aware of the socially constructed nature of audio-visual material and encourage them to make choices about how they wish to represent themselves. More crucially, Kindon destabilises the distanciated and disembodied researchers' gaze by repositioning their bodies within the frame of the videos, thus highlighting the corporeal aspects of researcher–subject relationships. Such innovative uses of visual data enable multiple and partial ways of looking and, as Kindon claims, provide new possibilities for the production of knowledge.

In my research, such 'new' methodological approaches are important because they enable a shift in the disembodied gaze of the ethnographer to participants' everyday mobilities in the city on their own terms. I do not suggest that participants' photographs are 'democratic' in depicting migrant urban life. Rather, my approach in this chapter is that they do not make claims to any single reality in migrants' lives. Instead, they provide 'spaces of vision and observation' (Crang, 1997, p. 368) that can be interpreted only through the researcher–participant relationship. Further, they help to overcome linguistic and often cultural boundaries through pictorial representations. In embodying the mobile migrant and the reflexive photographer as one and the same person, these photographs work as interview 'triggers' to stimulate discussion and reflection on the affective geographies in the city and of their mobilities. This becomes particularly significant when participants carry their cameras not only across urban settings in London but also across national territories in ways that connect urban mobilities to transnational migration, as we shall see in this chapter.

In this way, these photos act as 'prompts and personal mnemonics as well as powerful ways of capturing and conveying information in an accessible, economical and nonverbal way' (Sweetman, 2009, p. 502). This approach, then, is not engaged with theories of visuality; rather, with participants' emplaced mobilities across urban and transnational spaces, and the addressing of wider questions generated around movement and migration in the global city.

Thus, instead of aestheticised images, what we get are a set of photographs that are striking in their depiction of 'unspectacular' and often banal migrant lives in the city. They therefore present us with a different visual optics through which to understand and conceptualise transnational urban spaces, because they embody and embed participants' mobilities in spaces which they can often find hard to describe in words. In shifting the focus of these photographs from aesthetics to ordinariness, visual narratives therefore open up questions around migrants' embodied use of urban spaces during migration and mobility.

PHOTOGRAPHING EVERYDAY LIFE IN LONDON

London has long been a destination for migrants from across the world. The impact of an increasingly flexible global labour market in London has seen a rise in migrant numbers from across the world. This has made London one of the most diverse cities in the United Kingdom. In the 2001 Census, London showed evidence of its intense history of migration from all parts of the world, with ethnic minority groups making up 29 per cent of its population (CRE, 2007). This figure increased to 40 per cent when White ethnic minorities were taken into account. The most recent impact of migration into London, however, has been the accession of eight east European states to the European Union (EU) in May 2004, labelled as the A8 countries. Migrants from these states were required to register their employment details with the Workers' Registration Scheme (WRS) run by the Home Office in the UK in order to live and work here. During the following five years, 630,000 individuals registered with the WRS (Home Office, 2009), of whom nearly two-thirds (65 per cent) were from Poland. These migrants were primarily male (58 per cent), young (82 per cent between 18 and 34 years) and without dependants (93 per cent) in the UK (Home Office, 2009). In 2009 London had the second-largest concentration (15 per cent, 51,750) of WRS-registered workers in the UK (Home Office, 2009).

The presence of A8 workers in London had transformed the physical and social landscapes of the city during 2006–7 when this research was undertaken. In 2009 a total of 29,260 workers registered with the WRS were working in the skilled and unskilled manual trades in construction (Home Office, 2009), a high percentage of whom were Polish. A large number were also illegally employed in the building sector. Given the temporary nature of construction work and difficulties in accessing the housing market, these migrants are highly mobile in their housing arrangements, continuously moving in order to be close to their workplaces – the temporary building sites that also keep moving across London.

The visual narratives, as I call them in this article, are part of a wider project entitled 'Home, migration and the city'. I interviewed around 24 participants (one Bulgarian, two Romanians, one Ukrainian, one Latvian and the rest Polish) just after the expansion of the European Union in 2004 when they arrived in London. The participants in this study were mostly single men in the UK between 24 and 47 years of age, arriving during 1996–2006. Those who had arrived before 2004 had until then largely worked illegally – once they gained legal rights to work in 2004, they returned to their countries and entered the UK legally as EU migrant workers. They were all working for small-time building contractors on home refurbishment projects in London. The participants were contacted through snowballing and, after an initial information-gathering interview, were given a disposable camera to carry around with them for a month before they returned it. Participants were informed about the focus of the research in the first interview, but the brief for taking photos was purposely left very open as 'pictures of any aspect of living in London that they wanted to talk about'. Once the photographs were developed, we met again; this time, however, it was a more in-depth interview that was structured loosely around the issues and experiences that participants had captured in their photos.

The interviews were conducted after work or at weekends, sometimes in participants' houses, in the Polish community centre, cafés or pubs. Most of these interviews were conducted in English, apart from a few with the newly arrived Polish migrants, when this was done with the help of a Polish interpreter. The second interview brought wider issues to the fore and led to a greater reflexivity, using photographs as visual prompts. The participants had not just taken photos, but they were also reflecting upon the context, politics and meanings of the spaces portrayed in these photos. In that sense, these photos became auto-interpretative of their multiple positionalities in urban spaces.

This chapter then focuses on participants' photographs 'on the move'. By that, I mean that the photographs are taken during participants' daily routines of moving through the city to reach work, home or leisure; but they also suggest a form of wider 'move' of participants across national and regional boundaries. This can be seen in three aspects of this paper – firstly, in looking at how the disillusionment of migration is produced from particular physical landscapes of the earlier 'desired' city; secondly, in constructing a city from this disillusionment as a place of ordinary everyday life; and thirdly, in 'moving on' from the city in order to facilitate a return to the homeland.

'WHERE IS THE GLOBAL CITY?'

London's position as a global city has always been of particular importance in the social and cultural subjectivities of participants and it has shaped how participants made sense of their mobilities in London. During the socialist regime in their home countries, restrictions of access and control over their movements into the 'West' had shaped how London had been imagined. Until the fall of communism in 1989, most participants had never travelled to the 'West'. A few older participants had travelled within the Soviet bloc as tourists, but for them these countries had been part of a similar political system. In this context, London for many years had been the cultural symbol of the 'West', as a city at the heart of English 'culture' which had been largely forbidden during the socialist regime.

Before the EU expansion in 2004, then, participants' routes into London had been fraught with difficulties, since they were often denied entry when they arrived at the UK ports. However, since they had become part of the EU, the 'West' had at last opened up to them. London was now the financial capital of the world – participants would hear from others who had gone before them to London about the increased availability of jobs, high salaries and the general boom in its economy which would make way for individual 'success'. To come to London, therefore, was to become a part of London's past as the symbol of the 'West' and part of its present as a global city.

This imagined construction of London became the yardstick against which all real-life experiences were compared and made sense of. And this comparison first arose during their route into the global city as seen in the series of photos taken by Andrej (see Figure 1.2). His journey from Poland to the UK was by coach across Europe and finally by ferry across the English Channel from Calais to Dover. This is also the route he took when visiting his family during holidays when these photos were taken. They capture Andrej's mobilities across transnational spaces in order to access the 'global city'. They highlight his mobility between home and abroad, which allowed him to confront, in the interview setting, the expectations that were embedded in this route when he made the journey into London for the first time.

> What came to my mind is that ... a city that lost its integrity. It's not a typically English city but a city which is multi, multi, cultural. That's how I understand that. That's how I try to explain it to myself. And so, walking along a street in this city, you meet not only people, for example, only Englishmen or, but many nationalities ... It was strange for me. I couldn't get used to it for some time.

I have written elsewhere how such notions of 'strangeness' in a global city were a recurrent theme in most participants' discussions of their first encounters with London (Datta, 2009). I noted that these encounters with 'others' in London produced particular types of 'situated cosmopolitanisms' among my participants. It was their access to social and cultural capital in different spaces (public and private) in London which determined their attitudes towards 'otherness' in the city. While a detailed discussion of exclusion and otherness in the city is outside the scope of this paper, these attitudes towards otherness were pronounced because of the geographical proximity to deprived neighbourhoods in London which also housed a large number of ethnic non-White migrants.

A

B

C

D

Figure 1.2 Series of photos taken by Andrej showing his journey to London across the English Channel.

The next photo I wanted to talk about ... and present to you, are, actually this photo. These sights are, in east London actually, very common. And it is something that bothers me here, turns me against London. And I spoke with my friends who come to London, they imagined London differently, and it is different, like, you know, they land in Stansted, they come to, say, Ilford or to some sort of eastern area, and you know, something gets them.

Benedykt's photo (Figure 1.3) is taken to discuss the 'dirt' and 'filth' of a city which confronts those traversing a particular route into the city. His photo is produced from the dynamics of past experiences of socialism which framed a modern city in the 'West'. The photo of rubbish in an east London house speaks to this dynamic, because it portrays an antipode of the Western city – one that was expected to be sanitised and extraordinary, but that disappoints with its 'filth'. 'Where is the global city?', therefore, was a rhetorical question symbolic of both their journey into the heart of the 'West' and their search for an imagined iconic city.

Benedykt further highlights how their disillusionment was compounded by the landscape of their route into the city, which was often via land and sea like

Andrej's or via low-cost airlines into London's outlying airports like Stansted and Luton. It is at the same time geographical in terms of migrant roots (since migrants from Asia or Africa would come through Heathrow airport) and social in terms of their class and ethno-national subjectivities. As Benedykt points out, this route of entry into London is an important part of this disillusionment – it took them through London's suburbs straight into the heart of east London, a place with a high number of ethnic minorities. It bypassed the 'extraordinary' London with its historical monuments and iconic buildings and produced the first embodied confrontation with the 'global city' through its peripheral neighbourhoods.

Figure 1.3
Benedykt's photo of rubbish outside an east London house.

Figure 1.4
Mikolaj's photo of a train station in east London.

Mikolaj:	Looks like in Poland. Look like, looks like in Poland. The same like a village station somewhere in Poland. Like regular station in Poland.
Interviewer:	But it's not Poland.
Mikolaj:	No no, it's London. I never supposed to see that when I came to London. I hoped to see large buildings, everything clean and super but typical, usual, nothing special.

Mikolaj's picture of the train station (Figure 1.4) was taken when he was commuting to work in the city centre – this station was his everyday route into the city, a place which also reminded him of a 'village station' in Poland, rather than what he had expected. Mikolaj had come to London from Lublin, a small town compared with London or even with other Polish cities. He expected therefore to see physically larger spaces and buildings; he thought London would be grander and spectacular. Yet he, like other participants, also came into London via low-cost airlines that took him into east London. Living in east London reminded him of similarities rather than differences with Lublin; it produced a city that was 'nothing special'. The London of his imagination had been 'clean and super', but the everyday London of his experience was 'typical, usual' – an ordinary city, where he led an ordinary life.

Significant in this construction of the ordinary city were also those iconic spaces and buildings of London which were seen as disappointing.

Interviewer:	Do these remind you of any other place?
Mikolaj:	Yeah, like New York or something [laughs] no. Yeah but I expected it to be bigger or something.
Interviewer:	Why did you expect it to be bigger?
Mikolaj:	Because it's London, when you told people from Poland that you were in London they go, 'Wow! Really? You were in London? How is it?' But you would expect something bigger, something larger, something that's extra, yeah but it's nothing special really. You can get used to it. When you have works [sic] you don't really care about these things, don't care about commercials or something, I know because I work five days, yeah [laughs].

Mikolaj here takes a series of photos of different places in central London on a night out with his friends (Figure 1.5). Most of these are easily recognisable: they are in and around London's West End, places which capture the tourist gaze. Yet Mikolaj refers to them as ordinary and disappointing because he had expected these to provide him with an experience of a spectacular city. It is here, in the size of these buildings, that the disjuncture between the imagined iconic city and the real embodied city begins to creep in. This disappointment is also related to the wider marginalisation experienced by migrants like him who came without relevant skills and worked in the lowest labour hierarchies in the construction sector and lived in temporary accommodation (Datta, 2011). In this context, the visual narratives presented here take on a different kind of significance. They suggest that participants' imagined global city is not just disappointing on arrival, but it is

A

B

C

D

Figure 1.5 Mikolaj's series of photos during a night out in Piccadilly Circus.

also socially distant and hence irrelevant to their everyday lives. This does not mean that the global city is unimportant; rather, these visual narratives reflect their sense of separation and alienation from this global city.

Crucially, in this series of photos, Mikolaj includes one of himself with his friends where they are drinking while waiting for the bus. Mikolaj reflects upon this as 'embarrassing' since he feels that it reinforces the stereotype of the binge-drinking Polish migrant in the West. Thus his visual narratives not only situate his disenchantment during transnational mobility, but also provide scope to reflect upon how his location within urban settings might evoke representations of ethno-national subjectivities.

In capturing the mobile migrant within the frame of these photographs, Mikolaj therefore destabilises the traditional divides between observer and subject in much of urban photography and suggests how the observer, subject and image might relate to each other. Here, Mikolaj works as the observer in two distinctly different ways: firstly, as the everyday mobile observer-subject who has a corporeal experience of these urban places while he moves through them; and secondly, when he reflects upon these photographs with the researcher in an interview setting. The mobility embedded in his observation and the 'conceptualisation of the

Figure 1.6
Benedykt's photo of
Polish shops in London.

observer as among images rather than apart from them' (Crang, 2002, p. 21) in ordinary urban settings provide a different optics of understanding migrant sub-jectivity and 'otherness' in the city. They refer to disillusionment with their urban dreams, dilemmas of migration and the difficulties of leading a life beyond every-day survival in the global city.

'WELCOME TO POLAND'

I began this chapter with the photo taken by Mikolaj to situate visual narratives as a theoretical and methodological approach that challenges the notion of an iconic and global city. The discussion so far constructs a city that disappoints in its global credentials and is therefore largely irrelevant to migrants' everyday lives. Yet, as these visual narratives produce a sense of alienation from the global city, they simultaneously produce a heightened sense of locatedness and belonging within particular urban neighbourhoods (Datta, 2011). In this next set of visual narratives, participants reflect a 'positive reterritorialisation where culture and social relations are recuperated and refigured, rather than lost' (McKay, 2006, p. 275).

> And this photo [Figure 1.6] show [*sic*] the development of the Polish shops in London. So I am looking from the perspective of time, I am going back say six years, when getting a Polish product bordered on the miraculous, and now there is plenty of it everywhere. This is the one thing that makes me happy.

Rabikowska and Burrell (2009) note how the recent emergence of Polish shops selling Polish food has produced a notion of home among many of the migrants who arrived after 2004. They argue that, while Polish products were available earlier, these were largely geared towards middle-class interests in health foods and were more expensive. The new Polish shops which sell these products at affordable prices produce 'a feeling of belonging, recreate a feeling of home, empower its customers as citizens and mark ownership of territory' (Rabikowska and Burrell, 2009, p. 219). These Polish shops, recently established across east London, remind and connect Benedykt to everyday practices around Polish food which he was used to from living in Torun. This constructed for him a sense of belonging to particular neighbourhoods in east London where such shops were more abundant. Hence, when he recently moved home, he decided to live in east London so that he could be near these particular places which connected him to familiar sights, tastes and smells from his past.

What is striking here and what comes across in many visual narratives is what Ley describes as 'the continued relevance of the geographical building blocks of separation and difference in a putative world of growing proximity and sameness' (Ley, 2004, p. 162). The temporality of these processes in everyday life is captured in the spaces and places of the visual narratives. The localities and neighbourhoods in London are continually changing, developing, transforming, as new and different migrants move into them and make a living in London. Benedykt's visual narrative speaks of this continual transformation of London's urban spaces and places during the migration of east Europeans. In their transformation, they begin to provide continuity to migrants' transnational lives across different cities in their home and host countries.

Images then afford opportunities for 'attending to everyday ecologies of materials and things; for thinking through the rhythms of urban environments; and for producing affective archives' (Latham and McCormack, 2009, p. 252). As builders, participants' affective geographies were as much about traversing home and work as about transforming the material geographies of home, migration,

Figure 1.7
Tadeusz's photo of
a car boot sale in
London.

settlement and return. The construction of future homes in their homelands was seen by many participants as a way of performing their gendered roles, in sustaining the traditional Polish home and family through building (Datta, 2008). Yet this return was facilitated not necessarily through an alienation from London, but rather through a detailed knowledge of London's urban neighbourhoods in ways that could be harvested towards a productive material return.

> You know car boot sale? Yeah. I'm mad about car boot sale. I like very much. In 1989 when I started to go first time there, once mostly Sundays, I visited three of them – in Leytonstone, another in Shepherds Bush and another in Hounslow. And now, last two weeks ago I was in Basildon. Huge one, if you want to find something interesting, even pictures. I'm a fan of eh embroidery. I used to do. I'm fan of books. I'm buying books for my boy, for myself and sometimes small eh oil paints from like £1.50 or so and now because I started to build a house in Poland I need some equipment for house, mostly decorations for walls. In the time of four years, I have four big suitcases in Poland of these goods.

Tadeusz was in fact building his home during short trips to Poland on land gifted to him by his mother-in-law. This home had to be furnished, and Tadeusz collected items from car boot sales across London's neighbourhoods (see Figure 1.7). For Tadeusz, then, the photo captured his aspirations that would connect his past to the future. This was even more significant since, as Tadeusz claimed, antiques and historical objects that he could find in England were not available in Poland because the occupation by German forces had destroyed most of its historical goods.

Tadeusz's photo makes his movements across different neighbourhoods of London significant as a way of constructing a different kind of visual narrative of his future home – it captures the intent of displaying English historical objects in a Polish home to tell a personal story of migration and social mobility in his homeland. And his visualisation of the city through highly localised ties in order to facilitate return is starkly different from the aesthetic approaches of Biemann (2004), who deliberately flags distant ties between places in her videos. Tadeusz's picture is not concerned with aestheticisation or critique; rather, his sole intent is to show to the researcher those spaces and places related to his transnational, urban and social mobilities. These are the places that matter most to him.

CONCLUSIONS

In this chapter, I show how visual narratives can provide both methodologically and theoretically distinctive ways to understand migrants' lives in the city. As a combination of participant photographs and narrative reflection over these photographs, visual narratives challenge urban pictorial traditions in a number of ways. Firstly, they shift the gaze of the voyeuristic and disembodied observer to that of an observer-subject, manifested in the body of the migrant often framed in these photos. Secondly, they connect the migrant-subject to transnational and urban spaces through their multiple mobilities embedded in and reflected upon in the photos. Finally, visual narratives make a shift from aesthetic or documentary approaches to representing the global city. Instead, participants' emplacement in and observation of banal and ordinary places in the city and *en route* to their homeland suggest an assemblage of a mobile migrant-subject within everyday urban spaces.

One of these assemblages relates to the sense of disillusionment with the global city. The disenchantment participants express through their photographs reflects the disjunctures between the imagined city and the everyday city. This disjuncture, I have argued, is related to the roots of their construction of the global city as the seat of modernity and Westernisation juxtaposed against the routes that take them into the city's deprived neighbourhoods and the routes that they traverse every day between home and work. Yet, while the global and iconic city remains largely irrelevant to their lives, participants are able to find within London's rapidly changing neighbourhoods a sense of 'homeliness' and possible routes of return to the homeland.

One of the key assemblages of the mobile migrant, then, is from the ways that visual narratives induce discussions of movement, settlement and return. Participants' photos provide a visual frame for migrants to reflect upon their personal journeys to and from their homeland and link these to their personal histories and future aspirations. And in doing so, the visual narratives become a way for participants to become self-reflexive of the meanings and consequences of their own movements. Such reflexivity, I argue, allows researchers to pay attention to the highly subjective and temporal forms of migrant mobilities in everyday urban life.

While visual narratives connect the experiences of moving across transnational urban spaces to the practices of moving through, seeing and picturing everyday urban spaces they also provide opportunities for observation, reflection and transformation of migrants' mobilities. They bridge across spaces of transnational migration, urban mobilities and embodied experiences of the global city by encouraging participants to take affective charge of their mobilities. They make telling points about the experience of coming to and moving through foreign urban space and about the persistence of categories of near/far, home/abroad, migrant/other.

Examining the city through the visual narratives of migrants, then, opens up a diversity of spaces for reading, experiencing and narrating the city which are multiple and often contradictory, but which illustrate ways of making connections between the spaces and places of migrant pasts, presents and futures. These narratives are not authentic representations of transnational urban spaces; rather, they work as prompts to bring into 'view' (both conversationally and visually) those spaces in migrants' everyday lives from which the researcher is largely excluded. And these narratives can only be understood in the context of the researcher–participant relationship. While photographing the global city has been a highly aestheticised practice, participant-directed photographs construct a different version of the global city: one that is mundane, ordinary and relevant and one that is constructed through its relation to migrants' personal histories and their affective landscapes of mobility and migration.

NOTE

1 The eight countries were Poland, Latvia, Lithuania, Czech Republic, Slovakia, Slovenia, Estonia and Hungary. Rights given to their citizens to live and work in the UK were conditional upon registering with the UK Home Office on arrival.

FUNDING STATEMENT

The author wishes to thank the Suntory Toyota International Centres for Economics and Related Disciplines at the London School of Economics for the New Researcher Grant awarded to the author, without which this research could not have been carried out.

ACKNOWLEDGEMENTS

The author wishes to express heartfelt gratitude to the participants who kindly devoted their time to patiently answering questions and taking pictures. Thanks also to Katherine Brickell, research assistant, and Magdalena Maculewicz, Polish translator, for their valuable contributions towards the fieldwork. Finally, the author's gratitude extends to Andy Cumbers and the four anonymous referees for their helpful and insightful comments without which this paper would not have been completed. Any other omissions or mistakes are the author's own.

REFERENCES

Becker, H. S. (1995) Visual sociology, documentary photography, and photojournalism: it's (almost) all a matter of context, *Visual Studies*, 10(1), pp. 5–14.

Biemann, U. (2004) Touring, routing and trafficking female geobodies: a video essay on the topography of the global sex trade, in: T. Cresswell and G. Verstraete (Eds) *Mobilizing Place, Placing Mobility: The Politics of Representation in a Globalized World*, pp. 71–85. London: Rodopi.

Brickell, K. and Datta, A. (Eds) (2011) *Translocal Geographies: Spaces, Places, Connections*. Farnham: Ashgate.

Burrell, K. (2008) Materialising the border: spaces of mobility and material culture from post-socialist Poland, *Mobilities*, 3(3), pp. 331–351.

Crang, M. (1996) Envisioning urban histories: Bristol as palimpsest, postcards, and snapshots, *Environment and Planning A*, 28(3), pp. 429–452.

Crang, M. (1997) Picturing practices: research through the tourist gaze, *Progress in Human Geography*, 21(3), pp. 359–373.

Crang, M. (2002) Rethinking the observer: film, mobility and the construction of the subject, in: T. Cresswell and D. Dixon (Eds) *Engaging Film: Geographies of Mobility and Identity*, pp. 13–31. Lanham, MD: Rowman & Littlefield.

CRE (Commission for Racial Equality) (2007) *Ethnic Minorities in Great Britain*. Commission for Racial Equality Factfile 2 (http://www.cre.gov.uk/downloads/factfile02_ethnic_minorities.pdf).

Datta, A. (2008) Building differences: material geographies of home(s) among Polish builders in London, *Transactions of the Institute of British Geographers*, 33(4), pp. 518–531.

Datta, A. (2009) Places of everyday cosmopolitanisms: East European construction workers in London, *Environment and Planning A*, 41(2), pp. 353–370.

Datta, A. (2011) Translocal geographies of London: belonging and otherness among Polish migrants after 2004, in: K. Brickell and A. Datta (Eds) *Translocal Geographies: Spaces, Places, Connections*, pp. 73–92. Farnham: Ashgate.

Dodman, D. R. (2003) Shooting in the city: an autophotographic exploration of the urban environment in Kingston, Jamaica, *Area*, 35, pp. 293–304.

Emmison, M. and Smith, P. (2000) *Researching the Visual: Images, Objects, Contexts and Interactions in Social and Cultural Inquiry*. London: Sage.

Farrar, M. (2005) Photography: making and breaking racialised boundaries: an essay in reflexive, radical, visual sociology, *Sociological Research Online*, 10(1), http://socresonline. org.uk/10/1/farrar.html.

Harper, D. (2002) Talking about pictures: a case for photo elicitation, *Visual Studies*, 17(1), pp. 13–26.

Haywood, K. M. (1990) Visitor-employed photography: an urban visit assessment, *Journal of Travel Research*, 29(1), pp. 25–29.

Hirsch, J. (1981) *Family Photographs: Content, Meaning and Effect*. New York: Oxford University Press.

Home Office (2009) *Accession monitoring report May 2004–March 2009* (http://www.ind. homeoffice.gov.uk/sitecontent/documents/aboutus/reports/accession_monitoring_re port/report-19/may04-mar09?view=Binary; accessed 11 February 2010).

Kindon, S. (2003) Participatory video in geographic research: a feminist practice of looking? *Area*, 35(2), pp. 142–153.

Latham, A. (2003) Research, performance, and doing human geography: some reflections on the diary-photograph, diary-interview method, *Environment and Planning A*, 35(11), pp. 1993–2017.

Latham, A. and McCormack, D. P. (2009) Thinking with images in non-representational cities: vignettes from Berlin, *Area*, 41(3), pp. 252–262.

Ley, D. (2004) Transnational spaces and everyday lives, *Transactions of the Institute of British Geographers*, 29, pp. 151–164.

Markwell, K. (2000) Photo-documentation and analyses as research strategies in human geography, *Australian Geographical Studies*, 38, pp. 91–98.

McKay, D. (2006) Translocal circulation: place and subjectivity in an extended Filipino community, *The Asia Pacific Journal of Anthropology*, 7(3), pp. 265–278.

Pink, S. (2007) *Doing Visual Ethnography: Images, Media and Representation in Research*. London: Sage.

Rabikowska, M. and Burrell, K. (2009) The material worlds of recent Polish migrants, in: K. Burrell (Ed.) *After 2004: Polish Migration to the UK in the 'New', European Union*, pp. 211–232. Aldershot: Ashgate.

Rose, G. (2007) *Visual Methodologies: An Introduction to Interpreting Visual Materials*, 2nd edn. London: Sage.

Sontag, S. (1973) *On Photography*. New York: Farrar, Straus and Giroux.

Sweetman, P. (2009) Revealing habitus, illuminating practice: Bourdieu, photography and visual methods, *The Sociological Review*, 57(3), pp. 491–511.

Thomas, F. (2007) Eliciting emotions in HIV/AIDS research: a diary-based approach, *Area*, 39(1), pp. 74–82.

Tolia-Kelly, D. (2004) Materializing post-colonial geographies: examining the textual landscapes of migration in the South Asian home, *Geoforum*, 35(6), pp. 675–688.

Chapter 2: Edge of centre

Australian cities and the public architecture of recent immigrant communities

David Beynon

INTRODUCTION: NON-WESTERN ARCHITECTURE
IN AN AUSTRALIAN CITY

In the late 1990s, the author undertook a survey of the public architecture of non-Western immigrant communities in Melbourne (Beynon 2002). The survey was undertaken within a social context of rapid recent growth in non-Western immigration to Australian cities, coupled with a political context where at state and local level Australian governments were engaged in managing cultural diversity through multiculturalist policies. By the late 1990s, the number of overseas-born, or with overseas-born parentage, had become almost 40% of Australia's total population (Australian Bureau of Statistics 1998–89). Substantial numbers of such immigrants originated from outside the 'West'. Compared to other Australian cities, Melbourne had at the time of the survey the largest communities of certain birthplace groups: notably Sri Lankans, Malaysians, Turks and Somalis. The purpose of this survey was to see to what extent Melbourne's diversifying demography had changed its architectural landscape, and more broadly, what such changes in the built environment indicated about Melbourne's (and by extension Australia's) cultural identity.

The survey included the stated premises of every non-Western community organisation that could be found; places of worship, community centres, museums and clubs. The resultant list of around 400 entities constituted the public representation of over 50 distinct ethnic groups and 40 different religious groups. This collectively represented over 470,000 people, or around 16% of Melbourne's population (Australian Bureau of Statistics 1996; Walmsley *et al.* 1999). Around 100 of these entities occupied buildings that had been substantially altered or constructed for specific purposes, and these buildings provided the basis for more detailed analyses. A large proportion of surveyed new buildings were religious in purpose: mosques, Buddhist temples and Hindu temples, as well as Christian churches of Eastern denominations. Census data confirmed this aspect of demographic change, with non-Christian religions (Hinduism, Buddhism, Islam) all increasing in number at far greater rates than most Christian denominations.

It was noted at the time that many of the groups surveyed were made up of first-generation immigrants in provisional forms of inhabitation (e.g. use of a residence as a Buddhist temple while resources were gathered for construction of a purpose-built structure). However, the increasing numbers of immigrants raised questions of how the adaptations of existing buildings, let alone the planned new buildings, might transform, rather than be simply assimilated by, Australia's built environment (Beynon 2002, 2005, 2009). Due to the newness of much of this inhabitation and construction, it also became clear that with the passage of time transformative aspects of the built works might become apparent, and that now, some 15 years after this survey, would be a good time to test possible transformations by revisiting the surveyed buildings, in particular the seven buildings selected as case studies.[1] All the communities represented by these buildings are still occupying their sites for the same purposes and all have made at least minor alterations and extensions to enhance their purpose and land usage.

In six of the case studies, the communities are still using buildings today that are essentially the same as those previously surveyed, while the seventh, the Emir Sultan mosque, has been more substantially transformed. For this reason, this mosque will be discussed in more detail in this chapter, as it is not only indicative of a trajectory of establishment and site transformation but is also illustrative of broader social and political contestations over a period of time in which Australian cultural identity has moved from being framed as one of loss – the tyranny of distance between an emigrant people and their origins – to one of surplus – the overabundance of identities within a hybridising/localising populace of diverse origins (Papastergiadis 2006: 101).

This shift in framing underpins this chapter's discussion, as it is not only about the trajectory of a particular immigrant community that has come to be part of Australian society, but also about how the establishment of diverse immigrant communities has an architectural dimension – both from the literal need for specialised building typologies for peoples of diverse cultural or religious backgrounds and from a range of potential architectural modes and expressions brought by these new settlers.

THE MULTICULTURAL CITY: CRISIS OR OPPORTUNITY IN THE BUILT ENVIRONMENT

The initial survey was completed during a time when governmental rhetoric was largely multiculturalist, engaged (at least at a local and state level) with genuine attempts to harmoniously accommodate the new cultures that were coming to exist within the Australian nation. Such attempts were hardly unproblematic, as the author has outlined in previous writings on the subject of immigrant architecture (Beynon 2007, 2009). Critical dissection of Australian multiculturalism at the time exposed the contradictions and elisions inherent in governmental Australian attitudes towards local identity and its effects (Hage 1998, 2002, 2003, 2006; Ang 2001, 2006; Gunew 1990, 2004). At the time, it was hoped by some that such attitudes would be modified by the changing realities of Australian demography, as Hage put it at the time: 'Do we need an assimilation program to help ease them [whites] into the multicultural mainstream?' (Hage 1998: 247).

However, since the early 2000s, in the wake of ongoing conflicts between the U.S.A. and its political allies (e.g. Australia) and a succession of enemies (mostly identified with Islam), the notion of a 'multicultural mainstream' has become discredited. Instead, from various sides of the political/social spectrum, there is a growing body of global opinion that multiculturalism is now dead, or it has failed, or it should be reduced to a periodic celebration of food and festivals. Rhetoric has turned from enthusiasm about diversity to talk by the Left of the ecumenical secularity of the liberal state, and by the Right of clashing civilisations and (more chillingly) the importance of cultural purity. In Australia this notion has led to governmental pronouncements about the nation's 'Judeo-Christian' traditions (Patton 2014). As a result, immigrants are, as they were prior to the advent of governmental multiculturalism, again being asked primarily to integrate themselves into the assumed culture of their place of settlement, and it is within this shifting socio-political context that more recent social and architectural developments find themselves. This development has occurred despite (or perhaps because of) the 'overabundance of identities' that Papastergiadis has identified as the contemporary Australian condition. It is obvious on the ground that societies in Australian cities have remained definitively multicultural. Thus, rhetoric about multiculturalism's demise seems more an act of political wishful thinking than a statement of fact, betraying a governmental standpoint that Ghassan Hage has referred to as that of the 'domesticator', who seeks to classify otherness in term of axes of usefulness/uselessness and harmlessness/harmfulness (Hage 2006).

A critique of early 2000s multiculturalism – and one that also has a direct bearing on the religious nature of the more prominent new works of immigrant architecture in Melbourne's suburbs – is outlined in Tariq Modood's *Multiculturalism* (2013). Modood's main point is that liberal citizenship has certain assumptions in relation to society, and recent demographic shifts (in particular an increase in non-Christian religiosity amongst recent immigrants to Europe) present a clear challenge to these assumptions. A key assumption is that public life in Western liberal citizenship is based on individual rather than group identities. Thus, discrimination on the basis of certain individual characteristics – colour, gender, sexual orientation – is of concern to liberal citizenship as these are perceived to be innate, whereas issues of cultural or religious affiliation are considered to be matters of private individual choice (Modood 2013: 63). Following this line of thought, religions cause intrinsic conflict for liberal citizenship, firstly because they wish to have a role in the public realm, and secondly because they bring into that public realm their own views on individual characteristics. Religions especially present a problem for the essential secularism of multiculturalism if they provide particular views of the world that may be exclusionary and antithetical to secular conceptions of equality and individualism (Modood 2013: 66). Modood also emphasises the essential singularity of religious belief, though in this respect he seems to be taking a rather orthodox view. Nevertheless, a central issue is made clear.

ARCHITECTURE – IDENTITY AND THREAT

The production of architecture is significant, as it provides focal points for such posi-tionalities and arguments to be played out in the public realm. The history of buildings is a history of identity. The construction, alteration, and replacement of buildings have social and cultural significance in that an individual building's worth as architecture cannot be disentangled from its association with society. Because of this, new types of buildings are both the results of and the vehicles for negotiation and contestation over identity and culture when they are inserted into existing urban environments. The appearance of a building that is not just new but of an unfamiliar type adds to this contestation, as it does not fit into an assumedly fixed cultural context.

The process by which buildings come to be constructed is, of course, not just a matter for architects and clients but also for public and governmental scrutiny, as they involve practices and assumptions that are grounded in a particular view of how the public and private spheres should interact in space. In particular, follow-ing Modood's argument outlined earlier, the appearance of a new and unfamiliar religious building challenges the notion of a public sphere where 'normality' is rep-resented (Modood 2013: 50). Within a nominally Christian but practically secular Australian state, a non-Christian religious building is a visible manifestation of oth-erness, but an otherness that can be seen as incommensurate with the secular state.

On an instrumental level, what is interesting about these buildings is how they establish themselves within the broader realm of the city; how policies and prac-tices from the dominant centre impact on them, and how they contest and inflect such policies and practices. However, on a broader level, what do such buildings architecturally and culturally represent in relation to Australia's evolving identity? Previously the author has adopted Hage's term and referred to the buildings that represent non-Western immigrant communities as being 'third world-looking', implying that despite their evident presence in the Australian built environment, they are considered to belong elsewhere (Hage 1998: 18; Beynon 2005: 68–83). Moreover, this 'elsewhere' is often seen as being outside the civilisational lineage to which Australia imagines itself as belonging. The label 'third world-looking' provides comment on a tendency to regard non-Anglo-Celtic societies and cultures, despite years of diverse immigration and multiculturalist government policy, mainly in terms of how they have integrated into a pre-existing and presumably homog-enous society. However, these buildings are not peripheral to Melbourne's built environment, indeed they are central to the ways in which parts of the city are evolving. Thus, in terms of architectural or cultural identity, whose identity is being discussed here? Creating a dynamic environment and retaining a sense of the present locality (if this is desirable) demands both change and conservation, but the question, in a diversified and multicultural society, is how (and who) should decide what is significant? *Whose* cultures or histories should be preserved, altered or established anew, especially when there are conflicting needs and interests?

In Melbourne (as with other Australian cities), clear illustrations of these tensions are the number of recent public contestations at local and state government levels that have involved the construction of non-Christian religious buildings. The recently publicised planning controversies around proposed mosques in Bendigo, Victoria and Currumbin, Queensland are just the latest in a large number of such contestations (Spooner 2014; Moore 2014). In the state of Victoria, planning permission (development control) for most buildings is generally devolved to local government. As any architect working in the Australian planning system knows, the combination of ambiguous planning guidelines, a process of public advertisement and engagement and, when there is visible opposition to a new development, the involvement of elected councillors in decision making, means that even minor and apparently innocuous building projects can be refused planning permits. Issues such as increased traffic, worries about car parking, additional noise or general loss of existing amenity for surrounding residents and land users are brought up in relation to most new proposals. If proposed building works are denied a planning permit by a local metropolitan or rural council, the applicant can appeal the decision at the Victorian Civil and Administrative Tribunal (VCAT). As a result, the transcripts of the planning disputes involving ethnic minority religious buildings adjudicated by VCAT make for illuminating reading. Since 1999 there have been around 40 cases relating to mosques, 30 to Buddhist temples, 10 to Hindu temples, 50 to synagogues and 80 in relation to Orthodox, Coptic or other Eastern denominations of churches (*Victorian Civil and Administrative Tribunal: Planning and Environment List*: 1999–2014).

Some of the issues raised in objection to proposals are ostensibly those that might be applied to any new public or community usage or intensification of existing land use, but disputes in relation to non-Christian or non-Western places of worship often indicate deeper tensions. A glance at the public record of recent governmental planning decisions in relation to the construction or development of mosques, Buddhist temples and Hindu temples in Australia indicates the high degree of scrutiny and opposition faced by these types of building proposals, suggesting that some of the opposition to these buildings transcends normal levels of scepticism about new buildings into blatant mistrust, xenophobia and racism.

To give focus to both procedural as well as broader theoretical questions of multicultural contestation in relation to architecture the following section will provide a more detailed discussion of the Emir Sultan mosque, as an example of how a particular community, on a site it has not only occupied but architecturally developed over a period of 15 years, has both reflected and influenced demographic and political shifts over this period of time. Consequently, it provides an illustration of architecture's intersection with contemporary issues of immigration, difference, identity and belonging, showing how buildings physically manifest the cultural and religious diversification of the Australian suburban landscape.

EMIR SULTAN MOSQUE

for Muslims neither the Qur'an nor any visual Islamic display is a locus of contemplation; they are meant to initiate articulation and action.

(Qureshi 1996: 48)

The Emir Sultan mosque is situated in the northern part of Dandenong, a large and culturally diverse suburb some 25 kilometres to the southeast of the centre of Melbourne (Australian Bureau of Statistics, 2011). It is one of four mosques in the municipality of Greater Dandenong, and located on a minor thoroughfare surrounded by a mixture of residential and institutional uses. The mosque was set up in the 1990s by representatives of the local Turkish Islamic Society, Turkish-Australians being one of the larger Muslim communities in the Melbourne metropolitan area. Until 2009 the mosque was housed within an existing building that was originally a small public meeting hall (and whose previous occupant was an evangelical Christian group). This building consisted essentially of a single double-height space with a few ancillary rooms. Adjacent to the mosque was a small ex-residence used for community meetings and religious or language tuition.

While the mosque was housed in the old meeting hall its purpose was not obvious to the casual observer. There was no minaret, no dome and only discrete signage. The only physical addition to the plan of the building was a small semi-cylindrical extrusion in the centre of one exterior wall. Otherwise, the only noticeable alterations involved new windows with arched highlights and internal framing that was visible through some of these windows. Visually this collection of minor extrusions and alterations did not seem very substantial, but on entering the interior of the building, it became evident that they engendered a profound reorientation of the building's purpose. The side entrance led to a small vestibule with shoe-racks and a noticeboard, and from here a doorway led directly into the main interior space of the building. This space occupied two-thirds of the building and was orientated towards the wall where the semi-cylindrical protrusion can be seen from the outside (Figure 2.2). On the inside, this protrusion was revealed as a *mihrab* niche signifying *qibla* (the direction towards Mecca), though it was actually a few degrees misaligned, due to the pre-existing orientation of the building. As the most important physical attribute of the mosque, this wall was given special attention and finished in timber veneer. The other feature of the space, explaining

Figure 2.1 Main street view of the previous building (left) and new Emir Sultan mosque (right), Melbourne. Photograph by author.

Figure 2.2 *Qibla* wall view of the previous building (left) and new Emir Sultan mosque (right), Melbourne. Photograph by author.

the framing visible through the external windows, was that the back half of the main volume was covered by a mezzanine storey. This was the women's gallery, in keeping with Islamic precepts of gender separation during worship. The entrance to this mezzanine section was accessed separately via stairs to the foyer at the main street end of the building. The split entrance allowed two overlapping but separate inhabitations of the same space.

Now this building has been demolished and a new mosque occupies the site that is correctly aligned towards Mecca, and so about five degrees from perpendicular to its street frontage. Compositionally, the new building consists of two major volumes of roughly equal size in plan. The volume closer to the main road contains a reading room, the other the prayer space. This second volume is taller, as the area for female worshippers again occupies a mezzanine level, and the overall volume is defined as the focus of the site via its broad-domed roof. Between the two major spaces is a passageway with foyers to both the northern side (for male worshippers) and the southern side (for female worshippers). On the northern perimeter wall is a minaret, the top of which is accessible via a spiral staircase. Adjacent to the main structure are a few ancillary buildings, one containing a funeral parlour, another containing a *halal* food outlet and the third with a meeting room and small offices. In terms of architectural composition, the mosque is, as might be expected, the most visually dominant of the buildings on the site. The broad dome is counterpointed by the height of the minaret, with its green aluminium cladding reflected in the surface of the minaret's balcony and conical roof. However, while these elements provide a clearly Islamic character to the building, the architecture is otherwise reflective of the mosque's suburban surroundings. The mosque is constructed of brick veneer, with a skin of external beige brickwork concealing the steel and timber framing that spans its large internal volumes. The ancillary buildings are similarly clad and indistinguishable in character from suburban offices or classrooms in the surrounding area. In all buildings, aluminium windows punctuate the brickwork in a symmetrical but otherwise functional fashion, the only concessions

Figure 2.3 Side street view of the previous building (left) and new Emir Sultan mosque (right), Melbourne. Photograph by author.

to symbolic purpose being the curved heads of windows to the prayer space itself. Due to this subdued palette of materials, the overall effect is of suburban domesticity, despite the obvious symbols of dome and minaret, and it is the mixture of these overt symbols with the otherwise unassuming architecture that underlies the transformation of the site. From the occupation of an existing building, with only signage, regular usage and the slightly enigmatic protrusion of the *mihrab* to indicate its identity, a more extensive and permanent ensemble of entirely new structures and symbols now occupies the site. The purpose-built architecture of the mosque now establishes a clearly identifiable presence on the site. It provides a grounding of an immigrant culture in locality while rendering legible connections beyond the site. Local connections are made via the use of construction materials and techniques that predominate in the surrounding area. The dome and minaret, on the other hand, are symbols not just of Islamic identity, but also of particularly Turkish precedents, indicative of the mostly Turkish origin of the mosque's worshippers. While Turkish mosques have a great heterogeneity of size and composition, most are distinguished by a rectilinear arrangement of domed roofs (Ünsal 1959: 57–60). The Emir Sultan mosque could be considered as an example of the 'single-unit' small neighbourhood mosque typology in Turkey (Kuran 1968).

Overall, the new building displays a confluence of sources, values and architectural devices, its resultant whole responding to particular geographic and temporal circumstances. It provides for the physical imagination of differentiated futures, but not only for the small community that is its immediate user group. Its presence also provides ongoing questioning of the identity of its immediate suburban environment. While the adaptation of a meeting hall into a mosque reconciled architecture, difference and location in ways that were contingent and strategic, the newly constructed building is a more emphatic statement of place-making. Subtleties such as the slight realignment of the building away from the street towards *qibla* suggest the transcendence of sacred space over secular cartographic projection, overlaying a particular spatial imaginary on top of its quotidian

Figure 2.4 Street context view of the previous building (left) and new Emir Sultan mosque (right), Melbourne. Photograph by author.

presence. In both cultural and religious terms, this is not so much a simple changing from one identity (Anglo-Celtic/Christian) to another (Turkish/Muslim) but a more complex transformation, in which new cultural/religious elements are sometimes clearly delineated (the minaret) and sometimes blended with pre-existing aspects of the neighbourhood (the brick exterior walls). In this respect, the building does not so much illustrate a theory of cultural/religious transformation but embodies tangible and observable processes of physical and social negotiation. In being both more physically dominant and more explicit in identification than when it was housed within the ex-hall, the new mosque building suggests confidence in its purpose and a sense of belonging, while its use of local construction methods and materials embodies the simultaneous hybridising of its form in order to accommodate physical and social surroundings. In this respect, the development of the site partially illustrates Papastergiadis' notion of surplus identity, and how his 'overabundance of identities' can be accommodated through hybridisation and localisation.

The confluence of minority identity, religious purpose and community democracy is brought into focus by the planning process undergone by the new building complex, revealing the contestations that relate this particular site to broader questions of multiculturalism, liberal democracy and secular versus religious beliefs outlined earlier in this chapter. This process firstly involved the Dandenong Islamic Society applying for the demolition of its existing facility (the mosque and ancillary facilities within the existing hall and nearby residence) and the construction of its new mosque and associated facilities. The City of Greater Dandenong refused this application on the basis that the proposal was an 'overdevelopment' that would adversely impact the site's neighbours (characterised by the council as mostly residential). In its decision to refuse planning permission, the local council's position largely rested on procedural matters, focusing on the size of the proposed development compared to the existing, and its impact on car parking and noise for surrounding residents. It is arguable that any proposal for a new public building on the site would have encountered such issues. However, one point highlighted

Figure 2.5 Further street context views of the previous building (left) and new Emir Sultan mosque (right), Melbourne. Photograph by author.

by a representative of the local council in the later appeal hearing suggests other implications. This observation revolved around the nature of the existing building. As its previous occupiers had been Christian evangelists, the Dandenong Muslims had never been required to obtain planning permission to use the existing building. However, it was now suggested that they should not be automatically granted that right of usage in a new building, the main argument being that the existing building had actually been designed for secular purposes, though it was also implied that even if the existing building's purpose was religious, Christian worship was intrinsically different from Muslim worship.

Following the council's refusal to grant a permit, the Dandenong Islamic Society took its case to VCAT, and was represented by Ed Cuma, the architect of the proposed development (*Victorian Civil and Administrative Tribunal: Dandenong Islamic Society v Dandenong CC*: 2005). At the VCAT hearing it emphasised that the new mosque building would house only a small increase in worshippers (its ongoing status as a strictly suburban institution being reinforced by evidence that the same architect was designing a much larger mosque in the adjacent suburb of Keysborough that would service Melbourne's wider Turkish-Muslim community). Reference was made to the 'very multi-cultural' nature of the Dandenong population, and to the fact that the reading room and ancillary functions of the mosque would be open to all. Accepting these arguments, the VCAT tribunal gave a different reading than the council of the nature of the neighbourhood surrounding the proposed mosque, in which the presence of several other institutional buildings was noted.[2] This reading meant that, rather being required to 'fit in', there was considered value in the proposed mosque's becoming a local landmark, as well as meeting the needs of local Muslim residents for a nearby place to worship. It was also noted that the site was already used as a place of worship, the applicants producing evidence that in 1982 one of the previous titleholders to the site had listed his occupation as 'evangelist' and so worship activities had been happening on the site for much longer than 15 years. The tribunal then gave the view that there was no essential difference between Muslim and Christian worship for planning purposes. While not cited by the tribunal (perhaps because no further argument eventuated in this case), the VCAT judgement could have referred to the Supreme Court of New South Wales' judgement in 2000 that a proposed conversion from a church to a mosque was legally a continuation of an existing use (*Supreme Court of New South Wales – Court of Appeal: House of Peace Pty. Ltd & Bankstown City Council*: 2000). As a result, the council's decision was overturned.

CONCLUSION – OTHER PLACES AND LOCAL ARCHITECTURE

Despite the outcome of the VCAT tribunal, and the subsequent construction of the mosque, the fact that Muslim usage was suggested as different from Christian usage within a planning context is indicative of how shifts in demography can call into question received social and cultural definitions, and how the production of architecture can render these shifts physically tangible (since there seemed to be no public issue while the Muslims inhabited the previous building). As a transitory population is unlikely to make such a substantial and enduring investment, the appearance of new architecture from an immigrant community is a definitive statement of establishment. For instance, since there is no publicly audible calling to prayer allowed in Australia, the new mosque's minaret functions primarily as an element of architectural expression integral to the mosque typology and a symbol of Islamic presence. In this respect, its practical function is less important than the visceral sense of belonging that it imparts to Muslims, and the projection of Islamic presence that it imparts to others.

The Islamic nature of the new building intensifies issues of belonging and allegiance in the current Australian political climate, as the nation's public has come to see the Muslim *umma* as the greatest threat to its national narrative, with the increasing assumption/conviction that when this identity locates itself it inevitably displaces national space. While minority members of the *umma* in Australia may not disagree with this from their own standpoint of a transcendent Islam, for most there is a more delicate process of negotiation in process – whether or not such a process is actively desired or resisted. What the construction of a building such as the new Emir Sultan mosque indicates is the affirmation of place that is both of its immediate locality and also related to a transcendent sense of supra-national belonging. The political travails of the project through the planning process are evidence that the local governmental standpoint remains one of concern about this sense of belonging, in Hage's terms of the level of 'domestication' of the otherness that is embodied within such a building.

Given the nature of its identity as an Islamic building at this particular time and place in Australian history, it makes explicit a number of challenges to multiculturalism. Apart from its indigenous population, Australia's contemporary population is self-evidently multi-religious, multi-ethnic and multicultural. However, these attributes are not fixed categories but in a gradual process of cohabiting and intermingling. Notwithstanding the current rather regressive rhetoric about Australian identity, the main attribute that distinguishes Australia from European countries is the extreme newness of a great majority of its settlement. It is this newness that is Australia's great potential (and for some its great threat), as it implies that Australian identity is much more malleable than French or German or English identity. Over the long term, the descendants of present-day immigrants are as collectively likely to influence the future of the nation as those who arrived a couple of hundred years earlier, while of course, they are themselves unlikely to remain unchanged by their experiences of immigration and settlement. In a plural society, their way of life cannot avoid being compared with other ways of life. The impact of (Western) modernity and the access to different worldviews caused by globalisation, rendered tangible by buildings such as the new Dandenong mosque, have rendered problematic the simple handing down of received conventions, or any simplistic return to imagined pasts (Giddens 1994: 5). Some of these conceptions involve the invocation of a sense of cultural past, some appeal to an immanent religiosity and others relate to the local quotidian connections – but most importantly, as the Emir Sultan mosque indicates, they all coexist. Nevertheless, the establishment of a building such as the Emir Sultan mosque is also a claim for equality, not just privately, but as part of the framework of *public* space (Modood 2013: 50). Both process and product call into question static conceptions of place and make explicit the implications of ways of life that individuals (both inside and outside a particular minority community) might otherwise remain unaware of. Leaving aside issues of threat for the moment, the reception of other cultures can be a field for creative appropriation, in which the insertion of the unfamiliar into a largely familiar context allows for an expansion of the possibilities of a cultural space (Saalman 2006: 133).

Perhaps this is too idealistic, and in reference to Modood's position on the differing trajectories of theologically based cultures and secular liberalism within Western multiculturalism, tolerance of difference is as much as can be expected of a culturally, ethnically and religiously plural society, based on pragmatic needs for social cohesion rather than true empathy for the positions of others. Such acceptance can be based on the principle of agreeing to disagree, like Ashworth and Tunbridge's conception of 'dissonant heritage' in which they contend that the nature of places will always be contested as their definitions exist only via interpretation (Ashworth and Tunbridge 1996: 21). One does not have to read the opposing views of proposed developments brought to VCAT hearings for this to be readily apparent, though the architectural characteristics being argued over are indicative that Australian culture is being influenced by such buildings. A broader view would be to accept that a narrow territorial definition of identity is inadequate when the population derive a large part of their history from other places. As Hage has put it, the 'towns and villages from which Australia's migrant population has originated' provide ingredients that constitute the multicultural present just as much as any local built heritage (Hage 2002: 2). New buildings are always transformative. Sometimes this transformativity is minor, a matter of adjustments of scale or style. At other times it is more profound, involving transformations of purpose, usage and identity.

The lineage of a building such as the Emir Sultan mosque reveals a rich intermingling of sources: stylistic, structural, material, spatial and typological. Notwithstanding the contestations around this building's procurement and establishment, the short history of construction on its site in suburban Melbourne is illustrative of how its immigrant community's relationship to hierarchies of power and influence has gradually shifted from being entirely peripheral (an almost invisible presence within an existing building) to being visibly established (the newly constructed mosque becoming a local landmark). In this shift, some areas of contestation have been resolved. The architecture of the new building integrates a typology derived from a particular immigrant culture with local material expression. In an architecturally heterogeneous neighbourhood, its addition of another layer of cultural/religious identity is a public statement, evidence of a determination within the mosque's community to have a role within the neighbourhood's public realm. Perhaps, as this determination develops, Modood's concerns about the intrinsic incompatibility between religious desires and liberal citizenship will play out within this public realm. However, it seems more likely the building's contribution to its neighbourhood's, its city's and its country's 'overabundance of identities' is evidence that whatever the political rhetoric of the time, the living reality of Australia's future is multicultural and multi-religious. Whatever the future holds, this brief account of a single site in one of Australia's most culturally diverse regions is indicative of how architectural and construction processes can be transformative in the broader sense as Australia deals with the ongoing immigration and settlement of communities of diverse cultural and religious backgrounds.

NOTES

1 These case studies included the Chùa Phúóc Tuông (Vietnamese Buddhist temple) in Richmond, Emir Sultan mosque in Dandenong, Gurudwara Sahib (Sikh temple) in Blackburn, Dhamma Sarana Vihara (Sri Lankan Buddhist temple) in Keysborough, Cypriot mosque and community centre in Sunshine, Wat Buddharangsi (Cambodian Buddhist temple) in Springvale South and Sri Shiva Vishnu Hindu temple in Carrum Downs.
2 Both Dandenong District Hospital and Dandenong Technical and Further Education Institute are nearby, as well as the local public swimming pool and both primary and secondary schools.

REFERENCES

Ang, I. (2001) *On Not Speaking Chinese: Living Between Asia and the West*, London: Routledge.
Ang, I. (2006) 'Immigration and Everyday Multiculturalism in a Globalised World', *Everyday Multiculturalism*, Conference, Macquarie University Sydney.
Ashworth, G. and Tunbridge, J. (1996) *Dissonant Heritage: The Management of the Past as a Resource in Conflict*, Chichester: Wiley.
Australian Bureau of Statistics (1998–99) *ABS Migration 3412*, Canberra: Commonwealth of Australia.
Australian Bureau of Statistics (2011) *National Regional Profile: Greater Dandenong City (Statistical Subdivision): Population/People*, <http://abs.gov.au/ausstats/abs@.nsf/781eb 7868cee03e9ca2571800082bece/c73235081d0a7fc7ca2571cb000b1646!OpenDocum ent> (accessed 26 March 2015).
Beynon, D. (2002) 'Hybrid Representations: The Public Architecture of Non-Western Communities in Melbourne', unpublished PhD Thesis, University of Melbourne.
Beynon, D. (2005) 'Melbourne's Third-World-looking Architecture', in C. Long, K. Shaw and C. Merlo (eds) *Suburban Fantasies: Melbourne Unmasked*, pp. 68–83, Melbourne: Australian Scholarly Publishing.

Beynon, D. (2007) 'Centres on the Edge: Multicultural Built Environments in Melbourne', in S. Velayutham and A. Wise (eds.), *Everyday Multiculturalism Conference Proceedings: 28–29 September 2006*, Sydney: Centre for Research on Social Inclusion, Macquarie University, pp. 1–10, last accessed 21 August 2015, http://www.crsi.mq.edu.au/public/download.jsp?id=10572.

Beynon, D. (2009) 'Architecture, Multiculturalism and Cultural Sustainability in Australian Cities', *The Journal of Environmental, Cultural, Economic and Social Sustainability* 5, 2: 45–57.

Giddens, A. (1994) *Beyond Left and Right: The Future of Radical Politics*, Cambridge: Polity.

Gunew, S. (1990) 'Denaturalizing Cultural Nationalisms: Multicultural Readings of "Australia"', in H. Bhabha (ed.) *Nation and Narration*, pp. 99–120, London: Routledge.

Gunew, S. (2004) *Haunted Nations: The Colonial Dimensions of Multiculturalisms*, London: Routledge.

Hage, G. (1998) *White Nation: Fantasies of White Supremacy in a Multicultural Society*, Annandale: Pluto.

Hage, G. (2002) *Arab-Australians Today: Citizenship and Belonging*, Melbourne: University of Melbourne.

Hage, G. (2003) *Against Paranoid Nationalism: Searching for Hope in a Shrinking Society*, Annandale: Pluto.

Hage, G. (2006) 'On Everyday Exterminability', *Everyday Multiculturalism*, Conference, unpublished conference presentation, Macquarie University, Sydney.

Kuran, A. (1968) *The Mosque in Early Ottoman Architecture*, Chicago: The University of Chicago Press.

Modood, T. (2013) *Multiculturalism*, Cambridge: Polity.

Moore, T. (2014) 'Gold Coast Mosque Rejection "Common Sense"', *Brisbane Times*, 16 September, <http://www.brisbanetimes.com.au/queensland/gold-coast-mosque-rejection-common-sense-20140916-10ho4l.html> (accessed 26 March 2015).

Papastergiadis, N. (2006) *Spatial Aesthetics: Art, Place and the Everyday*, London: Rivers Oram.

Patton, C. (2014) 'Curriculum Review: Where Did "Judeo-Christian" Come From?' <www.theconversation.com/curriculum-review-where-did-judeo-christian-come-from-21969> (accessed 26 March 2015).

Qureshi, R. (1996) 'Transcending Space: Recitation and Community among South Asian Muslims in Canada', in B. Metcalf (ed.) *Making Muslim Space in North America and Europe*, pp. 46–64, Berkeley: University of California Press.

Saalman, G. (2006) 'The Encounter, Exchange and Hybridisation of Cultures', in D. Schirmer, G. Saalman and C. Kessler (eds.) *Hybridising East and West: Tales Beyond Westernisation. Empirical Contributions to the Debates on Hybridity*, Berlin: Lit Verlag.

Spooner, S. (2014) 'Bendigo Mosque Case Delayed for Months', *The Age*, 3 December, <http://www.theage.com.au/victoria/bendigo-mosque-case-delayed-for-months-20141203-11zhw3.html> (accessed 26 March 2015).

Supreme Court of New South Wales – Court of Appeal: House of Peace Pty. Ltd & Bankstown City Council: (2000) <http://www.austlii.edu.au/au/cases/nsw/NSWCA/2000/44.html> (accessed 26 March 2015).

Ünsal, B. (1959) *Turkish Islamic Architecture: in Seljuk and Ottoman Times 1071–1923*, London: Portland Press.

Victorian Civil and Administrative Tribunal: Planning and Environment List (1999–2014) <http://www.austlii.edu.au/form/search1.html?mask=au/cases/vic/VCAT> (accessed 26 March 2015).

Victorian Civil and Administrative Tribunal: Dandenong Islamic Society v Dandenong CC (2005) <http://www.austlii.edu.au/cgibin/sinodisp/au/cases/vic/VCAT/2005/2501.html?stem=0&synonyms=0&query=mosque> (accessed 26 March 2015).

Walmsley, J., Rolley, F. and Weinland, H. (1999) *Atlas of the Australian People 1996 Census Victoria*, Canberra: Department of Immigration & Multicultural Affairs.

Chapter 3: Indian-American landscapes in Queens, New York

Ethnic tension in place remaking

John W. Frazier

INTRODUCTION

Urban localities, neighborhoods, and boroughs incur change due to effects of global flows of information and images, arrival of new demographic groups and immigrants, fashionable ideas about buildings and houses, and consumption patterns. Visible components of the urban and built environment are associated with particular ethnic communities and can often be highlighted in this complex context of changing landscapes. These are perceived as the cause of undesirable changes, and neighborhood communities become divided along lines of ethnicity, race, and cultural identity. Queens, an ethnically diverse and dynamic borough, tends toward segregated settlements for many cultural groups, and has a history of ethnic tensions and racial issues (Frazier 2011). This chapter addresses the circumstances, processes and outcomes of Indian immigrants residing in Queens from a critical perspective about *place* and *place remaking*, and how remaking place by new ethnic groups incites protest from existing residents. Importantly, these protests coalesce around a particular architecture, building, or site in the neighborhood environment and the sites become instrumental in the trajectory of tensions. Despite similarities, Indian identity and settlement structures emerge differently across United States regions, including those that seek *in*visibility, as well as those that promote visibility, and sometimes present success through architecture. Ethno-architecture and ethnic functions play important roles in the transformation of *place*. Ethnic identity, European or Indian, contributes to the creation of a sense of place, but new associations in the process of *remaking* a landscape to enhance *belonging* for recently arrived groups also trigger a sense of loss and nostalgia for existing residents and this induces ethnic tensions.

This chapter will examine the responses of Queens' residents — including Indian residents, and Irish, Italian and German residents who identify as 'white' and 'European' — to new architecture. While some Queens' residents refrain from open statements, social media reveal latent, long-term, emotion-based issues in eastern Queens, Queens Village and Bellerose; each is a small, adjacent neighborhood. Figure 3.1 reports three response categories related to Indian ethno-architecture in Queens during 2013 and 2014, a decade after changes occurred. These responses were made by 'white' residents. The three social media-posting themes that prevail, including among educated and above-average-income residents, openly express feelings, good and bad, regarding social or physical space that has taken on the meaning of *place*. The quotes that appear illustrate that one theme is clearly racist and Indians are unwelcome unless they abide by rules established by the Irish and Italians, who have blended into a common sense of belonging in this context. The second theme illustrates the positive, non-racist view that cultural preferences vary and racist language is not helpful in addressing issues. These types of responses also suggest that some housing-style changes represent significant, positive investments because they curb a general decline in the economic situation of Queens, evident in lack of maintenance due to aging households and the departure of children seeking employment or more-preferred neighborhoods on Long Island (an observation also noted by our key informant, remodeler in these neighborhoods). The third theme presents a negative view of ethno-architecture, without reference to race or ethnicity, but predominantly contains postings made by neighborhood residents, or by those who have relocated but have remained attached to their previous neighborhoods. We will return to these themes later in the essay.

Negative: Racist	Positive	Negative: Non-Racist
"Was once a normal looking QV Archie Bunker style house, now INDIAN TAJ MAHAL.."	"It looks beautiful and clean. More than can be said for many other homes!"	"It doesn't look like a 'Taj Mahal' to me, just an incredibly oversized house for the property.
Indians are the ones or Middle Eastern or Towel Head, Dot Head, whatever you want to call them are doing this to their houses, not white Americans. They pay for these houses in cash.	"I don't think that hut is bad at all. But I'd change a few things... I'd lose the above balcony and do something like on the side entrance. Other than that I seen nothing really wrong with the house. It has nice brick work & windows."	"These homes have nothing to do with racism rather taste! The do not fit the character of the area, take the footprint of the property and eliminate all grass, trees, etc., and leave a large ugly, limestone or white brick monolith."
"Where would the stable be for the CAMELS ?"	"It is a cultural thing though. this stuff follows every ethnic group. The old joke in Elmont was there was no concrete in Elmont until the Italians moved in!!"	"It's an ugly McMansion, sadly Queens is being taken over by these houses that just don't fit into the neighborhoods in which they are being built. I don't care if the owners are purple and choose to worship a stuffed Giraffe. It's just UGLY and doesn't fit."
"Before we know it we will be living in India or China you pick."	"Racist language is more offensive than any house could ever beer. Disgraceful."	

Figure 3.1 'The Story of Queens Village' – an eastern Queens content-based social media webpage. The site is a group of more than 4,000 members from Queens Village and Bellerose, Queens. http://www.facebook.com/group/3386869/62320000. Last accessed 15 March, 2015.

A range of sources was used for the illustration and analysis of the architec-tural–cultural landscapes. The New York City Historical Archives provided historical images of infrastructure and Queens' houses. A method of observation used by the author resulted in photographic documentation of the present urban fabric. The United States Census Bureau website provided population data for multiple years. The individual comments of Indians and protesters came from two sources: journalistic reports that contained quotes, and comments made on social media sites. Data regarding the varied individual and collective viewpoints and opinions of Indian construction and the remaking of Queens' neighborhoods was sourced from both interviews and social media sites.

PLACE REMAKING

Space, often used in an abstract way to describe a bounded area and its con-tents, also reflects the processes that produce the space. Abstract space can be transformed into a place through movements and 'pauses' that permit the attach-ment of meanings (Tuan 1977). Place provides the setting for human actions 'as a rich and complicated interplay of people and environment – as a place' (Cresswell 2004: 11). In addition to sounds, odors, breeze, temperature, observations of use, textures, patterns, ornament, signs, and the material architecture and urban arti-facts form the urban landscapes as visualizations of culture.

Urban renewal is one form of place remaking, and its effect includes the displacement of class-based groups, and sometimes immigrant communities. Ley's study of Boston's West End illustrates the neighborhood as a 'communal home', bonded by place, identity, landscapes, and shared social life, highlighting the losses when slum clearance forced displacement of residents (Ley 2010). Ley summarized the definitions of neighborhood from Firey and Fried:

> A range of psychosomatic, stress-related conditions accompanied the prying apart of residents from a familiar and much-loved setting … [Referencing Firey 1945] … the tightly intertwined bonding of society and space, place, and identity … created neighborhood as a larger communal home … disrupted by external change agents.
>
> (Ley 2010: 176)

Place making and remaking (altering existing meaning attached to structures and landscape) occur within a matrix of power relationships, identity and rights, and sense of belonging. The idea of a contested place is framed as the change between new and old urban landscapes, and these are constituted through visual cues related to sites, buildings, signage and the visual presence of new resident groups. Ethno-architecture and new functions inserted into the urban landscapes express the presence and identity of a new migrant culture, especially through religious/cultural cues. The residents that identify themselves with the old 'neighborhood' or 'community' of the existing local culture react against the new insertions through support of the authority and law, protests, verbal attacks, print media, social media commentary, and even violence. Triggered by perceived changes in local places with embedded and nostalgic meanings, reactionary emotions rise to the surface. A line is drawn by residents who perceive themselves as longer-term members and believe they have established privileges, reinstating a host–guest structure to the local neighborhood and liberally expressing feelings of anger and resentment. In this structure, recent-migrant groups should assimilate into the existing landscape without making changes that do not 'fit'. Ethno-architecture, expressing a different set of cultural references, is perceived as not wanting to 'belong' to the existing environment, a form of defiance toward existing rules and regulations, and is unacceptable to the existing community. Conversely, the arriving residents view control of their behaviors as non-inclusive, a rejection of their presence, that they are not equal and not welcome. The difference between a position that wants to preserve the existing character and identity of a neighborhood, and a position that wants to insert new structures towards developing new relevant meanings gives rise to ethnic tension.

Shaughnessy, a neighborhood in Vancouver, British Columbia provides an example of landscape and ethno-architectural change. When Hong Kong Chinese feared the return of their investments to China in 1997, many wealthy residents invested in second homes in Vancouver. Their arrival in Shaughnessy caused ethnic tensions and disruption among the existing residents. David Ley characterized this place as follows:

> [This] 'anglophile landscape' of European-style homes surrounded by impressive vegetation suggested an 'elite identity of well-being and privilege', while providing 'the status of distinction and the comfort of belonging'.
>
> (Ley 2010: 177)

The Hong Kong Chinese were perceived as cultural intruders because they inserted their architectural preferences and fused them with the existing anglophile landscape, or replaced it entirely, rather than wanting to assimilate within the existing place and community. While not a clear case of urban renewal, this case exemplifies the collision of two cultures with different ideas of presenting status and wealth, one Anglo and one Hong Kong Chinese. Shaughnessy provides a context for examining place remaking among the European-based population in Queens, New York.

Both the Queens and Vancouver cases have an existing ancestry, Anglo in Shaughnessy and Irish, Italian, German in Queens, themselves historical migrants, but in those instances experiencing an influx of non-white immigrants with middle-class and higher status. Local regulations were strong in the Shaughnessy neighborhood and the local government acted quickly to pass additional regulations that limited architectural styles to ones that did not appeal to Chinese immigrants. But, although there were small protests by neighbors carrying signs, individual reactions by the Chinese and those of European ancestry did not emphasize racism in local media reports. One major difference between the two immigrant groups and the local settings was that the Chinese invested in Canada, selecting elite suburban neighborhoods for construction of new homes, but their migration and settlement to Shaughnessy was short lived – and perceived to be so, as there was imminent return to Hong Kong – and different from the Vancouver Chinatown. Queens, on the other hand, is not an elite suburb, and has a history of racial segregation and resistance to people of color entering white neighborhoods (McGovern and Frazier 2015). The ongoing presence of Indian immigrants in New York City and its suburbs presented a long-term rather than short-term settlement. For decades, Indian immigrant presence in New York City has been as a visible minority. Little India was established in Jackson Heights, Queens, as a commercial enclave and has attracted Indian immigrants who settled in Manhattan. The rapid Indian population increase after 1980 was due to the 1965 Immigration and Naturalization Act, and the rapid increase in H1B visas in the 1990s (and beyond) coincides with the rapid increase of Indians in Queens.

The intention to make permanent homes and to seek opportunities to build new lives in the United States in numbers much higher than for the Chinese entering Vancouver further differentiates the two forms of ethno-architecture. However, race is an intervening invisible factor in the case of ethnic tensions in Queens. The ethnic tensions encompass a variety of white responses, including statements to the press, protests against and occupation of private property, and statements placed on social media. Despite cultural differences in architectural styles, racism is a single but vital dimension in a complete understanding of ethnic tensions in Queens.

Other forces are part of this story, including economic forces, out-migration, availability of affordable homes in suburbia, and an Indian population seeking the American Dream, and have resulted in a dynamic environment in eastern Queens that differs from that in Vancouver in important ways.

INVISIBILITY AND VISIBILITY OF INDIAN MIGRANT COMMUNITIES IN THE U.S. AND IN QUEENS

Studies reveal conflicting evidence regarding Indian visual expressions of identity in America, including through architecture and place making that reflect significant differences in the formation of Indian-American ethnic identity. Clearly, conclusions by key scholars – Skop, Lessinger, and Khandelwal – differ regarding the material expression of this ethno-cultural group and its importance in shaping Indian-ness and identity.

Skop's thesis that Indian identities are shaped by the desire to remain invisible, but to stay connected through strong regional cultural associations as a part of heterolocalism, is supported by a growing literature. The theme of Indian *invisibility, including in their new locations and neighborhoods* employs descriptors 'not highly visible' (Dubey 2003), 'unnoticed minority' (Tinker 1977), 'imperceptible', 'invisible' (Skop and Altman 2003; Skop 2006), and 'invisible Americans' (Kar 1995). These studies argue that cultural and economic diversity in the Indian subcontinent leads to a lack of cultural affinities which fosters a similar division in the U.S., especially with regard to family and economic security (Lessinger 1995; Mitra 1996; Shankar 1998a, 1998b; Dave *et al.* 2000). It is argued that the racial history of the U.S. may contribute to a strategy of invisibility, avoiding racial concentration, and favoring dispersed suburban settlement, reflecting an absence of concentrated material cues and resulting cultural landscape (Skop 2012). Increasing numbers of Indians have settled in suburban gateway communities in a dispersed pattern (Zelinsky and Lee 1998), one that is reinforced by a similarly dispersed pattern found in a New York study in the 1990s (Lessinger 1995).

However, Lessinger points to the role of the material world in shaping ethnic identity, arguing that materialism and consumption were 'badges of ethnicity' for Indian Americans in New York. Lessinger reflected on the infrastructure, ethnic association, temples, and cultural societies and celebrations that amplified and supported Indian values and culture. Khandelwal (2002) similarly viewed cultural maintenance and diversity as significant for Asian Indians, identifying dress, including the *bindi* and gold jewelry, and the vital role of media and institutions in 'transplanting' Indian culture into an American framework. Khandelwal points to the media representation of the significance of religious structures:

> They came gradually, so at first we didn't notice, until now they are all over. It's just too much. They're taking over the neighborhood. We believe in the right to worship, as you want; I mean, Flushing is the birthplace of religious freedom. But what about our rights as residents? The churches don't even look like real churches. You know, a Hindu temple just doesn't fit into our architecture here.
> (Khandelwal 2002, p. 88, quoting from the *New York Daily News*, February 23, 1990)

The shift of an Indian population centered firstly in Manhattan, and then relocating to Queens, provides an historical backdrop for attraction to Queens. The context of Queens, its airport gateways (JFK and LaGuardia), the commercial Indian-ness in Jackson Heights, and the attraction of affordable home ownership in its neighborhoods clarify Queens as social, cultural, and economic opportunity. Both Lessinger and Khandelwal discuss the transplantation of Indian cultural elements to the U.S. and New York City. In this sense transnationalism is a process of 'becoming American', parallel to the evolution of bicultural identity: Indians express 'Indian-ness' in multiple ways. One such way is through Indian homeowners' modification of architecture and houses and the replacement of existing homes with larger homes.

VISIBILITY AND INDIAN-AMERICAN IDENTITY IN QUEENS

Indian-owned religious, commercial, and residential properties in the eastern Queens' neighborhoods have increased. This visibility brought about public outcries by local residents, including racist comments that lend little to welcoming and multiculturalism. Other complaints were couched in terms of property rights and legal rights of zoning. Examination of the changes that triggered tensions between those of white ancestry and the Indian immigrants are provided.

Maps in Figure 3.2 illustrate the changing Indian density for the period between 1990 and 2010. The darkest patterns represent neighborhood areas that have the highest Indian densities when compared to Queens overall. It is obvious that the

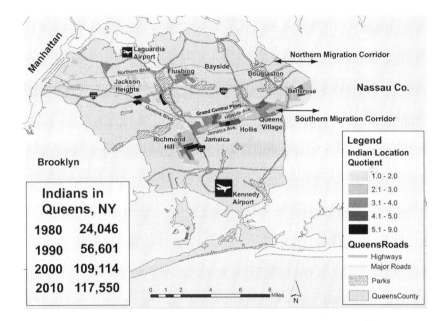

Figure 3.2a
Indian location
quotient, Queens,
New York, 1990.
Source: Census Data
1980–2010. Image by
Brendan McGovern,
7 January 2015.

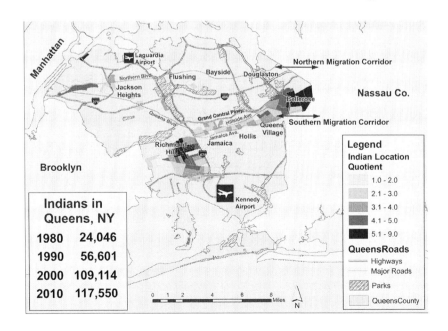

Figure 3.2b
Indian location
quotient, Queens,
New York, 2010.
Source: Census Data
1980–2010. Image by
Brendan McGovern,
7 January 2015.

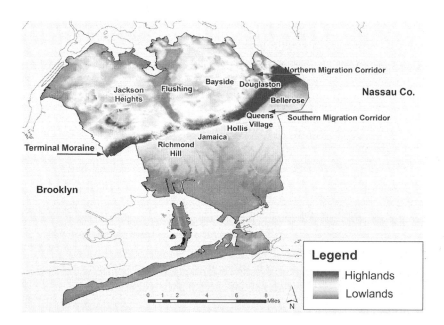

Figure 3.2c
Queens physical geography shaped by the last Ice Age retreated some 12 to 14 thousand years ago, their farthest southern advance was marked by a high ridge, or thermal moraine. Today that moraine forms a 'spine' of high ground that spans across Long Island and divides Queens into northern and southern halves. Image by Brendan McGovern, 21 April 2014.

Asian Indian Population of Eastern Queens by Census Tract

Census Tract	2000			2010		
	Asian Indian	A.I. Percent	Total Pop	Asian Indian	A.I. Percent	Total Pop
478	444	7.95%	5,586	577	10.90%	5,294
484	685	12.97%	5,282	843	16.93%	4,979
492	391	7.48%	5,227	403	8.48%	4,750
542	892	15.62%	5,709	905	17.84%	5,074
552	445	12.60%	3,531	450	14.69%	3,064
554	498	20.38%	2,444	363	15.76%	2,303
556	412	19.12%	2,155	486	22.57%	2,153
558	287	14.61%	1,964	281	16.22%	1,732
1301	545	13.63%	3,998	785	20.71%	3,791
1551	1,328	17.06%	7,786	1,242	15.17%	8,185
1571	1,606	22.37%	7,178	2,236	30.99%	7,216
1579.1	1,057	21.94%	4,817	1,612	33.58%	4,800
1579.2	1,125	30.49%	3,690	1,502	39.16%	3,836
1579.3	847	22.05%	3,841	1,184	30.02%	3,944
1617	465	10.67%	4,359	573	13.33%	4,297
1621	1,099	17.78%	6,181	1,550	25.01%	6,197

Figure 3.2d
Asian Indian population of eastern Queens by census tract.

Source: Census Data 1980–2010. Image by Brendan McGovern.

increasing densities occur along the Southern Migration Corridor and are highest in Richmond Hill and Bellerose-Queens Village. The analysis in this essay focuses only on the latter neighborhoods because they have become the center of highest Indian visibility. Figure 3.2 lists the Census counts for Bellerose-Queens Village neighborhoods for 2000 and 2010. Those numbers indicate that 14 of 16 neighborhoods increased their percentage of Indians relative to their total population.

Seven of these neighborhoods had 20%+ of their population as Indian, while four exhibited 30%+. These seven can be considered as evolving Indian ethnic enclaves containing homeowners and families with children.

The number and density of Indian commercial activities have become concentrated and visible, as in Figure 3.3, which shows the three main commercial

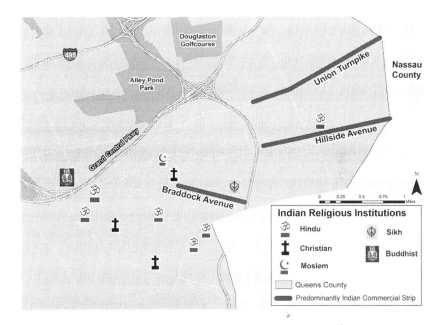

Figure 3.3a
Indian commercial landscapes and religious institutions in eastern Queens, New York. Image by Brendan McGovern, 18 September 2014.

Figure 3.3b
Gurdwara Sant Sagar, New York. Photograph by Brendan McGovern.

Figure 3.3c
Satya Sanatan Dharma
Mandir, New York.
Photograph by
Brendan McGovern.

Figure 3.3d
St John's Mar Thoma
Church, New York.
Photograph by
Brendan McGovern.

strips – Union Turnpike, Braddock Avenue, and Hillside Avenue – which border the increasingly dense Indian settlements in these two eastern Queens' neighborhoods. The figure also indicates the scattered and diverse Indian religious institutions, including a Sikh Gurdwara, a Hindu Temple, and a Christian church (the Buddhist and Muslim structures are not shown). Many of the commercial and religious structures illustrate architectural designs, building remodeling, a new pastel color palette, and other features that make them different from the Catholic churches that once dominated the landscapes.

NOSTALGIA, RACISM AND INDIAN PLACE REMAKING IN QUEENS

In order to detail the role of ethno-architecture and ethnic tension this section will elaborate on two events that occurred in Queens and received extensive media coverage. They indicate the importance of nostalgia in images of place and also contain clear verbal linkages between nostalgic place and volatile emotions toward migrants, who are unwelcome unless they conform to architectural design and economic functions of a bygone era. Figure 3.4 portrays the sites of these incidents.

The first event was related to the loss of a favorite bakery, Reinwald's Bakery, which had served two generations of children and parents of European Americans. Those who spent their formative years in this neighborhood have enshrined particular places with a nostalgic yearning for the lost pleasures of what they seem to collectively remember as a simpler, more pleasant time.

> I remember going to Reinwald's for my mom on Sundays and I loved the Braddock Avenue deli, [where] my friend Paul worked. And of course there was Jobar's Meat Market and my mom use to buy coke syrup from the candy store.
> (*The Story of Queens Village*, a webpage 2013–2014)

> … Reinwald's, it was more than just a bakery.
> (*The Story of Queens Village,* a webpage 2013–2014)

Reinwald's Bakery was part of a strip development that became a meeting place where neighbors waited in line to purchase crumb buns after Sunday mass and hamburger meat for the evening dinner. While waiting, they discussed neighborhood news and shared the intimacies of their daily lives. This nostalgia recalls a prosperous time, different from the aging population and business area in decline of their present reality.

Those stories are memories of childhood. The reaction of the Irish, Italian, German [European] community has ranged from a sense of sadness, a mourning for this lost special space, to an anger that is focused on the ethnic groups that have replaced them and are now producing different meaning through ethno-architecture in this same location. The bakery was replaced by the Tandoor Indian Restaurant and Bar. Social media became active with the drive of nostalgia related to loss of a sense of place and expressions of anger toward Indian people and their places.

> Heart breaking! … Not the same anymore!

> Tragic … what they did to that landmark. Now it's an Indian restaurant!!!

> What a shame. Our kids are dying in the Middle East to try and keep peace so the Middle East can walk in peace on Braddock Avenue. We gave up our neighborhood *to those people.*
> (*The Story of Queens Village*, a webpage 2014)

Figure 3.4 Changing functions and meaning in architecture, 1974–2014. Nostalgic meanings and their loss as triggers for racial remarks. Photographs by Brendan McGovern.

The second case involves the Frozen Cup Ice Cream, another special social space which was lost after serving the eastern Queens' neighborhoods for generations. Like Reinwald's, it provided the trigger for nostalgic memories of a different time. Illustrated in the 1974 photograph (Figure 3.4), taken long after it had opened, and serving work-ing- and middle-class families in the neighborhood for decades, the 'Cup' was a place of social gathering. Despite a significant attachment, there was no interest to purchase it. In fact, the *only* interested buyer of the property was Mr. Patel (see Chapter 9 in this volume), who purchased the property with the intention of demolishing the building and constructing a motel – a reasonable investment in an area in transition. Motels are often symbols of South Asian ownership in the U.S.

The tensions created over Mr. Patel's proposal were reported in the *New York Times* on February 22, 2009. Arguments and viewpoints were expressed differently. The viewpoint of the residents who had memory associations was expressed as protecting the neighborhood 'character' and saving a histori-cal landmark, while Mr. Patel's position argued that he was being progressive and moving a neighborhood forward economically in a capitalist society. Local protesters recalled a time that had long passed. Mr. and Mrs. Augugliaro, two retired workers of Italian descent, spoke of this 'beloved neighborhood spot' as the 'last place left in Bellerose *where our kids used to go*' (Angelos 2009). They reported that they had watched other places erased from their neighborhood: a bowling alley and a movie theatre, and a motorcycle shop replaced by a Sikh temple. Like the Frozen Cup, these vestiges of a bygone era had little economic value and limited appeal on the resale market. Rather than attribute such changes to economic decline in the area, these residents interpreted new ethnic and religious activities as invasive, destructive, and unwanted. To residents, their sense of place was challenged by decline and their familiar cultural landscapes were being eroded. Mr. Patel argued that local residents (non-Indian) were non-progressive and racist.

Objections to the Indian visibility became louder and more explicitly racist: 'They're turning the neighborhood into a third-world country and destroying an historical landmark for money and a 44-room motel that will be like their Floral Park motel that stands out like the Taj Mahal and be rented to their people' (Angelos 2009). Yet there is no outward display of Indian-ness at the Quality Inn.

Mr. Patel struck back verbally at the loud public protest. He termed the complaints as being based on 'a kind of jealousy … They feel we are coming from out of country and we move forward (progressive), and they move back' (Angelos 2009). He openly challenged the protesters and the response as racist: 'If they have so much feeling, let them buy it.' No one did and the 'Cup' was demolished and replaced. Mr. Patel saw the protest not as an issue of neighborhood change, but as one of people stuck in a previous time and racist in their actions. The Taj Mahal, an architectural destination for people from many diverse cultures and highlighted by architects and academics, is a strange reference of the local neighborhood community wanting to point out the negative and undesirable aesthetic sense of the Floral Park hotel.

These ethnic clashes, couched in legalities, become blurred when comments are racist or related to cultural differences. Suspicion leads to stories such that it is difficult to assess what is true and, more importantly, what is of benefit to the neighborhood. One was the publicly stated suspicion that a newly planned Indian business was going to be a 'hot sheet motel' (Costella 2012). This may be part of a white racial ideology that has been termed the race–place connection (Anderson 1987; Frazier 2014). The use of language is important. Negative references to Indian symbols such as the Taj Mahal, which attracts millions of visitors annually, to the smell of food, and to hygiene, create an environment of exclusiveness, racial dislike (or hatred), and barriers to immigrant belonging to American society.

The remodeling and replacement of existing single-family homes (e.g. Cape Cods and Colonials) in eastern Queens' neighborhoods also created prolonged outcries from neighborhood residents. One key informant, a local owner of a remodeling company who had worked almost exclusively for Indian clients in recent years, described attributes of 'Indian-style' housing. He indicated that the cues included architecture, color, and house features:

> Look for changes in the facades, the soft colors, ornamental decorations, marble stairs, concrete replacing grass, and stainless steel fencing. There are other obvious cues of Indian occupancy, including removal of grass and other vegetation from the front of the structure and ornamental decorations. Facades are changed such that they have different architectural slopes and angles that alert you to architectural differences from surrounding homes. They are certainly distinctive.
> (Key informant interview, November 10, 2008)

A survey of residential streets in eastern Queens shows many examples of sometimes dramatic modifications and replacements in Queens Village and Bellerose. As Lessinger observed, home ownership is a symbol of success sought by Indian Americans, but the modifications and enhancements to facades and architectural changes also represent a 'badge of ethnicity'. This indicates that Indian residents in Queens desire to demonstrate their success of being Indian American and visibly illustrate 'Indian-ness' through a unique expression of place remaking using housing. In response to why Indians find this particular style of architecture and house appealing, one professional Indian informant was typical:

> Home ownership is a symbol of class and success in India. That carries over to America. The enclosed yard by fencing reflects and reminds of home. It is recreated here. The remainder – the architecture, animal decorations, the colors, the glass and the facades – are all displays of beauty. The concrete replaces grass because home owners in India do not care for their own lawns. Here it is viewed as a necessary waste of time.

This presents the differential related to aesthetics, and the Indian residents expressed the idea of living with beauty while demonstrating material success. Indian migrants have marked places with an Indian-American identity, developing neighborhoods of their own, as the Irish, Italian, and German immigrants did before them. The *remaking* occurs in neighborhoods of differing levels of socio-economic status (SES) and the level of investment made by the Indian homeowner varies accordingly. Figure 3.5 illustrates the decorative and architectural changes on a single property in Queens Village. Pictured are 1980s archive photos (City of New York, n.d.) and a recent photo (2012) of the same house now occupied by an Indian family, illustrating an example of substantial modifications in décor and architectural style. On streets with households of lower SES, investments may include only stainless steel railing and an elephant figure in concrete in the front yard. The second of the two photos in Figure 3.5 represents an increasingly frequent process started in the early 2000s whereby an Indian family purchases and then demolishes a house and replaces it with a new, much larger home on the same property.

The residents with strong place attachment to Queens from decades ago perceive the new houses as 'out of place' and as having caused the destruction of other homes considered to be beautiful. This idea of 'out of character with the

Figure 3.5 Changing existing residential architecture, 1980s–2014. Lower right as an example of "McMansions". Photographs: 1980s – NYC Municipal Archives; 2000s – Brendan McGovern.

neighborhood' and many houses built in unwanted new styles was given the name 'McMansions'.

Examples of modifications as well as reconstruction exist in eastern Queens. In 2006, housing concerns were directed at Indian-owned construction corporations. Dissatisfaction was expressed and demands made of New York City's Department of Buildings. One example reported by the media focused on legal violations and property rights of homeowners. Then Senator Padavan demanded the revocation of building permits and demolition orders for the units in question, stating:

> The blatant disregard by the developer of both building code and zoning resolution is one of the most outrageous examples I have ever observed.
>
> (Rhoades 2006)

The violations pertained to set-back rules, out-of-compliance curb cuts that were 500% larger than allowed, inadequate parking (due to parking on the streets), and paved-over front yards after removal of vegetation. He termed the structures abominations and wanted them demolished. Non-Indian residents felt pushed out of their homes by the changes in the neighborhood and the loss of neighborhood character.

> It's partly an aesthetics issue, but it also affects our lives. We don't want to be pushed out of our community.
>
> (Rhoades 2006)

It is somewhat difficult to interpret the phrase 'pushed out'. Is it architectural difference and aesthetic appearance? Or home size? What is pushing residents from the neighborhoods? Is it the growing number of Indian residents? Other housing issues include upsizing houses to multiple-family and also renting basements in what were one- and two-family home neighborhoods. These legal issues remain contentious more than a decade later (Costella 2011; Costella 2012; Gannon 2013a; Gannon 2013b; McGovern and Frazier 2015).

There is some evidence that Indian residents simply being present in the neighborhoods is the real issue, regardless of architectural styles. An incident in 2014 supports this contention. When a newly arrived Indian family moved into a house next door, an elderly neighbor posted pornographic pictures in his front window, apparently to provoke the Indian family and to let them know they were unwelcome. It was captured by Channel 7 News, which reported:

> The photographs can be seen clearly from the public sidewalk. They are so vile, so intentionally pornographic, that just about anyone would be offended by their public display, especially, the father of the 4-year-old boy who lives right next door.
>
> (Dolan 2014)

Sanjeev Aggurawal and his family are the neighbors at which the pictures were directed. He, justifiably very disturbed, told the reporter:

> My son! He's four! My nephews are 7 and 9 and they come over and they see this. This is ridiculous it has to stop. He's upset because some Indian guy moved in next door.
>
> (Dolan 2014)

While changes in housing style and size trigger protests and criticism, it is the presence of the Indian residents that generates the racist reaction.

This points to both the complexity of the problem and the often too-loaded reaction. First, houses sizes have continued to expand since the early twentieth century and have become especially large in the suburbs, while lot sizes have become smaller (Mason 2012). Second, similar changes to the character and size of housing in nearby ethnic neighborhoods occurred long before Indian residents began building 'McMansions'. Italian residents were known for extravagant stone- and cement-work on their houses in Queens. There was little objection expressed in the media. Italian families were viewed as outwardly displaying their socio-economic status. In response to postings expressing negativity about a current Indian McMansion located in Queens Village, a local neighborhood woman reminded complaining residents of this situation in social media:

> Apparently none of you have been to Howard Beach ... enormous overdone homes (built by Italians) have been there for years and no one ever complained about them.
>
> (*The Story of Queens Village*, a webpage, 2014)

Her point was that landscape changes among ethnic groups are not new. This, of course, raises questions about the motivations, racial attitudes, and targeting behaviors of some residents of eastern Queens' neighborhoods toward Indian residents. What role does the architecture have in relation to the presence of Indian residents? Ethnic tensions are triggered by architectural tastes and changing neighborhood conditions but, in some cases, these are fueled by protests and explicit racist expressions. One group, with place-attachment related to a past reality, yet perceiving their right to control the landscape, will protest against change and attack a new resident group that remakes a place, seeking to keep them out of the neighborhoods.

CONCLUSION

Queens provides an opportunity to examine the processes and outcomes of place making by a culture that has sought invisibility in many suburbs in the United States. Although Indian immigrants have resided in New York City since the 1970s, their direct settlement in the suburbs upon arrival has occurred largely since 1980. Indian visibility contributes both to a unique Indian-American identity and to ethnic tensions in eastern Queens neighborhoods due to *place remaking* that reshaped the local landscapes.

Ethno-architecture and ethnic functions provide triggers for ethnic tensions that can spill over into confrontation, protests, and racism when a sense of place is felt to be jeopardized or lost. Several examples have been provided to illustrate how the place remaking process in Queens' neighborhoods led to ethnic tensions between different ethnic groups – Indians and local residents of mixed European ancestry. Ethno-architecture is perhaps the most important trigger because this type of cultural landscape change in place remaking is symbolic and semi-permanent. Considering that Queens' neighborhoods had suffered some decline, economically and culturally, the arrival of a dynamic immigrant group made manifest changes in physical and visual ways. This triggered a loss of valued places that challenged ethnic pride and nostalgic memories, as well as a loss of power by one group to another. Cultural and racial differences have always mattered for many Americans and have led to the racialization of members of society (California News Reel 2003). This case study illustrates an implicit long-term conflict in American society. Americans promote a 'melting pot', but have witnessed racial prejudice and discrimination continuously for centuries.

Of course, not all people in Queens are racist. Neighborhood responses suggested that difference matters but many comments were not racist in nature. However, it is equally clear that these triggers of ethnic tensions in eastern Queens' neighborhoods brought racist feelings to the surface in some cases. Because architecture manifests one form of belonging it disturbs the sense of belonging that existed in a time past. Also, racialization and racist behaviors remain barriers to immigrants' cultural inclusion and belonging. There is little evidence that institutions have responded in any fashion other than to address the legal issues surrounding property. Local government hearings and meetings focusing on legal code violations are unlikely to provide an adequate forum for the problems described here. Perhaps when residents of European and Indian ancestry find a means for open dialogue and interaction that includes but goes beyond the issues of law (Fredman 2011) and addresses structural change without stigma and stereotypes, then Queens' neighborhoods will evolve into places that welcome and support inclusion and dignity for all residents.

ACKNOWLEDGEMENTS

Thanks are due to Professor Wei Li (Arizona State University) for her encouragement to write this chapter, and to Professor Norah F. Henry and Mr. Brendan McGovern for comments on a draft of this manuscript. Mr. McGovern also created the graphics. I also wish to thank the editor for her guidance and suggestions and two reviewers who made suggestions that improved this manuscript.

REFERENCES

Anderson, K. (1987) 'The Idea of Chinatown: The Power of Place and Institutional Practice in the Making of a Racial Category', *Annals of the Association of American Geographers* 77: 580–598.

Angelos, J. (2009) 'The Great Divide', *New York Times*, 20 February 2009, accessed 20 February 2009, http://www.nytimes.com/2009/02/22nyregion/22froz.html.

California News Reel (2003) *Race – The Power of an Illusion. Episode 1: Difference Between Us*. Executive Producer Larry Adelman. 56 minutes. California News Reel.

City of New York (n.d.) in 'Queens 1980s Tax Photo' folder, NYC Municipal Archives, accessed 8 July 2014, http://nycma.lunaimaging.com/luna/servlet/view/search/who/CITY+OF+NEW+YORK?q=mediaCollectionId%3D%22RECORDSPHOTOUNITQUE~1~1%22&os=0.

Costella, A. (2011) 'No Creedmoor Vote; Bribe Claim', *Queens Chronicle*, 13 October. www.qchron.com/editions/www.qchron.com/editions/eastern/nocreedmoor-vote (accessed 7 November 2011).

Costella, A. (2012) 'DOB Gives Updates on CB 13 Problem Spots', *Queens Chronicle*, 2 February. www.qchron.com/editions/www.qchron.com/editions/eastern/dob-gives-updates (accessed 15 March 2012).

Cresswell, T. (2004) *Place. A Short Introduction*, Oxford: Blackwell Publishing.

Dave, S. et. al. (2000) 'De-Privileging Positions: Indian Americans, South Asian Americans, and the Politics of Asian American Studies', *Journal of Asian American Studies* 3, 1: 67–100.

Dolan, J. (2014) 'Queens Man Posts Porn in Windows to Bother Immigrant Neighbors with Children', *BC13 Houston*. ABC Eyewitness News. New York City, 13 November 2014.

Dubey, A. (ed.) (2003) *Indian Diaspora: Global Identity*, Delhi: Kalinga Publications.

Firey, W. (1945) 'Sentiment and Symbolism as Ecological Variables', *American Sociological Review* 10: 140–149.

Frazier, J. (2014) 'The Race–Place Connection in Teaching Ethnic Geography', in L. Estaville, F. Akiwumi and E. Montalvo (eds.) *Teaching Ethnic Geography in the 21st Century*, pp., Washington D.C.: Washington D.C. National Council for Geographic Education.

Fredman, S. (2011) *Discrimination Law*, Clarendon Law Series, Oxford: Oxford University Press.

Gannon, M. (2013a) 'Council Approves CB 13 Zoning', *Queens Chronicle*, 3 July. www.qchron.com/editions/www.qchron.com/editions/eastern/popular-zone-change (accessed 10 July 2013).

Gannon, M. (2013b) 'Popular Zone Change Gets Closer CB 13', *Queens Chronicle*, 21 March. www.qchron.com/editions/www.qchron.com/editions/eastern/popular-zone-change (accessed 2 July 2013).

Kar, S. (1995/1996) 'Invisible Americans: An Exploration of Indo-American Quality of Life', *Amerasia Journal* 21, 3: 25–52.

Khandelwal, M. (2002) *Becoming American, Being Indian: An Immigrant Community in New York City*, Ithaca: Cornell University Press.

Lessinger, J. (1995) *From the Ganges to the Hudson. Indian Immigrants in New York City*, Upper Saddle River: N. J. Allyn and Bacon Press.

Ley, D. (2010) *Millionaire Migrants*, West Sussex: Wiley-Blackwell.

Mason, M. (2012) www.moyak.com/papers/house-size.html.

McGovern, B. and Frazier, J. (2015) 'Evolving Ethnic Settlements in Queens: Historical and Current Forces Reshaping Human Geography', *Focus on Geography* 58, 1: 11–26.

Mitra, A. (1996) 'Romantic Stereotypes: The Myth of the Asian American Khichri-Pot', in S. Maira and R. Srikanth (eds.) *Contours of the Heart: South Asians Map North America*, pp. 421–431, New York: The Asian American Writers' Workshop.

NY Times.com (2009) 'The Great Divide. Queens Ice Cream Stand at Center of Ethnic Divide', 22 February. http://www.nytimes.com/2009/02/22/nyregion/thecity/22froz.html?pagewanted=all&_r=0.

Rhoades, L. (2006) 'Housing Violations in Bellerose to be Fixed', *Queens Chronicle*, 21 December. www.qchron.com/editions/north/housing-violations (accessed 15 January 2007).

Shankar, R. (1998a) 'Foreword: South Asian identity in Asian America', in L. Shankar and R. Srikanth (eds.) *A Part, Yet Apart*, pp. ix–xv. Philadelphia: Temple University Press.

Shankar, R. (1998b) 'The Limits of (South Asian) Names and Labels: Postcolonial or Asian, American?', in L. Shankar and R. Srikanth (eds.), *A Part, Yet Apart*, pp. 49–66, Philadelphia: Temple University Press.

Skop, E. (2006) 'Asian Indians and the Construction of Community and Identity', in edited by I. M. and C. A. Airriess (eds) *Contemporary Ethnic Geographies in America*, 2nd edition, pp. 271–290, Lanham, MD: Roman and Littlefield.

Skop, E. (2012) *The Immigration and Settlement of Asian Indians in Phoenix, Arizona 1965–2011*, Lewiston: Edwin Mellon Press.

Skop, E. and C. E. Altman. (2003) 'The Invisible Immigrants: Asian Indian Settlement Patterns and Racial/Ethnic Identities', in J. W. Frazier and F. M. Margai (eds) *Multicultural Geographies of the United States*, pp. 309–316, Binghamton: Global Academic Publishing.

The Story of Queens Village, Facebook (public forum), accessed 15 March 2015, https://www.facebook.com/groups/338686916232000/

Tinker, H. (1977) *The Banyan Tree: Overseas Emigrants from India, Pakistan, and Bangladesh*, London: Oxford University Press.

Tuan, Y. (1977) *Space and Place: The Perspective of Experience*, Minneapolis: University of Minnesota Press.

Zelinsky, W. and Lee, B. (1998) 'Heterolocalism: An Alternative Model of Sociospatial Behavior of Immigrant Ethnic Communities', *International Journal of Population Geography* 4, 4: 281–298.

Chapter 4: Security, surveillance and the new landscapes of migration

Mark Gillem and Lyndsey Pruitt

Nationalism is a sentiment unifying a group of people who have a real or imagined common historical experience and a common aspiration to live together as a separate group in the future.

(Shafer, 1955: 4)

INTRODUCTION

In the small town of Joplin, Missouri an arsonist targeted a local mosque in 2012 and succeeded in completely destroying the building. At the time, a member of the Islamic Society of Joplin said that "This incident should not stop us from worshipping our God. We are going to find a place probably to continue our service to God" (Smith, Calhoun and Imam, 2012). Two years later, in July of 2014, they found that place and opened their new $2 million mosque. At the opening, Iftikhar Ali, president of Joplin's Islamic Society said, "Getting the mosque back is like getting our home back" (Fowler, 2014). Muslims immigrating to the United States have the right to build their own houses of worship, but in post 9/11 America that freedom has come under attack. As immigrating Muslims move into small towns and suburbs across the United States, they are following a model of dispersion rather than concentration, stimulating anxiety in closed communities. While the model of concentration was the norm for generations of immigrants to the United States such as the founders of Chinatown and Little Italy, the model of dispersion is becoming more commonplace. Immigrant communities are now rarely grouped together in tight-knit communities with what planner Kevin Lynch would call clear edges, nodes, and landmarks (Lynch, 1960). Rather, members of many of these communities are scattered in the sprawling suburbs of American cities. Immigrants are still drawn to certain cities, but the physical embodiment and enclave model of their nation is no longer an identifiable community. In addition to localized and visual ethnic markers, there are symbols of national reference that attract attention – the mosques and marketplaces – sites that stage cultural and religious practices. The repercussions from this model can be profound, and are not just in the form of attacks on religious symbols but also in the new state of surveillance that immigrants – especially Muslim immigrants – now endure. In fact, a federal judge ruled in 2014 that the New York Police Department's (NYPD) surveillance of mosques in order to identify "budding terrorist conspiracies" was legal (Associated Press, 2014).

The issue of security and surveillance that these and other incidents represent is a new reality for many immigrants in the twenty-first century. They are part of an ever-changing landscape of immigration that this chapter will explore. Traditional socio-spatial settings occupied by immigrants to the United States have evolved from identifiable and concentrated communities that transported and translated the architectural language of the homeland to more dispersed settings where immigrants meld into American suburbs and towns. Architectural references to the aesthetic and built-form traditions of the homeland still appear in socio-spatial organization and settings for cultural and ceremonial practices, but in localized and micro insertions, rather than in geographically bounded enclaves. But, in these new environments, architectural icons are visible landmarks of difference that are targets of surveillance and, in some cases, retribution. The chapter follows the experience of three immigrant communities to trace how the models of concentration and dispersal materialize in the urban fabric of historical and contemporary settings: Chinese immigrants in San Francisco, California; Ethiopian immigrants in Atlanta, Georgia; and Muslim immigrants in Detroit, Michigan. The chapter concludes with a cautionary note about the backlash that can result from the more recent model of dispersal in an increasingly frightened nation.

Regardless of their country of origin, immigrants have been essential actors in American urban history and their experiences are tied to a national identity of a hard-working society with members who optimistically believe their efforts will yield benefits to future generations. This shared notion both binds Americans who would otherwise have no common ground and acts as an advertisement for hopeful believers lacking economic opportunities. Yet, despite the promise of Lady Liberty, numerous challenges over the last two centuries, from the onset

Figure 4.1 Locations of the three case studies in this chapter: California, Michigan, and Georgia. Maps by authors.

of restrictive legislation to oftentimes unwelcome shifts in foreign-born population demographics, point to a parallel narrative. As immigrant communities turn
over to the next generation, realizing aspirations of economic prosperity, integration, and identity, they frequently meld into middle-class America. The shift
from a concentration to a dispersal model comes with corresponding material and
spatial aspirations of gentrification or rejection of self-imposed segregation. In the
twenty-first-century American melting pot, place-based immigrant communities
like San Diego's Little Italy, Seattle's Chinatown-International District, and even
New Orleans' French Quarter are giving way to a more dispersed network of immigrant communities.

Regarding the model of concentration, an appropriate lens to view immigrant experiences is through Rapoport's concept of cultural landscapes (Rapoport,
1992). Rapoport's basic thesis is that cultural norms as represented by, for example, religious practices, building traditions, and artistic forms take shape in the built
environment in a variety of ways that in part represent that culture to others and
set apart that culture from others. In the United States, a plethora of cases exist
that support this theory as it applies to immigrant cultures. Each is unique, yet each
contains similar elements, from hope and freedom to racism and segregation. The
concentrated districts of early immigrants represent clear cultural landscapes that
provide a sense of familiarity in an unfamiliar world.

Cultural identity is marked through differences that are continuously under
construction (Hall, 1990), such that once immigrant communities stabilize, new
generations recast their identity, and do not typically pursue such clearly delineated place-based geographies. They are just as likely to be dispersed and integrated
into the socio-spatial fabric of their host metropolises. In the second decade of
the new millennium, new generations are expressing the ability to operate under
simultaneous identities; in effect, globalization permits society *not* to choose one
ethnicity, one culture, and one identity. This fragmentation and integration con-
trasts with the patterns of previous generations of immigrant communities that at
one time imported their culture and established spatial artifacts to ground their
society and reaffirm their identity in the new place. The Chinese experience in
San Francisco is a representative example.

THE CHINESE IMMIGRANT EXPERIENCE IN SAN FRANCISCO

The year 2012 was the 150th anniversary of California's Anti-Coolie Tax, "an act
to protect free white labor against competition with Chinese Coolie labor, and
to discourage the immigration of the Chinese into the state of California" (Anti
Coolie Act, 1862). The Coolie feud sought to curtail the mass influx of Chinese
labor into America for the construction of the first transcontinental railway across
North America. The flagrant and public hostility of the people of California toward
incoming Chinese to San Francisco contributed to the growth of San Francisco's
Chinatown – thirty blocks of dense mid-rise apartments and shops on the eastern
slopes of Nob Hill.

Figure 4.2
The cacophony of signs, storefronts, and symbols energizes the bustling streets of San Francisco's Chinatown c. 2014. Photograph courtesy of Tyler Preston.

It can be argued that the intent to repatriate, combined with the hostility of the competing American workforce, motivated Chinese in the region to maintain their cultural identity through place-based geographies. For over seventy years, Chinatown supported temporary opportunity for economic advancement, mostly for Cantonese men. To support their ambition of return and to protect themselves from the onslaught of bigotry by several vehement politicians encouraging hate crimes, they sought introversion and the exclusion of an American identity (Norton, 1913: 292). Over time, Chinese immigrants relied on their community for customer loyalty to bolster their intradependent economy (Adler and Gielen, 2003: 86). As the Chinese population grew, Chinatown became robust, and the community's economic and physical security stabilized.

The resilience and autonomy of the Chinese community in San Francisco was resented among the German and Italian immigrants, as the Chinese were able to solicit work for lower wages since they were predominantly single men living in shared houses (Gyory, 1998: 221). In 1892, responding to violent outcries for border control, Congress passed the Geary Act, a precursor to the modern green card, which required Chinese legally present in America to carry a certificate of residence. Potentially of greater significance than the Chinese economic threat was the fear of identity invasion that swept across America in 1911 (Rupert, 1911). Madeline Hsu, Director of the Center for Asian-American Studies at the University of Texas, frames how the 1892 Chinese Exclusion law began a national trend of distinguishing and allotting differential rights to people on the basis of their immigration status. Further, she notes that it was a considerable turn in a country that considered itself democratic, a country that has a Constitution embedded with notions of equality for all. It was the symptom of American xenophobia:

> We have to remember at this time period that Charles Darwin had published his famous book, and many people's [fears] about racial difference were affirmed scientifically by what they understood of evolution and social Darwinism. Ideas of racial difference, competition between the species, the ideas that some species evolve and survive, whereas others were meant to go extinct, were in fact very real. When you couch this sense of competition against Chinese who were seen as fundamentally racially different, incapable of exercising citizenship on fully equal terms in an American republic ... Chinese were believed not suitable to become U.S. citizens ...
>
> (Rose, 2014)

Hsu elaborates further by describing what she terms the "yellow peril," or fear of Orientals taking over America. This imagined assault on American values was possible only because of the self-segregation of incoming Chinese so as to retain their identity; an identity that stood in stark contrast to the previous immigrants conceptualized as pioneers. The incited parochialism was expressed in the dense urban form of San Francisco's Chinatown. The multi-story shop houses with curved eaves, recessed balconies, and a distinctive oriental style were rebuilt after the 1906 earthquake (American Memory, 2003) and, in part, replicated a memory of the villages of Canton. This is not unusual in the immigrant experience, where architectural typologies, signage, parks, and streetscapes borrowed patterns from distant homelands. The growth of identifiable neighborhoods emerged out of a push–pull duality. The "pull" of a place where social networks, employment opportunities, and familiar cultural markers could be found was strong. But this pull had a dark side where ethnic divisions among seemingly similar immigrant groups were exploited for economic gain and political power. Concentrated immigrant districts provided a starting point but were yet another place of exploitation. The pull of association, for better or worse, was also augmented by the disturbing fact that immigrants were also pushed into these neighborhoods out of fear, envy, and anger (Guest, 2003). Professor of History at Indiana University Bloomington and author of *The Color of Success: Asian Americans And The Origins Of The Model Minority*, Ellen D. Wu argues, "In the broadest strokes, Chinatowns were products of extreme forms of racial segregation ... Beginning in the late 19th century and really through the 1940s and '50s, there was what we can call a regime of Asian exclusion: a web of laws and social practices and ideas designed to shut out Asians completely from American life" (Goyette, 2014). In effect, these practices and policies pushed Chinese immigrants into concentrated and spatially identifiable districts.

Since the new millennium, this pattern has changed, in part as a result of the fact that San Francisco's Chinatown is in the midst of a revitalization process. The area has undergone gentrification and is a mecca for young entrepreneurs demanding proximity to the adjacent financial district and the uniqueness the district provides (Greenberg, 2013). In 1960, two-thirds of the Chinese population in the San Francisco Bay Area resided in Chinatown (Lee, 2013). Pedestrians patronized the shops, traded with the street vendors, and socialized in these urban settings. Restaurants were open until 3 a.m. and Chinese grocers, family associations, and the four Chinese movie theaters drew people from the suburbs. As of 2010, fewer than 1% of the Chinese population in the San Francisco Bay Area live in Chinatown (from U.S. Census data, 2010 and San Francisco Planning Department, 2011). Many of them have moved to outlying suburbs and to other locations in San Francisco.

The San Francisco housing shortage of the 1980s and the 1989 earthquake greatly influenced the Chinese urban-to-suburban migration. First, new immigrants joining their families in America were able to quickly purchase a home inside Chinatown within a few years of establishing themselves (Lee, 2013). As the population increased, pressure for housing did too. Many Chinese families capitalized on the market and moved to other districts in San Francisco including Richmond, Sunset, and the Mission. Second, the earthquake of 1989 damaged the freeway leading to Chinatown and city officials had the elevated freeway demolished. While the dispersed Chinese community members were still coming to Chinatown for social support and cultural reaffirmation, they found the longer route inconvenient and some began going elsewhere (Lee, 2013).

As globalization integrated cultures and allowed for the interchange of perspectives, modernity reinforced the individual and freedom of choice. It has become commonplace in the early twenty-first century for an Indian-American to want dim-sum for lunch and for teenage boys to ask for *The Legend of Qin* boxed set for Hanukkah. Product followed the demand, and stores like Panda Express achieved over 1,653 locations in the United States as of 2014 (Darcy, 2014). Because access to culture increased across the city and access to Chinatown decreased, many of Chinatown's Chinese restaurants began shutting down (Lee, 2013). Without patrons coming from dinner, and with fewer residents, Chinese theaters were forced to close: in 2001 the last theater, the Great Star, finally shut its doors (Lee, 2013). It was not that the increasing population of Chinese-Americans no longer had a taste for Chinese dishes or entertainment; rather, the increasing homogenization of globalization made access convenient in other locales and neighborhoods grew more accepting of diversity within previously segregated suburbs.

THE ETHIOPIAN IMMIGRANT EXPERIENCE IN ATLANTA

The pattern of concentration and dispersal in America underwent little change between the early eighteenth century and the late twentieth century. One of the most recent cases did not occur until the late twentieth century. In 1980, the U.S. Congress amended the Immigration and Nationality Act by adding provision for the immigration of refugees of special humanitarian concern. Refugee immigrants have significant motivational, emotional, and nationalistic differences when compared to economic migrants, but they also reside in communities for security and economic gain, and they establish a shared identity through place-based geographies.

Similar to Vietnamese and Serbian refugee communities, Ethiopian refugees came in large numbers in the 1980s immediately after the United States changed its immigration law. Initially, the U.S. Immigration and Naturalization Service (INS) granted Ethiopians refugee status to escape the repressive political tactics of the Mariam regime, which exercised violence and religious division against opposition groups and controlled the media in order to maintain power (Clay and Holcomb, 1986). A famine had spread across Northern Africa and many Ethiopians migrated to the Khartoum region of Sudan. Most of them were unemployed and relied on remittances for support or lived in resettlement camps. For political reasons the U.S. opened its doors to refugees of Marxist Africa and many transplanted Ethiopians in Sudan chose a second resettlement in America (Haines, 1996).

Like earlier migrants, for a variety of reasons, many Ethiopians settled in one area. The major cities receiving Ethiopian refugees were Washington, D.C. (due to the large service sector), Atlanta (due to a culture of African empowerment), and New York (due to the large sector of immigrants). In Atlanta, this area was the suburb of Clarkston – a typical Southern town until the INS designated it a refugee resettlement site in the 1990s. Author Warren St. John describes the sudden change in the Southern town as exotic spices, cloaking robes, and a rainbow of children flocking to the only activity available: soccer (John, 2009). The Ethiopian Community Association promoted Ethiopian holidays and experiences to affirm cultural identity, supporting the construction of the Debra Bisrate St. Gabriel Ethiopian Orthodox Tewahdo Church in Clarkston. The significance of the Orthodox Church as one of the few yet prominent representations of Ethiopian culture supports prominent urban historian, Nezar AlSayyad's conclusion that a robust resurgence of religion is a major force in shaping contemporary life in many parts of the world. And, like the North End (Italian immigrant community) in Boston or Chinatown in San Francisco, immigrants also brought their culinary experiences to their new communities. For example, a Google search in 2015 returned nine Ethiopian restaurants/grocers in the greater Atlanta metropolitan area, of which eight were in Clarkston. Most of these restaurants have a traditional section with the *mosob* (table-plate from which all members eat).

Thirty years later, Ethiopian refugees are moving out of Clarkston. According to Sue Chovanec of World Relief Atlanta, a non-governmental organization that provides resettlement and support services, many Ethiopians are now re-establishing and integrating into the wider Atlanta community (telephone discussion). As the refugee generation ages, their children, raised and schooled as Americans, pave the way towards dispersed forms of integration, propelled through advancement in economic class. As a patriarchal culture in which generations live as a cohabitating family unit, the second generation typically stays proximate. However, opportunities for the children to have higher-earning jobs lie in downtown Atlanta, not in Clarkston. Thus, the trend is for parents to follow children, either to Atlanta or to another metropolitan city. The family unit overshadows the solidarity that was required of the Ethiopian social network immediately upon resettlement. In just two decades, the refugee community has transformed its identity from "displaced Ethiopian" to "Ethiopian-American," and a dispersed spatial model manifests this shift.

DETROIT'S LEBANESE-AMERICAN COMMUNITY

Among the many ethnic groups in the United States, controversy has surrounded the demographics of Arab-Americans because they have never been counted as a single racial group (documented predominantly as White or Asian) in demographic surveys. However, even conservative counts place the ratio of Arab-Americans in Detroit as one of the highest in the United States. Arabs began coming to Southeast Michigan in the late nineteenth century, mostly from Lebanon and Syria. Immigration increased at the start of the twentieth century with the industrial explosion of Detroit's auto industry (Cwiek, 2014). Since 2000, the United States has increased the number of special visas for Arabs and in 2000 there were an estimated 4.2 million Arab-Americans in America (Arab-American National Museum, 2015). As part of the application process, many immigrants act as "sponsors" for other family members or people they know from back home: "And so the chain migration phenomenon repeats itself, with whole families and even small towns relocating from the Middle East to Michigan" (Cwiek, 2014). As whole communities resettle in the suburbs of Detroit, they bring spatial order, networks, and artifacts of their urban geography. Some of the physical associations are remnants of political and philosophical hardships. For example, the prohibition on commercial activity in Lebanon, and the cultural freedom to own a commercial business in America, is evident in "a stereotype that Arabs own most of the gas stations and liquor stores in metropolitan Detroit. … that goes back decades and decades to the early Syrian and Lebanese immigrations" (Cwiek, 2014). Religious establishments are also prominent in the suburbs. In 2005, the Islamic Center of America opened in Dearborne, Michigan, effectively the largest mosque in the United States. The Lebanese-American community that commenced the project has operated a mosque in Dearborne since 1949 (Norris, 2005). The community of Dearborne has adopted an Arab identity: "Along Warren Avenue, the nexus of Arab Dearborn, Lebanese flags flutter everywhere. Nearly every sign is in English and Arabic. Some bear familiar names. The Shatila Bakery is named after an infamous Beirut slum" (Raz, 2006).

Analyzing the patterns of Arabs in Detroit, Ethiopians in Atlanta, and the Chinese in San Francisco shows that concentration is not the objective of immigrants to the U.S. Rather, America is appealing as the nation founded on immigrants. The intention for new immigrants includes becoming American through dispersal into American communities. The road to integration is often paved with strife, especially when cultural artifacts are politically controversial. The *Take on Hate* campaign seeks to ease this transition for both Arabs and the receiving community. Nadia Tonova, director of the National Network of Arab American Communities, the organization heading the *Take on Hate* campaign states,

> So we're looking to target very specific communities which might have changing demographics, where Arabs and Muslims may be new to the community. And start right there with the children, who can pass that on to everyone in their home.
>
> (Wells, 2014)

In Michigan, you could see everything from billboards and ads, to heritage and cultural events like movie screenings and community dinners, to teacher-training guides sent out to classrooms in communities where Arab-American families are moving.

Every immigrant community rebuilds its identity by tying cultural artifacts from its past with its new freedom as Americans. In the Ethiopian and Chinese cases tension with the existing local community was rooted in the fear of change: that the immigrant culture would influence the established community and render it un-American. Yet, the fears in Detroit regarding Arab-Americans have changed, due to memories of terrorist attacks stemming from religious fears and political tensions. In 2010, three Christian missionaries incited tensions through video-recording attempts to debate Muslims at the Arab American Festival in Dearborn. In addition to costing the community $300,000 for security, to the outrage of conservative Christian groups, the conflict became the foundation for an inhibiting increase in liability insurance for the festival organizers. Over the next three years (to the time of writing) the anti-Islamic climate has cancelled one of the largest gatherings of Arab-Americans in the United States (Brush, 2014).

In 2015 the state of affairs regarding immigration, especially from the Middle East, points to some problems with the resettlement models of immigrant communities. As dispersal becomes the norm, place-bound migrant districts are diminishing and some have slowly disappeared. The ubiquitous Chinatown and the counterpart ethnic enclaves continue, but the priority of economic class as the basis of concentration in the United States is eroding these bounded districts. Immigrant communities have moved into established suburban neighborhoods and small towns across the United States, but this does not mean that the architecture and urban settings of their neighborhoods are abandoning all cultural markers.

THE MOSQUE

Religious institutions and marketplaces that mark an immigrant culture are still being built and are still generating controversy. The concern now seems to be more about the growing fears of terrorists and the impact on "national security," and the backlash this presents to immigrants – specifically Muslim immigrant communities. The most obvious cases are the attacks against mosques since 2010 as a result of sentiment since 9/11 and the Arab Spring. As symbols and signs of a culture and a community, mosques have become targets in America's culture wars. While U.S. soldiers have been trying to help build stable democracies in the Middle East through the construction of schools, community centers, clinics, and infrastructure, some Americans back home have been damaging and destroying the most obvious symbols of those same communities in cities and towns across the United States; in fact, the arsonist of the Joplin mosque was an Iraq war veteran (Fowler, 2014).

The 2012 attack on the Joplin mosque may be the most egregious recent example, but it is not the only case of post 9/11 backlash. In 2012, six Sikh worshippers were killed in an attack in Oak Creek, Wisconsin. In the twelve days following that attack, eight other cases of violence were documented by the Arab Anti-Discrimination Committee (Huss, 2012). This is a story of blowback against Muslims in America that represents a clear and present threat to religious liberty and the ideal of the cultural melting pot. While Chalmers Johnson's series of books examining the consequences of the American Empire culminated in a powerful but notional blowback largely against American policy (Johnson, 2004), immigrant blowback is against spatial practice.

Figure 4.3
The smoldering remains of the Joplin mosque, Missouri are one unfortunate sign of the blowback that Muslim immigrants have had to face in post-9-11 America. Courtesy of Fox2Now.

In addition, this blowback is not just against established buildings. There has been blowback against proposed buildings that can support Muslim communities. The case of Park51 in New York is a good example. Muslims had a presence in Lower Manhattan for many decades prior to the 9/11 terrorist attack: "In fact, Islam in New York began near Ground Zero. One of the first Arab-American enclaves in New York City was located on Washington St. in Lower Manhattan – the very area in which the World Trade Center was later built. Founded by Arabic-speaking Christians and Muslims from Ottoman Syria in the 1880s, it was called Little Syria" (Curtis, 2010). At the time of the attacks, two mosques were located in the vicinity of the World Trade Center and several Muslim prayer rooms existed within the World Trade Center building. Originally named the Cordoba House, the development Park51 was a planned 13-story Islamic community center in Lower Manhattan proposed in 2011. Controversy surrounded the development. The developer, SoHo Properties, said the center represented, "an American dream which so many others share ... We are Americans — Muslim Americans. We are businessmen, businesswomen, lawyers, doctors, restaurant workers, cab drivers, and professionals of every walk of life, represented by the demographic and tapestry of Manhattan" (Hernandez, 2010). The opposition was firm in advertising that it was promoting transparency only as a security concern (in regard to finances). The Anti Defamation League, an influential Jewish organization, joined the fray under concerns about respect for the loss of lives. Polling of the American public at the time showed that Americans believed the proximity of the center to the site of the World Trade Center in 2001 (the attacks were on religious ground) to be in bad form (Barbaro, 2010). During this period, national media, especially news editorials, largely influenced the

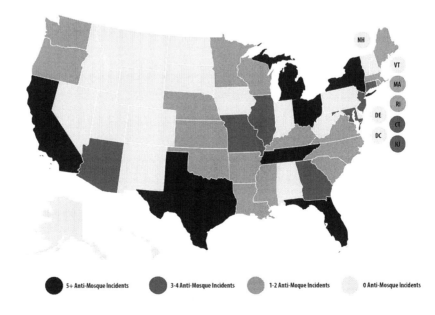

Figure 4.4
Map of attacks on mosques across the United States, 2005–2014. Map adapted from American Civil Liberties Union Nationwide Anti-Mosque Activity Map.

5+ Anti-Mosque Incidents   3-4 Anti-Mosque Incidents   1-2 Anti-Moque Incidents   0 Anti-Mosque Incidents

perspectives of Americans both collectively and individually (Griffin, 2008). Editorials carefully positioned their reporting to imply a disrespectful infiltration of opposing cultural values, rather than accounting for the fact that Muslims, like other American immigrants, had established communities, and lived in the borough of ground zero.

While overt attacks on the built symbols of Muslim immigrant communities grab the headlines, a more subtle form of blowback can be found in the surveillance practices of a nation struggling to find a way forward from the attacks of 9/11. The surveillance of New York mosques briefly discussed in the introduction is just one example. Regarding the federal court's support of the NYPD surveillance program, Baher Azmy, the Director of the Center for Constitutional Rights, argues that "by upholding N.Y.P.D.'s … Muslim surveillance practices, the court's decision gives legal sanction to the targeted discrimination of Muslims anywhere and everywhere in this country, without limitation, for no other reason than their religion" (Associated Press, 2014). The actual surveillance protocol was quite robust. According to Apuzzo and Goldstein, the police's 'Demographics Unit' created maps that identified where the targeted Muslim immigrants ate, shopped, and congregated (Apuzzo and Goldstein, 2014). This powerful role of surveillance mapping is a tactic that can be used to subjugate an entire community. But the NYPD is not alone. According to documents released by Edward Snowden, the National Security Agency (NSA) conducted surveillance on prominent Muslim Americans as part of its own data-collection efforts (Miller and Nakashima, 2013). When viewed together, these cases are another take on Foucault's interpretation of Bentham's panopticon. Bentham's concept of circular buildings for prisons, schools, and hospitals with their central observation towers is not needed for societal control when thousands of cameras track and record at will of municipal surveillance. Foucault's disciplinary society (1995) is much closer to a generic and social reality made possible by a widely available surveillance technology that has resulted in an estimated 30 million cameras lurking across the United States (Vlahos, 2009). This technology can easily target immigrants placed on a government blacklist, thereby infiltrating the urban fabric of democratic and economically advanced societies in the twenty-first century.

The United States is not above using surveillance data to further political ends. There appears to be a troubling similarity between the recent approach used by NYPD and the historic NSA Executive Order 9066, issued in 1942 by President Franklin D. Roosevelt (FDR). FDR's Executive Order authorized the internment of Japanese-Americans for reasons of national security. Japanese-Americans were located through active surveillance measures and rounded up from America's Little Tokyos and Japantowns in large numbers and then sent to what military commanders designated as "military areas" in the California interior (Robinson, 2001). It was not until President Jimmy Carter appointed the Commission on Wartime Relocation and Internment of Civilians to investigate the constitutional misuse of incarcerating U.S. citizens that the exclusion order was legally denounced, reparations were authorized, and findings were published stating that it was based on "racial prejudice, war hysteria, and a failure of political leadership" (Commission on Wartime Relocation and Internment of Civilians, 1983: 18). While an argument could be made that the model of dispersal may hamper race-based round-ups, as

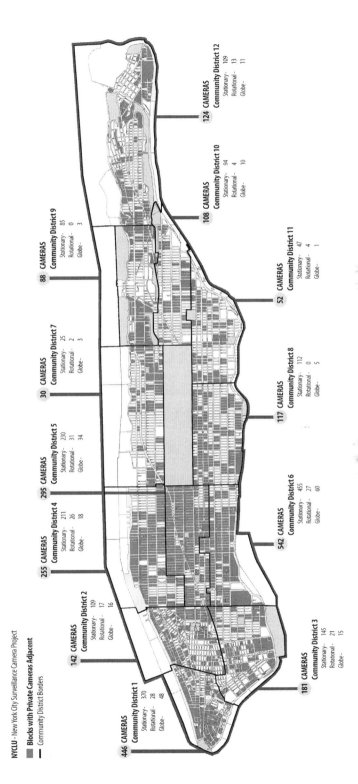

NYCLU - New York City Surveillance Camera Project

▨ **Blocks with Private Cameras Adjacent**
— Community District Borders

446 CAMERAS
Community District 1
Stationary - 370
Rotational - 28
Globe - 48

142 CAMERAS
Community District 2
Stationary - 109
Rotational - 17
Globe - 16

181 CAMERAS
Community District 3
Stationary - 145
Rotational - 21
Globe - 15

255 CAMERAS
Community District 4
Stationary - 211
Rotational - 26
Globe - 18

295 CAMERAS
Community District 5
Stationary - 230
Rotational - 31
Globe - 34

30 CAMERAS
Community District 7
Stationary - 25
Rotational - 2
Globe - 3

88 CAMERAS
Community District 9
Stationary - 85
Rotational - 0
Globe - 3

542 CAMERAS
Community District 6
Stationary - 455
Rotational - 27
Globe - 60

117 CAMERAS
Community District 8
Stationary - 112
Rotational - 0
Globe - 5

52 CAMERAS
Community District 11
Stationary - 47
Rotational - 4
Globe - 1

108 CAMERAS
Community District 10
Stationary - 94
Rotational - 4
Globe - 10

124 CAMERAS
Community District 12
Stationary - 109
Rotational - 13
Globe - 11

Figure 4.5 CCTV cameras are widespread in Manhattan and represent a new reality in the surveillance state. Map adapted from New York City Surveillance Camera Project 2014.

compared to the old model of concentration, the surveillance state, with its security cameras, drones, and wiretaps is no longer limited by a place-bound geography.

CONCLUSION

The historical model of immigrant communities in America, such as the Chinese-Americans of San Francisco's Chinatown and the Ethiopian Refugees of Atlanta, was to concentrate in selected neighborhoods and build familiar environments in unfamiliar settings. Over time, American immigrants establish and re-assimilate by economic class. Chinatowns and their counterparts, enclave place-bound geographies, are joined by dispersed models of integration. This does not mean that enclaves will disappear; rather, they may become augmented by a more dispersed network of communities located throughout a metropolitan area. As immigrant communities disperse into the broader urban fabric of cities, they construct spatial and urban settings that support their cultural patterns. Mosques and Ethiopian marketplaces, for instance, will become more widespread but will remain visible. This visibility presents its own set of issues. Mosques become targets of misplaced retribution – either blocked before construction or attacked after construction. Ethnically identifiable architecture thus exposes the attitude of "guilt-by-association" used by racist, reactionary, and radical groups and individuals to justify their attacks in this post 9/11 era of conflict that merges the local with the global.

AlSayyad (2014) argues that globalization has established a new platform for traditions. First-generation immigrants had adapted tradition so as to fit in with the host nation. A new generation, that has no actual context or experience with the homeland tradition but is longing for symbols, produce imagined traditions to define a perceived identity. The mosque is a marker of identity, as much as is the marketplace.

Immigrants, including refugees, have historically lived a diaspora experience and have tried to define themselves by reference to their distant homeland. In effect, they help to create what Benedict Anderson refers to as "imagined communities" (1983). They have attempted to reconcile differences through the creation of "cultural landscapes" (Rapoport, 1990) because they have built, occupied, or deployed urban spatial strategies to construct environments that are familiar, connected, and comfortable. They built the familiar in the enclosed district of Chinatown and the traditional *mosab* tables of Clarkston's Ethiopian restaurants. These nested communities are places where the first generations of migrants found refuge, relationships through a common identity, and hope as they embarked on new lives in the self-proclaimed "melting pot" that is demographic and ethnic diversity in America. When immigrant communities stabilize, the new generation recast their identity within the economic context of a globalized and modernized world. But this approach still engenders blowback. The dispersed icons of immigrant communities make easy targets for arsonists and vandals with little interest in tolerance or diversity. Landscapes of migration, impacted by wars of choice sold under the guise of national security and watched by a growing surveillance state, represent yet another chapter in the complicated story of America's immigrant experience.

REFERENCES

Adler, L. and Gielen, U. (2003) *Migration*, Westport: Praeger.

AlSayyad, N. (2014) *Traditions: the "Real", the Hyper, and the Virtual*, New York: Routledge.

American Memory (2003) 'San Francisco's Chinatown – Architectural Space', The Chinese in California. http://memory.loc.gov/ammem/award99/cubhtml/theme3.html (accessed 12 February 2015).

Anderson, B. (1983) *Imagined Communities: Reflections on the Origin and Spread of Nationalism*, 2006 edition, New York: Verso.

Anti Coolie Act (1862) 37th Congress of the United States (1862) Sess. II, Chap. 27; 12 Stat. 340.

Apuzzo, M. and Goldstein, J. (2014) 'New York Drops Unit That Spied on Muslims', *New York Times*, 15 April.

Arab-American National Museum (2015) 'Coming to America', Online. http://www.arabamericanmuseum.org/Coming-to-America.id.18.htm (accessed 12 February 2015).

Associated Press (2014) 'Judge Finds Surveillance of Mosques Was Allowed', *New York Times*, 20 February.

Barbaro, M. (2010) 'Debate Heats Up About Mosque Near Ground Zero', *New York Times*, 30 July.

Brush, M. (2014) 'Arab American Festival in Dearborn Cancelled Once Again,' Michigan Radio, 30 April. Online. http://michiganradio.org/post/arab-american-festival-dearborn-canceled-once-again#stream/0 (accessed 20 June 2014).

Clay, J. and Holcomb, B. (1986) *Politics and the Ethiopian famine, 1984–1985*, Cambridge, MA: Cultural Survival Inc.

Commission on Wartime Relocation and Internment of Civilians (1983) *Personal Justice Denied*, Washington DC: U.S Government Printing Office. Online. http://www.archives.gov/research/japanese-americans/justice-denied/part-2-recommendations.pdf (accessed 15 March 2015).

Curtis, E. (2010) 'Islam Has Long History Downtown: Why the 'Ground Zero Mosque' Belongs in Lower Manhattan', *Daily News*, 23 July. Online. http://www.nydailynews.com/opinion/islam-long-history-downtown-ground-zero-mosque-belongs-manhattan-article-1.202169 (accessed 22 March 2015).

Cwiek, S. (2014) 'What Explains Michigan's Large Arab American Community?' *Michigan Public Radio*. Online. http://michiganradio.org/post/what-explains-michigans-large-arab-american-community (accessed 12 February 2015).

Darcy, N. (2014) 'Panda Express', *Transcript of Panda Express*. Online. https://prezi.com/f3d1s_udzxdi/panda-experess/ (accessed 22 March 2015).

Foucault, Michel (1995) *Discipline and Punish: The Birth of the Prison*, translated by A. Sheridan, 2nd edn, New York: Random House.

Fowler, L. (2014) 'Joplin's Muslims Rejoice After Reopening of Mosque After Fire Blamed on Arsonist', Online. STLToday.com. http://www.stltoday.com/lifestyles/faith-and-values/joplin-s-muslims-rejoice-in-reopening-of-mosque-after-fire/article_9113b16b-e2e3-548b-9ec8-34ca0f8e3a63.html (accessed 15 November 2014).

Goyette, Braden (2014) 'How Racism Created America's Chinatowns', *Huffingtonpost*, Online. http://www.huffingtonpost.com/2014/11/11/american-chinatowns-history_n_6090692.html (accessed 17 November 2014).

Greenberg, I. (2013) 'I Left My Home in San Francisco: The Rise of the White, Middle-Class Anti-Gentrifiers,' *New Republic*, April 12, Online.. http://www.newrepublic.com/article/112886/san-franciscos-gentrification-problem-isnt-gentrification (accessed 20 July 2014).

Griffin, David R. (2008) 'Was America Attacked by Muslims on 9/11', Online. http://davidrayg-riffin.com/articles/was-america-attacked-by-muslims-on-911/ (accessed 12 February 2015).

Guest, K.J. (2003) *God in Chinatown: Religion and Survival in New York's Evolving Immigrant Community*, New York: NYU Press.

Gyory, A. (1998) *Closing the Gate*, Chapel Hill: University of North Carolina Press.

Haines, D.W. (ed.) (1996) *Refugees in America in the 1990s*, Westport: Greenwood Publishing Group.

Hall, S. (1990) 'Cultural Identity and Diaspora', in J. Rutherford (ed.) *Identity: Community, Culture, Difference*, London: Lawrence & Wishart.

Hernandez, J.C. (2010) 'Mosque Near Ground Zero Clears Key Hurdle', *New York Times*, Online. http://www.nytimes.com/2010/08/04/nyregion/04mosque.html?_r=0 (accessed 17 November 2014).

Huss, K. (2012) 'Attacks on US Mosques Prompt Muslim Security Concerns', *NBC News*, Online. http://usnews.nbcnews.com/_news/2012/08/17/13321512-attacks-on-us-mosques-prompt-muslim-security-concerns (accessed 12 November 2014).

John, W.S. (2009) *Outcasts United: An American Town, A Refugee Team*, New York: Random House Publishing Group.

Johnson, C. (2004) *The Sorrows of Empire: Militarism, Secrecy, and the End of the Republic*, New York: Metropolitan Books.

Lee, P. (2013) 'Reflections on the Last 50 Years of San Francisco Chinatown', *AsianWeek*, Online. http://www.asianweek.com/2013/11/04/reflections-on-the-last-50-years-of-san-francisco-chinatown/ (accessed 9 November 2014).

Lynch, K. (1960) *The Image of the City*, Cambridge: The MIT Press.

Miller, G. and Nakashima, E. (2013) '"Officials" defensess of NSA Phone Program may be Unraveling', *Washington Post*, Online. http://www.washingtonpost.com/world/national-security/officials-defenses-of-nsa-phone-program-may-be-unraveling/2013/12/19/6927d8a2-68d3-11e3-ae56-22de072140a2_story.html (accessed 18 November 2014).

Norris, M. (2005) 'Largest U.S. Mosque Opens in Michigan', *All Things Considered*, National Public Radio, 12 May. Online http://www.npr.org/templates/story/story.php?storyId=4650047 (accessed 12 February 2015).

Norton, H. (1913) *The Story of California from the Earliest Days to the Present*, Chicago: A.C. McClurg and Co.

Rapoport, A. (1990) *The Meaning of the Built Environment*, Tuscon: The University of Arizona Press.

Rapoport, A. (1992) 'On Cultural Landscapes', *Traditional Dwellings and Settlement Review* 3(2): 33–47.

Raz, G. (2006) 'Lebanese Americans are Angry and Anxious', *All Things Considered*, National Public Radio. Online http://www.npr.org/templates/story/story.php?storyId=5627457 (accessed 12 February 2015).

Robinson, G. (2001) *By Order of the President: FDR and the Internment of Japanese Americans*, Cambridge: Harvard University Press.

Rose, C. (2014) 'Episode 16: The First Illegal Aliens?', *15 Minute History*, podcast, http://15minutehistory.org/ (2 November 2014).

Rupert, G. (1911) *The Yellow Peril*, Choctaw: Union Pub. Co.

San Francisco Planning Department (2011) *San Francisco Neighbourhoods. Socio-Economic Profiles*. http://www.sf-planning.org/Modules/ShowDocument.aspx?documentid=8501 (accessed 17 November 2014).

Shafer, B. (1955) *Nationalism: Myth and Reality*. New York: Harcourt, Brace.

Smith, M., Calhoun, D. and Imam, J. (2012) 'Missouri Mosque Destroyed in Second Fire in a Month', *CNN*, Online. http://www.cnn.com/2012/08/06/us/missouri-mosque-burned/ (accessed 17 November 2014).

Vlahos, J. (2009) 'Surveillance Society: New High-Tech Cameras are Watching You', *Popular Mechanics*, Online. http://www.popularmechanics.com/technology/military/4236865 (accessed 18 November 2014).

Wells, K. (2014) 'Take on Hate Campaign Targets Anti-Arab Prejudice in Detroit', *Michigan Public Radio*, 23 June, Online. http://michiganradio.org/post/take-hate-campaign-targets-anti-arab-prejudice-detroit (accessed 12 February 2015).

Materialities of home

Chapter 5: Putting Vista Hermosa 'on the map'

Migrant boosterism in distant homelands

Sarah Lopez

Today in Mexico there exists a fierce energy. What was once difficult to realize is now being realized.

(Daniel Gutiérrez, Jalisco, Mexico 2007)[1]

Vista Hermosa in the south of Jalisco, Mexico is one pueblo among literally thousands worldwide undergoing accelerated built-environment change, due to endemic migration.[2] The story of what will be called 'the remittance landscape' (a built environment in which the flow of dollars becomes the driving force behind both visible change and social and economic processes) is a story about migrant-initiated building projects as well as the transformation of migrant and nonmigrant subjectivities.[3] The remittance landscape in Vista Hermosa is a landscape whose production speaks to the remaking of oneself and one's pueblo in an era of transnational migration. Complex financing orchestrated by individuals, groups, and the Mexican government, is supporting a new public infrastructure in this once-'provincial' town.

This chapter briefly outlines how remittances influence discourses on migration, planning, and place, using a research method that blends a material history of the built environment with place-based interviews, as well as studies of how macro policy influences local contexts. The evidence presented tells the story of Vista Hermosa's remittance boom and explores the implications for remittance spaces in rural Mexico more generally. Remittance space is a larger conceptual framework of which the remittance landscape, the physical built environment altered by dollars, is a subset. Remittance space is defined as the sum of all micro and macro processes, subjectivities, spatial practices, and the institutional and environmental changes associated with remitting as a way of life (Lopez 2015: 20). Remitting – an economic term defined as transferring money across distances – is also a fundamental social and psychological process that places hope for one's future elsewhere; to remit money to emigrant villages is to repeatedly enact hope in their vitality.

Migrants 'from below' – unskilled wage-laborers – as well as those who once occupied such jobs but have since achieved varying levels of economic success are working together to implement large-scale public building projects in their home-towns (Smith and Guarnizo, 1998: 3). Mexican gardeners, construction workers, and small business owners in the US have become de facto planners, developers, and economic boosters of rural Mexican pueblos or villages investing in hometown improvements. Migrants who maintain close ties to home and whose economic, social, and political projects are rooted in multiple places that cross national boundaries are referred to as transnational or transborder migrants. The building projects these migrants are implementing can be thought of as 'development from below', in that migrants are non-experts who (according to migrants themselves) are ushering in *progress* in the form of new amenities, better facilities, and needed infrastructure to rural places. Rather than significant institutional or governmental support, migrants rely on community resources, social networks, and extended familial ties to enact material change.[4]

Long-distance, cross-border migrant boosterism, however, raises important questions about the purported goals of transnationalism, how we think about development and planning discourses, and how we study places. While the transna-tional discourses spearheaded by sociologists and anthropologists are reminders that migration is not a unidirectional movement toward assimilation or acculturation into a singular host society (Levitt 2001; Cohen 2004; Smith 2005; Smith & Bakker 2007; Fitzgerald 2009), long-distance building projects expose persistent problems associ-ated with constructing a coherent, viable, socio-spatial life in more than one place with limited resources.[5] Under what conditions, and at what cost, can a transborder life be achieved? And what are the goals of collective transborder action? Rather than viewing the migrants in this case study as transnational migrants, we can think of them as migrants for whom migration and remitting is (has become) a way of life (Lopez 2015: 13). This distinction opens a line of inquiry into the identity and role of migrants continually investing in hometown improvements.

Migrant boosterism also complicates development and planning discourses (both academic and professional). Such discourses have been dominated by the description of 'first world' frameworks being used to lift 'third world' or devel-oping nations out of poverty, cronyism, or corruption. The World Bank relies on planning and policy experts to enact material transformation. Development and planning strategies have been critiqued as imposing societal norms from the West onto 'the Rest' (Roy 2011: 10). Responding to top-down development, new forms of expert engagement and participation with local communities harness develop-ment and planning as a social process and critique rather than a Western ideology. Even so, long-distance migrant boosterism does not fit into current models of development and participatory planning. Here, once-community members return to hometowns to realize new visions of and for the community that have been forged elsewhere – or, more precisely, forged in the spaces of migration. Thus, it is important to examine how a range of remittance projects are produced in order to see what drives migrants, when and how their own instincts to alter the hometown might be influenced by development debates and global theories, and when their beliefs and actions have their own logic. Beyond improvement or modernization, analyzing remittance landscapes allows us to view the work (cultural, social, and psychological) that building projects do.

The remittance landscape also challenges the way that architectural and urban historians study place and its constituent parts. Just as Anthony King's study of the bungalow revealed that London could not be understood without research-ing the bungalows produced (in part) by English remittance men colonizing India in the eighteenth and nineteenth centuries, US cities cannot be understood by examining the buildings and plans that shape them alone (King 1995). To under-stand US cities and migrants' roles in them, analysis of the buildings that migrants produce with US dollars but that are located in distant places is required. These buildings are invisible from US soil, yet they shape migrants' investment strategies as well as how migrants dwell in American cities.

Studying the architecture and landscape of the hometown allows us to glean the extent to which migrant spatial practices are geared toward place making in the hometown itself. By building in their places of origin migrants assert con-tinuing membership in their hometowns even while remaining physically absent from the pueblo. But, even more startling is the impact migrant building projects are having on nonmigrants who have never left the pueblo, who often express the feeling that they too have migrated. Migrants' investment in building projects positions them as primary place makers from a distance, shaping the daily lives of nonmigrant community members (as well as those of subsequent generations).

Rural Mexican place making is orchestrated in US cities, by migrant networks beyond the reach of the nongovernmental organizations, global capital from above, or public-private investment institutions that have historically driven devel-opment in the global South. It is the cosmopolitan and global reach of emigrant villages that motivates local change. The migrants' view of Vista Hermosa places the hometown on equal footing with – not as ancillary to – the host location. Rural Mexican localities are far from remote; they motivate the migrant narratives play-ing out in US urban centers, forging global connections between sites.

STUDYING THE REMITTANCE LANDSCAPE

Long-distance migrant boosterism resists categorization. Rather, the richness and complexity of such actions are revealed by empirical case studies that document what is occurring and under what conditions; such studies contribute to new theo-ries of built-environment change in these rural towns shaped by migration as a way of life. The purpose of this research has been to uncover new sites for schol-arly study, which will contribute to a re-theorization of the goals of migration itself, and the role of migrants in globalizing economies.

In keeping with George Marcus's call to follow the person, follow the thing, follow the metaphor (1998: 90–95) when conducting ethnographies in a globaliz-ing world, this study follows the flows of dollars from their sending regions to the actual built projects they finance. On the one hand, the individual narratives of people involved in the production of space contextualize migrant building projects. On the other hand, a material and institutional analysis including the form, construction, subsequent use and inhabitation of buildings, and the institutions that support their implementation, contextualizes individual stories. Blending ethnographic and architectural methods has the advantage of showing relationships between scales (local, state, transnational) and types of information (objective, material, and anecdotal), building a bridge between individual experience and macro policies and processes that influence place making. These multi-sited methods are critical because analysis of the built environment and the material world both at points of departure and at places of arrival provides a material analog, an index, that tells the hidden story of social change not told in the conscious narratives of individuals and groups. Frequently, it is the disjuncture between migrant narratives, their stated aspirations and intentions, and the resulting material form and use of a building that reveals the complexity, ambiguity, and ambivalences of remittance construction as a strategy.

In high-emigration regions in Mexico, where in 2010 remittances reached $22 billion, and where the Mexican government's *Tres Por Uno* (also referred to as both Three for One and '3×1') program quadruples migrant dollars geared toward development with matching municipal, state, and federal funds, the remittance landscape is historically layered and discernable patterns have emerged.[6] The state of Jalisco is one of four Mexican states – alongside Michoacán, Guanajuato, and Distrito Federal – with the highest rates of remittances. Almost two billion dollars of formal transactions were recorded in Jalisco in 2008 (Banco de México, 2009). While this work focuses on a public remittance project in Vista Hermosa, Jalisco, the project is contextualized in the remittance landscape at large.

To research the built environment of Vista, I traveled periodically over a span of five years from 2007 to 2012, interviewing migrants in California and Jalisco, as well as nonmigrants, professionals in development and planning, and Mexican politicians. This chapter focuses on key entrepreneurs and building motivators to better understand the aspirational nature of migrant projects. An extended examination would next address community members who have not migrated, as well as a larger group of migrants who contribute to remittance projects but do not spearhead them.

AESTHETIC AGENDAS: MEASURABLE PROGRESS

In the south of the state of Jalisco, Vista Hermosa or 'Beautiful View' is situated at the foot of the El Calaque mountain, overlooking a green carpet of sugar cane that stretches over the valley floor. Unlike some of its neighbors, the town was never an indigenous settlement; rather, industrious Europeans settled the then Santa Cruz del Cortijo, harnessing energy from its waterfall, extracting limestone and clay from its soil, and processing sugar cane, beginning in the 1620s. A large Hacienda, built adjacent to the main plaza, and a water-power plant still in operation attest to this early period. As Vista's key cement, wood, and sugar-processing factories closed, downsized, or relocated to the nearby *cabecera* (similar to a county seat) of Tamazula in the second half of the twentieth century, the town shrank and grew poorer. Its economic booms and busts are evident in the built fabric, which has been built incrementally using low-cost, locally available materials and local labor: one-story fired-brick or concrete block homes are joined in a series with shared party walls, forming continuous façades of painted, unpainted, or exposed brick, concrete, and, sometimes, adobe. These alternately richly colored and highly worn walls line hilly, partially paved roads with discontinuous sidewalks. Vista's only two-story buildings (excluding the church) abut the main plaza and are inhabited by mercantile families who have lived in Vista for generations. At 3,490 people in 2012, down from approximately 6,000 in 1980 and 14,000 in the 1970s (INEGI), the town's natural growth is occurring elsewhere, in both Mexican and US cities where individuals have relocated to find work.

The building of shared infrastructure in small Mexican towns has occurred through ongoing coordinated group efforts. Generations of men from Xocotla, a pueblo in the Mexican state of Veracruz, conducted physical labor from 1945 to 1976 to build a five-mile road that connected their mountain pueblo to the main highway below, creating pathways of mobility for the village's youth who subsequently migrated to Mexico City and beyond (Quinones 2007: 20). Finished as recently as 1995, in the pueblo of Los Guajes, Jalisco, it took locals 40 years to build a similar road connecting their pueblo to the municipality only 11.8 kilometers away, reducing a day's journey to a fifteen-minute drive. In addition to road building, ongoing community efforts have been required to erect new churches, jardíns (plazas), quiscos (gazebos), and municipal water and electricity infrastructure in pueblos. Vista Hermosa is no exception. Roads and sidewalks, water mains and sewer systems are partially completed as a variety of players invest in a patchwork of improvements. Weak and inconsistent financial support from the Mexican government has shaped these patterns. Today, migrant investors respond to this legacy by relying on incremental and communal building practices to implement built-environment change from afar.

While migrants have invested remittances in building projects in Vista for decades, today the 'fierce energy' exhibited by migrant boosters results, in part, from both grass-roots efforts and macro-policy shifts. For decades, informal Hometown Associations (HTAs), or migrant social clubs, have formed, disbanded, and re-formed in US cities. Today they are formalizing and their numbers have expanded from 570 registered clubs in 2006 to 2,474 in 2015 (Instituto de los Mexicanos en el Exterior). There are several factors that contribute to this. Migrants who came to the US in the 1960s and 1970s, many of whom are now retired, have benefited from decades of hard work during a period of steady growth for the middle class and the expansion of the welfare state. Some have become owners of thriving businesses and have the financial capacity to manage remittance investments. Migration from Mexico has greatly increased since the 1980s. An agricultural crisis in Mexico, starting in the 1960s and exacerbated during the 1980s economic recession, was followed by change in US policy. In 1986, the Immigration Reform and Control Act granted citizenship and residency to millions of undocumented Mexicans, facilitating continuous travel between home and host places. Ongoing engagement between the Mexican diaspora and Mexico's government has resulted in programs and policies ('3×1' is the program most directly influencing hometown associations) that have catapulted these clubs into a new transnational limelight. Additionally, the Catholic Church in Mexico has been involved in organizing its emigrants residing in the US since at least the 1940s (Fitzgerald 2009: 82).

Producing public remittance-funded places in migrant hometowns is a hierarchical process whereby key migrants (often defined by those who organize fundraisers in the US or donate substantial funds) make major decisions that influence the daily lives of nonmigrant villagers. For public projects, a large pool of individual migrant donations usually supports boosters' decisions. Two key players in the production of Vista's remittance landscape are Javier and Ruby Villaseñor, once undocumented migrants who now have US residency papers and who have achieved success and prosperity. Approximately 30 years after they moved to Napa to work as laborers on a vineyard, they now own their own vineyard, and launched their own California wine in 2014.[7] Another longtime migrant, Jorge Rosales – the manager of a building maintenance crew – has been a leader of Club Vista Hermosa. Since 1995, Club Vista Hermosa has consisted of a group of eight organized migrants who hold periodic fundraisers and potlucks to raise cash for long-distance projects.[8]

The success of implementing remittance projects depends upon strong relationships between migrants and those who have never left or have returned to the hometown. *Comadre* and *copadre* relationships (bonds between individuals that are formalized by the Catholic Church into familial-like ties) that carry both formal and informal duties extend across borders, cementing the relationships that bind migrant developers and boosters, and nonmigrant community members, together. In Vista, key migrants have worked closely with their *copadre*, Daniel Gutiérrez, who has managed projects on the ground on a daily basis and is heavily invested in the wellbeing and future of his pueblo. In the early 2000s, this small group created a bi-national building team performing the roles of speculator, developer, and contractor.

In Vista Hermosa, migrants' first public, collectively funded remittance projects were beautification projects, upgrades, and remodels. In 1995, migrants who formed Club Vista Hermosa initiated the remodeling of the town's main plaza. Club organizers would hold two fundraiser events each year in California, for some 300 migrants from Vista. It took seven years of what Jorge Rosales described as a 'continuous sacrifice' for migrants to save enough money to repave the plaza, install new planters, wrought-iron benches, and lampposts, plant trees, and build public bathrooms. Scaling up, the next migrant-sponsored project was to build an elegant *portico* or colonnaded walkway nearby the plaza to create a uniform aesthetic. This project required a higher level of coordination and design; building owners whose façades were adjoined to the portico had to agree to, and contribute to, the project. Without participation or donations from other migrants, the

Villaseñors built out and landscaped an intersection to 'create a European like sitting experience with a beautiful view of the whole town' and upgraded the entry into town by paving the street and adorning it with an elegant lighting system.[9]

Every migrant-sponsored project becomes a pedagogical process. And, over time, migrants experience a learning curve about how to manage and execute beautification projects that improves their level of satisfaction. While the plaza's transformation is viewed as a success, the Villaseñors noted that the three benches and two lampposts in the main plaza 'do not match'. According to Javier and Ruby, decisions were made about how to spend money that they had personally donated without their direct oversight or approval. The Villaseñors personally managed the execution of the next project, the colonnaded walkway, directing the architect hired for the job to study the colonial columns in the nearby town of Sayula, asking for a 'European, slender rather than fat', style. As a testament to the benefits of their direct involvement, the Villaseñors recall: 'Now in his portfolio he doesn't show his other columns, he only shows the Vista Hermosa ones.'[10] Their travels in both the US and Europe have cultivated an architectural sensibility that is directly influencing the aesthetics of remittance development.

FROM ORNAMENTATION TO SPATIAL TRANSFORMATION

Beyond beautification improvements, migrant boosters are experimenting with ways to bring about social, spatial, and economic transformation in the pueblo. Migrants' trajectories from organizing to beautification projects, to larger economic and socio-spatial transformations are a defining characteristic of remittance space. During a heated discussion about Vista's future that lasted for several hours, Javier Villaseñor's question: 'How do we convert a pueblo that is decaying and old

Figure 5.1
The portales in Vista Hermosa, Mexico's most elegant urban feature, have recessed lighting built into the floor, and cover up the different materials, heights, and styles of the houses behind them. Photograph by author.

into growth?', revealed his belief in Vista's future, a reconceptualization of his own role in its future, as well as the limits of remittance capital when used for ornamentation alone.[11] Economic decline and outmigration threaten the town's future, and the outcome and vitality of beautification projects. Who are these projects for if the pueblo as a whole is in a perpetual state of decline?

Boldly, Vista's migrant boosters believe, and hope, that remittances can reposition the town on the global stage. The pueblo just needs to be discovered; this logic is embedded in Javier's next question: 'How do we put Vista Hermosa on the map?'[12] Vista Hermosa, he explained, is located in a landscape that has 'natural amenities, such as a waterfall and rolling hills', and 'looks very much like Napa Valley'. Vista's migrants believe that the town's privileged geographic location near the ocean and mountains, and its natural beauty, can make it a tourist destination. The Villaseñors discussed several possible projects passionately – from converting the derelict Hacienda into a 'world-class' spa to building 'world-class' wineries. Migration has resulted in both place-awareness through comparison and self-awareness, a desire to produce and inhabit world-class spaces in hometowns and participate in the global tourism industry. But, where is the map located? While Vista's trajectory does not directly cohere with Saskia Sassen's global cities argument, urban theories and discourses about urban control nodes, and first-world elite urban centers, have – albeit indirectly – influenced how migrants think about their hometowns (1991). As Jennifer Robinson notes, promoting the idea of global cities and urban control nodes does damage by producing a 'regulating fiction' as the world's cities attempt to tailor their economies to the standards set by London, Hong Kong, and Los Angeles (Robinson 2002: 545). Migrants' confidence in the ability of first-world amenities to put Vista on the map motivates certain aspects of their decision making and influences their investment strategies. Importantly, it is not just the subjectivities of migrants that are shaped by the spaces of migration and discourses of global capitalism and tourism. By transforming the built environment, migrants influence the sensibilities of those who have never left, attempting to replace small-town provincialism with migratory cosmopolitanism.

In addition to economic duress, migrants (and nonmigrants) from Vista Hermosa are witnessing a 'hopelessness and decaying morale in the youth'. Daniel Gutiérrez explained that the youth in Vista, and men in particular, need something to occupy their time. They are 'alcoholics' and moreover 'they will have to leave and the pueblo will deteriorate'.[13] Demographically shrinking pueblos, and the visible evidence of young men (and teenagers) in the 'prime of their lives publicly drinking in the middle of a work day' inspires strong action amongst migrants. Migration scholars argue that emigration can breed hopelessness among those who remain, even while inspiring hope of a better future somewhere else – until one exits, that somewhere else is not lived daily. Migrants who once left are particularly attuned to this problem, and their remittances are invested in 'something for the people to stay here, so that they don't leave'.[14]

The material manifestation of migrants' newfound understanding of themselves as responsible for bringing social, economic, and spatial transformation to the hometown, and perception of the hometown, is the state-of-the-art sports complex. The quest for 'world-class' places in Vista influenced migrants' plans for the sports arena:

> If we do a sports center conventionally then it will be more of the same. We need to do something that grabs people's attention, so that people from outside Vista come and see how competition works, and are motivated. So the project is intended to be a first class space, First World. So that the boys feel that they are doing sports in a dignified place and feel proud of this space.[15]

Far exceeding the scope and ambition of earlier remittance projects, migrants started construction of the complex with land donated from the *cabecera*. Migrants have taken pride in the fact that they built dedicated courts and fields for different sports. Gutiérrez explained, 'rather than overlapping uses [characteristic of spaces of play in Vista], we have seven games so we will have seven courts'.[16] The first phase, completed in 2007, includes multiple courts for basketball, tennis, and volleyball, and monumental poured-in-place concrete stairs that serve as bleachers. While the project is currently much larger than any other public facility in the town (including the plaza), sponsors still imagine adding a gymnasium, sand volleyball court, indoor and outdoor soccer field, picnic area, bath and locker rooms, and outdoor café. The completed sections are comprised of expensive finishes and flooring,

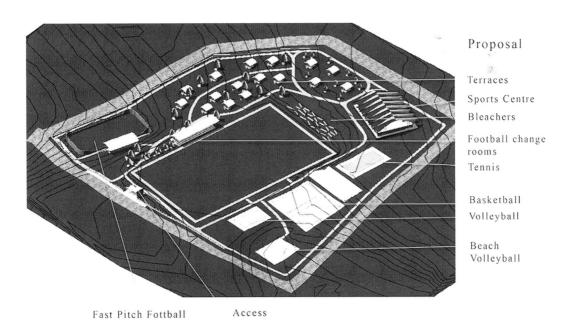

Proposal

Terraces

Sports Centre

Bleachers

Football change rooms

Tennis

Basketball

Volleyball

Beach Volleyball

Fast Pitch Fottball   Access

Figure 5.2 Architect's rendering of sports complex in Vista Hermosa. By 2007, the volleyball, basketball and tennis courts were finished. In 2015, construction began on the smaller *cancha de fulbol* (soccer field). A multi-purpose indoor gymnasium, outdoor seating, retaining walls, bleachers, bathrooms, locker rooms, and sand-volleyball court envisioned in the architect's plan await future investment. Image courtesy of Dante Lepe Gallardo.

Figure 5.3
State of the art
basketball courts in
Vista Hermosa and
productive sugar
cane valley below.
Photograph by author.

including basketball hoops that can be height-adjusted for different age groups. The arena is built for a growing future that some locals have trouble imagining.

The complex is intended to ignite economic development by attracting a regional or even national audience for competitive sports. Gutiérrez hopes the complex will be used for tournaments, and that '500 to 800 people will come visit each weekend'. The project sponsors found inspiration from other sports complexes in the universities of Monterrey and Guadalajara (Mexico's second- and third-largest cities). Gutiérrez thought: 'if they have one, why not our pueblo?'[17] Furthermore, running and managing the facilities will create local jobs, and the center could be rented to professional teams to generate revenue for the town. With endless possibilities, migrants imagine several ways in which the center could generate resources that will minimize the town's dependency on remittances.

In addition to attracting revenue, Vista's sports complex is intended to have a direct impact on the social and moral fabric of the town. A common sport in the region is bull-riding or the *jaripeo*. Gutiérrez notes that bull-riding breeds a drinking culture, as the challenge is to test men's strength and bravado, not their capacity to work in teams. Through building facilities for competitive sports, migrants hope to provide opportunities for young men and boys to better themselves, learn versatile skills and a work ethic, and to place them at the center of a new regional sporting culture.

Migrants conceive every aspect of the sports complex as demonstrative of the values that can save the town from its social and moral decline. Envisioned as Vista's first pay-to-participate space, each visit to the arena would cost a modest two to five pesos. The money would be used for maintenance, and is intended to instill a sense of ownership in users. While minimal, this payment represented a radical break from common spatial practices of the hometown. In pueblos, shared spaces are not commonly controlled with entry fees, curfews, or prohibited activities. Beyond the plaza, and possible rodeo arena or pool hall, built civic and public gathering places are rare; there is no theatre, library, or public playground, and the town's commercial spaces are limited to a few familial restaurants, taco stands, and corner stores. In this context, the sports complex cultivates knowledge about exclusive public venues.

As spectacular as the complex seems when put in the context of a town with surprisingly few public amenities, the sports complex is just one example of many large-scale remittance projects throughout Jalisco designed to transform local economies as well as social and cultural behaviors. In the nearby pueblo of Lagunillas, a rodeo arena intended to be an economic engine was built to seat over 2,000 people in a town populated by fewer than a thousand. Still, that is modest when compared to the 400-person village of San Miguel de Hidalgo, less than an hour away, whose arena boasts seating for some 7,000 (Lopez 2015: ch. 3). Rodeo-arena building is in part inspired by places like the Pico-Rivera sports arena in Los Angeles, where migrant clubs have organized formal mega-rodeo events to raise thousands of dollars for projects in Mexico.

ASPIRATIONAL PROJECTS, AMBIVALENT OUTCOMES

Despite the best intentions, the partially completed sports complex has failed to materialize as a force for change in Vista, or even as a useful amenity for the town. Since the first construction phase ended in 2007, the sports complex (which became a '3×1' project in 2004) has been unmaintained and unused. Until migrants began building the soccer field in 2015, it was deemed a failure by local politicians and governmental officials working with the '3×1' program. This has been a tremendous disappointment for migrants who have invested untold hours organizing, working overtime, and traveling to Vista, not to mention the thousands of dollars some have personally donated. By 2012, severe deterioration marked the complex, which is built on the side of a large hill. Time is also exposing defects in the design and construction of facilities, as court foundations have shifted; substantial cracking already mars the monumental concrete stairways that connect the various courts. Water and sand have damaged the surfaces of the courts themselves, and scratched and cracked the fiberglass backboards of the basketball hoops. Unfortunately, the damage is not attributed to heavy use. Rather, the abandoned mega-project is a daily reminder to villagers of the hubris and disappointments associated with remittance promises.

Completing remittance projects is difficult in the absence of a clear hierarchy or system for incorporating migrants and their dollars into local building processes. In the case of Vista, migrants blame the project's failure on the local municipality, which they believe should give them more funds to complete it. Municipal officials

Figure 5.4
Top: Tennis court,
unused since
2007. Lower: The
monumental stairs
connecting the tennis
courts to basketball
courts have cracked
as the leveled ground
beyond is poised
for construction.
Photographs by
author.

have voiced their frustration at migrants for not always producing their portion of
the budget in a timely manner. According to an official government document of
the '3×1' program's spending over time, migrants have paid their portion of the
project cost. The main records of all '3×1' projects do not expose any tensions or
failed payments for the parties involved. Nonetheless, rumors persist, and although
Rosales estimates that more than $200,000 have been spent by migrants and
the Mexican government on the sports complex alone, $300,000 more will be
required to finish the project.

Longstanding relationships between small towns and their *cabecera* are undergoing a painful restructuring. Small towns have been dependent on *cabeceras* for all public funds and improvements. The flow of migrant remittances to small pueblos has in some ways inverted this relationship. Now, the *cabeceras* depend on migrant remittances. In 2008, the ex-municipal president of Vista's *cabecera*, Tamazula, defined remittances as 'indispensable', and he warned that it would be 'deadly' if migrants stopped sending them. This is a dangerous, unstable condition, since migrant remittances are inconsistent, often tethered to the unpredictability of diasporic familial life. Now more than ever, the government's role in the maintenance and growth of the pueblo is needed to create robust alternatives to emigration, as well as continuity and dependability for the people of the pueblo.

Migrant intervention into local building processes is also changing the order of state development; that is, how projects happen and for whom. Gutiérrez notes that the sports complex has angered residents of Tamazula. Government officials in Tamazula (with a population of almost 38,000) are upset that it was not built there, asking why Vista should get such a large complex as well as a portion of the public budget. While the *cabecera* president in 2008 did not voice any objection to the sports project ('the idea is that the people of Vista will play sports, if it attracts others, great') he was not eager to invest municipal funds and remained uncertain of the project's capacity to attract a regional audience.[18] Disagreements result from the fact that remittances direct government funds to places where they have not historically gone.

Both migrants and local politicians have failed to perceive the ways in which building remittance landscapes in the context of a remittance space that encapsulates all of rural Jalisco changes the meaning and stakes of their projects as they unfold. While Vista builds the sports complex, other groups of migrants from other towns are strategizing ways to put their town on the map too. Rather than generating new revenue, competition between towns is oriented toward attracting migrant dollars for investment and thus, paradoxically, it is the continuing emigration of young people that becomes a possible strategy for the town's future economic growth. In Lagunillas, Ejutla, and San Miguel new migrant-sponsored rodeo arenas compete to attract audiences whose spending power is often tied to dollars earned abroad. Rather than a sign of hope, building arenas might be a race to the bottom as migrant boosters fight for limited audiences and their dollars.

The spaces of migration also produce local disparities and differences that result in jealousy and personal conflict for migrants, and between migrants and nonmigrants. According to Ruby Villaseñor, 'Our pueblo is divided. The people in the hometown see us as "*los nortenos*."' She explained: 'a woman worked with Club Vista Hermosa in California but she quit, she can't handle it anymore', *it* being the 'animosity' that grows from misunderstandings between people who live at either end of the migration stream.[19] Her relationships with townspeople are defined by their acknowledgement of her benevolent role, but often expressed acerbically: 'there comes the *vieja loca* (crazy old lady). She's gonna do it for us. She's gonna clean the streets.' Rather than thanking the Villaseñors for their investments and consistent efforts, Ruby notes: 'People [locals in Vista] are saying the town is not worth it.'[20]

In light of this communal reception, the Villaseñors must work at maintaining a flexible narrative to explain why they keep investing dollars in Vista. In addition to their investments in public infrastructure, they built an opulent four-story house – where their US-born children want to 'bring friends' to enjoy the private movie theater, bathtub jacuzzi, and game room floor – and view it as 'a gift to the town'. Javier explains, 'my philosophy of life is that you have to have a vision, you have to be seventy years ahead of your time, to see the future. We are not building for the present but for the future, like the owners of the hacienda. They came and built the hacienda in the middle of nothing, they imagined a future, and now

Figure 5.5
A remittance house in Vista Hermosa towers over the one-story and two-story adjacent buildings. The wrought iron fence, drive-in garage, and new concrete electrical pole erected next to the old wooden one bring security, convenience, and powerful electricity to this eclectic-European style façade. Photograph by author.

the hacienda is the most beautiful building in town. The house is out of love, not an investment. If we wanted to invest, we would take our money elsewhere.'[21] Here, Javier creates a false dichotomy between love and financial interest, but his motivations involve his love and gratitude for the pueblo, on the one hand, and his need for its continued existence and stable meaning, on the other. Javier builds out of necessity, it is through his ongoing relationship with the pueblo that he understands his place in the world, and it is in the pueblo where he feels at home. This sentiment is echoed by Ruby: 'the hometown, that is where I feel important, that is where people know me'.[22] Their extravagant home, the plaza, the portico, the sports complex, and more, are products of thirty years of maintained distance from the place where one feels important, and where one feels known.

The current state of remittance-financed projects in Vista Hermosa illustrates the ambivalent outcomes common to remittance landscapes throughout rural Mexico. On the one hand, migrants' changing fortunes allow them to envision and implement change in hometowns: this change can empower local people to improve their everyday environments and future prospects. On the other hand, unintended consequences, many of which result directly from the distance inherent to migration itself, call into question the narrative of independence and self-improvement.

Individual and collective remitting is motivated by several complex factors. Migrants witness the unraveling of their town's social and moral fabric as depopulation contributes to a real sense of hopelessness among the population's youth. Remitters are faced with new challenges to achieving upward mobility in the US as ladders from service-sector and menial labor jobs to managerial positions disappear and the gap between the rich and the poor in the US rapidly grows. Migrants are also aware of the Mexican government's continued disinterest in rural populations in Mexico, and the US government's continued inability to reach consensus about immigrant rights. All of these factors contribute to the extent to which migrants feel that remitting is not a choice but a necessity.

Migrants investing in building projects are driven by a repositioning of oneself and one's town vis-à-vis the spaces of migration. For Javier and Ruby Villaseñor, who went from rags to riches and have 'traveled to Europe several times', it is their personal transformation that allows them to perceive their pueblo as 'off the map'. Javier and Ruby are building to keep their own hope alive for a future that they can imagine, and in the meantime they are creating spaces that challenge some nonmigrants' normative understandings of the pueblo, of economic disparity, and the social relations that define it.

Beyond migrants' subjective transformation, one of the most important findings from this view into Vista's remittance landscape is the way in which the landscape is changing the personal horizons of Vista's nonmigrants. Gutiérrez remarks, 'They [the Villaseñors] have affected the way I think about what is possible for Vista Hermosa. I see how they do things, like their house, and learn about what is possible.'[23] After working with migrants to build several remittance-funded projects, Gutiérrez embarked on his own peso-investment in a grocery store modeled – according to him – on supermarkets in the US.

Vista Hermosa's built environment, from Gutiérrez's store to the sports complex, reveals that Vista is currently at a tipping point. The space of migration increasingly displaces bounded geographical context as a driver of spatial production, and its interpretation and use. The pushback of existing social worlds and material conditions against this new logic of place making defines the remittance landscape.

Migrant (and now increasingly nonmigrant) aspirations to put Vista on the map are aspirations to reposition the town vis-à-vis the global economy. Migrants seek to generate global capital – tourist dollars and foreign investment – from their pueblo, which they currently see as geographically and economically separate from global networks of power and wealth. However, the complex transnational economies that support pueblos make them global places, and reposition these towns in relation to the global economy in important and unusual ways. Migrants, whose aspirations are forged in multiple locations, are building for a global audience. Their confidence in the ability of first-world amenities to put Vista on the map motivates certain aspects of their decision making. Extra money is spent to make things that can compare to the world's powerful and elite centers, at the expense of other possible uses for limited funds, as the solution to reversing a town's fate is understood to be a formal one. Building first-world places, however, will not reverse Vista's economic decline. Rather, they are strong symbols of the promise of migration that breeds future migratory ambitions, while simultaneously being emblematic of the shortcomings of migrants' capacities alone to rewrite the fate of historically neglected places and peoples.

ACKNOWLEDGEMENT

Throughout this piece, pseudonyms are used; real names are used for public figures, including Federation of Jalisco presidents.

NOTES

1 Daniel Gutiérrez, interview by author, Jalisco, 2007.
2 Mexico is the fourth-largest remittance-receiving country after China, India, and the Philippines, but the U.S.–Mexico migration corridor is the largest in the world.
3 Remittances are defined by the World Bank as the portion of international migrant workers' earnings that is sent back to family members in their countries of origin. For up-to-date information on remittance flows see Migration Policy Institute (2010).
4 The Mexican government does financially support migrants through '3×1'. However, the program has reached only a small percentage of migrants who remit.
5 Multi-sited methods to study migration have their roots in a five-volume study by W. I. Thomas and Florian Znaniecki, entitled *The Polish Peasant in Europe and America: Monograph of an Immigrant Group*, where research took place in migrant host and home lands (Thomas & Znaniecki, 1920).
6 The government formalized the '3×1' program in 2001. From 2002 to 2009, the federal government increased its annual spending on the program from approximately $15 million to $50 million. See SEDESOL (2010, 52).
7 The success of the Villaseñors reflects a regional trend in Napa. See Patricia Leigh Brown, 'Latino Winemakers Rise in California, Through the Ranks', *New York Times* (Brown, 2013).

8 Club Vista Hermosa entered the Federation of Jaliscienses in 2005.
9 Javier Villaseñor, interview by author, California, 2007.
10 Ibid.
11 Ibid.
12 Ibid.
13 Gutiérrez, interview by author, Jalisco, 2010.
14 R. Villaseñor, interview by author, California, 2007.
15 Gutiérrez, interview by author, Jalisco, 2010.
16 Ibid.
17 Ibid.
18 Municipal president of Tamazula, interview by author, Jalisco, 2008.
19 Ruby Villaseñor, interview by author, Jalisco, 2007.
20 Ruby Villaseñor, interview by author, California, 2007.
21 Javier Villaseñor, interview by author, California, 2007.
22 Ruby Villaseñor, interview by author, California, 2007.
23 Gutiérrez, interview by author, Jalisco, 2008.

INTERVIEWS

Gutiérrez, Daniel (2008), interview by author, Jalisco.
Gutiérrez, Daniel (2010), interview by author, Jalisco.
Municipal President of Tamazula (2008), interview by author, Jalisco.
Rosales, Jorge (2014), interview by author, California.
Suarez, Sergio (2012), interview by author, Jalisco.
Villaseñor, Javier (2007), interview by author, California.
Villaseñor, Ruby (2007), interview by author, California.
Villaseñor, Ruby (2007), interview by author, Jalisco.

REFERENCES

Banco de México (2009) 'Las remesas familiares en 2008', 27 January, www.banxico.org.
    mx/documents/%7BB7CBCFAF-AB7D-BE65-F78F-6827D524C418%7D.pdf (accessed
    16 November 2013).
Brown, P. L. (2013) 'Latino Winemakers Rise in California, Through the Ranks', *New York
    Times*, 9 September.
Cohen, J. (2004) *The Culture of Migration in Southern Mexico*, Austin: University of Texas
    Press.
Fitzgerald, D. (2009) *Nation of Emigrants: How Mexico Manages Its Migration*, Berkeley:
    University of California Press.
INEGI http://www.inegi.org.mx
Instituto de los Mexicanos en el Exterior http://www.ime.gob.mx/directorioorganizaciones/
    (accessed 9 March 2015).
King, A. D. (1995) *The Bungalow: The Production of Global Culture*, Oxford: Oxford University
    Press.
Levitt, P. (2001) *The Transnational Villagers*, Berkeley: University of California Press.
Lopez, S. L. (2015) *The Remittance Landscape: The Spaces of Migration in Rural Mexico and
    Urban USA*, Chicago: University of Chicago Press.
Marcus, G. (1998) *Ethnography Through Thick and Thin*, Princeton: Princeton University
    Press.
Migration Policy Institute (2010) 'Global Remittances Guide', http://www.migrationpolicy.
    org/programs/data-hub/global-remittances-guide. (9 March 2015).

Quinones, S. (2007) *Antonio's Gun and Delfino's Dream: True Tales of Mexican Migration*, Albuquerque, NM: University of New Mexico Press.

Robinson, J. 'Global and World Cities: A View from off the Map', *International Journal of Urban and Regional Research* 23, 3: 531–554, 546.

Roy, A. (2011) 'Urbanisms, Worlding Practices and Theory of Planning', *Planning Theory* 10, 1: 6–15.

Sassen, S. (1991) *The Global City: New York, London, Tokyo*, Princeton: Princeton University Press.

SEDESOL (2010) *Cuarto informe trimestral de SEDESOL, 2009*, January 52, Online. www.sedesol. gob.mx/archivos/110/file/Cuarto_Informe_Trimestral_2009.pdf (16 November 2013).

Smith, M. P. & Bakker, M. (2007) *Citizenship Across Borders: The Political Transnationalism of El Migrante*, Ithaca, NY: Cornell University Press.

Smith, M. P & Guarnizo, L. (1998) *Transnationalism from Below*, New Brunswick: Transaction Publishers.

Smith, R. C. (2005) *Mexican New York: Transnational Lives of New Migrants*, Berkeley: University of California Press,.

Thomas W. I. & Znaniecki, F. (1920) *The Polish Peasant in Europe and America: Monograph of an Immigrant Group*, Boston: The Gorham Press.

Chapter 6: *Arquitectura de remesas*

'Demonstration effect' in Latin American popular architecture

Christien Klaufus

Rapid urbanization is one of the consequences of cultural and economic globalization. In Latin America, not only metropolises but also smaller cities have become part of global networks. The subsequent change in consumption patterns is visible in the landscape. This chapter addresses landscape transformations in the urban periphery by focusing on a trend in the architecture of houses related to transnational migration and remittances that started to appear in the 1990s. The trend is known under different names in different places, but in this chapter it will be referred to as *arquitectura de remesas*, remittance architecture. Remittance architecture is conceptualized as a 'spectacular cultural performance, a means for people ordinarily excluded from the political, economic, and social mainstreams of [Latin American] society to force themselves […] onto the public eye' (Goldstein 2004: 3).

Based on three complementary ethnographic case studies, the chapter discusses the values of architectural representation, the spread of remittance architecture and the concomitant social transformations. The first case study is based on research conducted between 2001 and 2013 in Cuenca (Ecuador), where a massive outflow of labor migrants resulted in a local construction boom and new architectural expressions due to remittance financing. Second, research conducted in 2008 in Quetzaltenango (Guatemala) showed similar forms of urban growth due to the impact of remittances (Klaufus 2010). The third example describes metropolitan Huancayo (Peru) based on fieldwork in 2011–13. The chapter aims to show that, although at first glance remittance architecture seems to be a localized hybridization of cultural repertoires established by individual agents, similar patterns are guiding the process across the region.

Since the 1960s Latin American urban studies have addressed the aspirations of the urban poor, their vulnerability and limited opportunities as self-builders. John Turner (1968) sketched an optimistic scenario for the consolidation of informal settlements but longitudinal studies highlight that their improved housing situation has not led to access to education, and high levels of unemployment and violence continue (Moser 2009; Perlman 2010). Transnational migration has taken on massive forms in Latin America between the late 1990s and 2013 and has been called a parallel political economy (Moser 2009). This chapter regards remittance architecture as a material and visible act, but also a cultural act. Older forms of 'bottom-up urbanism' in Latin America such as the 'organic' human-based urban growth have contributed in innovative ways. Remittance architecture highlights the mechanism through which groups challenge the cultural models of the old oligarchy and claim their right to the city as a self-conscious new (lower) middle class.

The first generations of migrants immediately started investing foreign currency in their hometowns, especially in new housing and the improvement of existing homes. The first boom of newly built houses developed into a catalyst for more construction activities, which gradually resulted in a densification of the built environment in peri-urban areas (UN-Habitat 2012). As an informal social movement, remittance architecture helped transnational families to claim citizenship, but also created new challenges for urban planning. The rise in self-help house building aesthetically challenged the dominant architectural models. Consequently, discussions on urbanism predominantly focused on aesthetics and not on compliance with regulations on zoning or density. Tensions primarily arose not over compliance – after all, Latin American elites had often managed to circumvent those regulations themselves – but over the power of architectural design in those changing landscapes.

The concept of 'demonstration effect' is used to analyze non-verbal communication through architecture and its geographical distribution. The analytic focus will be on the forms and symbolic values of houses to point out what remittance architecture means to different groups. According to local authorities and professionals, for example, it involves a loss of valuable rural landscapes and communal traditions. According to residents involved in the construction of their houses, it signals individual socio-economic success, whether or not this success is real. First, the academic debate on popular and vernacular architecture will briefly be summarized.

ARCHITECTURE AS A SOCIAL MEDIUM

In social sciences, architecture is both a medium (process) and an outcome (artifact) of social relations. In other words, built forms are instilled with meanings that can influence people's experiences and behavior in space. Two analytic approaches have long dominated the social-scientific studies of architecture: North American culturalists and French structuralists regarded architecture primarily as a *model of* social life (Fernandez 1974; 1992; Csikszentmihalyi and Rochberg-Halton 1981; Chambers and Low 1989; Carsten and Hugh-Jones 1995), whereas functionalists regarded it as a *model that shapes* behavior (e.g., Jacobs 1961). But architectural forms cannot be read passively as society, nor can human behavior be steered directly by built forms. Relationships between forms, meanings and human behavior have since been acknowledged as being complex and multiple (Parker Pearson and Richards 1994).

Moreover, architectural artifacts are constructed within stratified societies. 'Architecture' refers to an academic discipline or canon in which historical knowledge about building techniques and aesthetic preferences influence spatial design (Norberg-Schulz 1980; Frampton 2002); or to culturally embedded traditions of building and inhabiting (Rapoport 1969; 1988; Oliver 1975; 2003). The dichotomy between high-brow and popular architecture used implicitly in most societies is *not* based on the distinction between planned and unplanned buildings, or between formal and informal construction processes, but between academic and non-academic design traditions (Glassie 2000; Klaufus 2012a). Remittance architecture responds to the architecture valued by academically trained local architects, and its non-verbal message of noncon-formity contributes to the social impact of the architectural idiom.

DEMONSTRATION EFFECT

The producers of architectural design of Latin American urban peripheries are self-builders from lower social strata and people considered to be part of a new middle class who can afford to hire professional expertise. Dissecting the individual act of demonstration, and in the context of social status hierarchies, Fisher (2004) came up with a trajectory of three different behavioral stages: first an individual observes the behavior of a higher-status person and then weighs this information against the existing situation. The person then decides if it is useful and possible to copy that behavior and, finally, he or she acts upon that decision (Fisher 2004).

The term 'demonstration effect' is attributed to the economist Nurkse, who based his assumptions on Veblen's theory of 'conspicuous consumption' and stated in the 1950s that exposure of the poor to 'modern products' would lead to imitation behavior (James 1987). Qualities of successful products worth copy-ing are: visibility, superfluousness (Veblen, 1953 [1899]: 73) and adaptability (James 1987; Pezo 2009). In political science, 'demonstration effect' refers to the effect of political mobilizations across various spaces or countries (Horowitz 1985: 279). In tourism studies, the notion describes acculturation processes induced by contacts between Western tourists and receiving populations in developing countries (Fisher 2004). In housing studies the term is used to inter-pret how imitation in house design influences social stratification (Turner 1968; Georges 1979: 209; Holston 1991; Walmsley 2001). This last approach is the one used in this chapter.

Holston (1991) agreed that self-help housing demonstrates awareness among self-builders of the social prestige that design can generate: 'informed quotation and combination' of architectural forms in house building (Holston 1991: 460). This resembles the Western concept of the 'housing ladder' as the stratification of house types within a given society (Husock 1996). People who want to climb the social ladder attempt to climb the housing ladder by relocating or improving their houses (Klaufus 2012b). In both concepts, gaining power of self-representation and access to the symbolic capital of architecture are processes that can alter a society's social stratification.

This process can theoretically follow three possible scenarios. First, the copier can make an exact imitation of the appreciated original. In the Latin American urban periphery, this is usually not an option; residents are expected to add a personal twist to the design (Holston 1991; Klaufus 2012a; Klaufus 2012b). Second, the copier can also make an inexact imitation, either deliberately or accidentally. In informal settlements where individuality counts, color schemes in the façades are indeed deliberate inexact copies. People search for an example that they like and change the color scheme, by reversing foreground and background colors for instance. Accidental inexact imitations occur if the necessary products are not available. For example, a pastoral worker in Cuenca noted some years ago that a migrated member of his parish, living in the United States, had sent home a picture of the Sydney Opera House, requesting his wife to copy the design for their new home. The design was seen as a toolbox of forms to be copied and adapted for local living. It would never become an exact copy. A third process occurs when it is financially or technically impossible to copy altogether. In that case, people try to reach the same result by other means. For example, one Cuencan family, who could not afford to remodel their house, tried to achieve a cosmopolitan image of an international lifestyle by encouraging their son to use the internet, Facebook and learn French. In academic literature, this scenario is called 'social learning' (Fisher 2004).

Once people start imitating examples and adapt them to their own situation, a chain is set in motion. A house is copied, each neighbor non-verbally commenting upon the results of the others. Certain architectural designs are copied more often and become more successful. Individual acts of demonstration repeat, and a collective behavior, or an informal social movement, evolves, transforming the socio-spatial environments on a larger scale. Below, three case studies are presented to analyze the demonstration effect of remittance architecture in different parts of Latin America.

THREE CITIES, SIMILAR TENDENCIES

Cuenca, Ecuador's third-largest city, with 330,000 inhabitants, is situated in the southern highlands (INEC 2011: 7). Popular architecture started to attract attention at the start of the twenty-first century when transnational migrants began to invest massively in house building in the urban periphery. For most of the twentieth century, residents in the Latin American urban periphery relied on self-help housing. In Cuenca, self-built houses were small and usually made of adobe blocks and wood, with tiled roofs. They consisted of multifunctional spaces organized around the storage of products. Farming and the manufacturing of so-called Panama hats were important livelihoods. When the Panama-hat trade stagnated halfway through the twentieth century, small traders started to use their transnational trade connections to migrate. At the end of the twentieth century, when Ecuador faced a deep political and economic crisis, transnational migration numbers suddenly rose in an unprecedented way (Jokisch and Pribilsky 2002). Along with the outflow of people, money sent home by transnational migrants in the US and Europe entered the country, especially the Cuenca region.

Generally, the majority of remittances are spent on daily needs. In Cuenca approximately 5 percent is spent on house remodeling or the acquisition of land or a new house (Bendixen and Associates 2003). Notwithstanding the relatively small percentage of those investments, the effect is enormous, as remodeled houses communicate success, whether or not this is actually true. The myth of success is one of the main pillars in the daily lives of transnational migrants: 'Although not all migrants met with success abroad and were able to send back large remittances or return with sizeable savings, those who did presented young villagers with powerful images of possible success and markers of status that were hard to ignore' (Pribilsky 2007: 127). Regardless of setbacks, transnational families try to 'keep up appearances' and housing plays a central role in that story.

The myth of success is especially important to families in the urban periphery. As residents of informal settlements or villages, they often suffer from marginalization or ethnic discrimination (Miles 1997; Kyle 2000). A (fabricated) successful migration journey through a well-designed house communicates a move out of poverty. Remarkably, many migrant houses are not even in use. They stand empty, since all residents have migrated abroad. Yet, the power of architecture as non-verbal communication is reinforced: the houses serve as examples to be copied, spreading the message of success whether or not the houses are occupied.

In Cuenca's periphery, a new architectural idiom began to appear in the late 1990s (Klaufus 2006). The houses of migrants seem to avoid any association with the aesthetic patterns of elite urban housing or rural vernacular and show rather a non-conformist and hybrid language, in which all sorts of contemporary elements are combined. Houses of transnational families are considerably larger than other

Figure 6.1
Family building with neo-classical elements in Checa, near Cuenca, 2011. Photographs by author.

Figure 6.2
Migrant house in
Chiquintad, near
Cuenca, 2011.
Photographs by
author.

houses, and have roofs with various slopes, rims and roof openings. Ground-floor openings are closed off with roll bars to protect the acquired consumer goods against intruders, and neighbors look after empty houses. Many houses in villages with high migration rates stand empty, and streets often acquire a rather inhospitable appearance. New industrial materials, such as colored and glued windowpanes without frames, are widespread and demonstrate the homeowner's familiarity with the latest technological possibilities and a cosmopolitan sense of modernity (Pribilsky 2007: 116). Neo-classical elements such as columns, frontons, cornices and rims on façades are used in non-constructive ways for decoration purposes (Figures 6.1 and 6.2). Professional architects associate these elements with the US and regard them as foreign house types unsuitable for Cuenca. Arched window frames with grille patterns are also popular. The color of the façade changes continuously. The latest trends were soft green and salmon pink. The cultural elite, who once had a monopoly over architectural representations, oppose the increase in large houses with bright color schemes, and regard them as a visual deterioration of the landscape (Klaufus 2006).

Transnational families in Cuenca combine a livelihood based on remittances with agricultural or manufacturing activities. This influences the use of domestic space – the rooftops of such villas can be used to store or dry produce. That combination of old and new habits is scorned in the city, where a myth circulates about a migrant house used in the 'wrong way'. The house in the story has five floors and an elevator. The elevator is used as a stall for guinea pigs or to transport the pigs to the roof. Obviously, the story is told to ridicule migrant families from the periphery who aspire to a cosmopolitan lifestyle but do not use modern equipment in a 'proper' way. As will be described below, similar stories are told in Huancayo, but with different interpretations.

The second case involves Quetzaltenango, the second-largest city in Guatemala. It is situated in the central highlands and counts approximately 150,000 inhabitants (Arriola Quan and Escobar 2011: 4). The larger metropolitan area 'de Los Altos' counted 240,000 urban and 107,000 rural residents in 2002, but the urban areas have expanded considerably during the period 2002–12 (Mancomunidad de Municipios 'Metrópoli de Los Altos' 2007: 54). Like Cuenca, Quetzaltenango is the core of a region with high numbers of out-migration to the US. Out-migration started during the internal war of the 1970s and continued into the twenty-first century, when large numbers of the population used existing migration networks to leave the country or to otherwise profit from their transnational contacts (e.g. illicit trafficking of people, drugs, weapons). Approximately 40 percent of the population receives remittances (INE 2008). In peripheral areas such as Cantel and Zunil, people have invested remittances in house remodeling, thereby transforming the landscape into a densely built and colorful area.

Most migrant homes in the periphery of Quetzaltenango have two or three floors. Windows are made with reflective, colored windowpanes that are often framed with arched shapes (Figure 6.3). Houses have colored balusters that contrast with the color of the façade, and ground-floor entrances are closed off with roll bars. On the underside of balconies, decorations of flowers and animals can be found. Those typical decorations and contrasting balusters do not appear in Cuenca or Huancayo. Sometimes decorations directly refer to migration, such as those bearing the American flag or the Virgin of Guadalupe, who is said to guard over safe travel (Piedrasanta 2010). Surprised by the spread of this new architectural idiom, a group of researchers and architects from Guatemala, El Salvador and Honduras made a traveling exhibition and published a book with the title *Arquitectura de Remesas*. Remittance architecture is distinct from the adobe houses with tiled roofs that used to dominate the countryside and from the colonial and republican buildings in the center of Quetzaltenango, and one author has stated that 'the non-styles have been converted into the norm' (Taracena Arriola 2010). As in Cuenca, many houses remain uninhabited for most of the time or are rented out. The empty houses are considered to be a social problem because they create a general sense of insecurity as well as demographically skewed local populations (McBride 2007).

The third example is Huancayo, Peru, an intermediate highland city. The city shelters approximately 392,000 inhabitants and projections for the metropolitan area mention over 400 thousand inhabitants (MPH 2009; Haller and Borsdorf 2013). Due to the internal political violence in Peru in the 1980s, Huancayo received large numbers of internally displaced families and the city grew accordingly. Many of the families that moved to the city tried to survive by sending a family member abroad (Tamagno 2003). 'Being mobile' has become a form of capital (cf. Sheller and Urry 2006) and a general characteristic of Huancayo's families who constantly travel between their villages of origin, Huancayo, Lima and abroad. Their flexible attitude

Figure 6.3
Above: Façade with flower decorations and reflective windowpanes in Zunil, Quetzaltenango 2008. Below: Decorated façade in Llanos de Pinal, Quetzaltenango, 2008. Photographs by author.

enables them to adapt to difficult circumstances. Ten percent of the families have at least one family member abroad and 17 percent of the urban residents receive remittances. On average, remittances are sent nine times a year, from 50 to 200 US dollars (Bendixen and Associates 2005; INEI 2008). Spurred by the investment of remittances in home improvement, the urban periphery started to change over a decade ago, when the first colorful, three-story houses appeared amidst corn and potato fields alongside adobe homes. The difference in comfort level between the houses of migrant families and those of families without members abroad is visible in elements such as hot running water, TV and telephone connections.

Migrant houses consist of two or more floors. Glued, colored or reflective glass panes are used as windows. Windows are often curved (Figures 6.4 and 6.5) or the frames have one or more curved corners. Façades are painted in bright colors or are covered with shiny tiles in contrasting colors. Decorated façades are less common in this region, but diamond shapes or references to agriculture do occur. The openings at ground floor are closed off with roll bars. Finally, satellite dishes or telephone poles show that inhabitants are connected to communication networks. Although the *arquitectura de remesas* is not as widespread in Huancayo as in the two other cities – in part because new building materials reached Huancayo only between 2000 and 2011 (Catyl Rosales, personal communication, 3 March 2011) – it is as visibly outstanding as elsewhere. Locals immediately associate this architecture with transnational migration. Again, many of these houses stand (partially) empty.

In 2012, in a hidden street in Huancayo, several new migrant houses, consisting of four or five floors and split into separate apartments, were constructed. These belonged to migrant families from the nearby village of Chaquicocha. Several apartments were rented out, as the men were living abroad and the women came to Huancayo only during weekends to sell agricultural products at the market. The response of one resident to the question whether transnational families have special architectural preferences was that they just 'copy other transnational families'. This resident, the wife of a migrant and co-owner of a construction firm, noticed

Figure 6.4
Composition of reflective pane with round corners and curved façade, Huancayo, 2011. Photographs by author.

Figure 6.5
Tiled façade with curved window in Cochas Chico, Huancayo, 2012. Photographs by author.

that they are prepared to spend large sums of money on technical innovations, for example new window types. At the same time 'they do not deny their identity, because they use wooden doors as they do in the villages, and use the flat roof or patio to breed small animals' (Catyl Rosales, 3 March 2011). In her interpretation, specific architectural elements signify a connection to rural life and local identity. Those 'local' elements are integrated into cosmopolitan models. This interpretation differs from the urban myth circulated in Cuenca, in which hybrid models exemplify the loss of a local identity. People in Huancayo, in turn, are prone to stress a continuation of local values, traditions and place attachment, even if that message is incorporated in contemporary construction technologies.

VISIBLE NON-CONFORMITY

More than the functional organization of houses, which can still be agricultural, remittance architecture pays attention to form and aesthetic imagery in order to demonstrate success:

> Those houses combine the necessity to act out spatially, to demonstrate the aspirations to flee from poverty, to maintain old habits/points of view and ways of living, as well as catching up with modern functionalities.
>
> (Taracena Arriola 2010)

Imitations in remittance architecture tended towards the appearance of variations and development of a general idiom also used by non-migrants aspiring to a higher social status (Walmsley 2001). The process of inexact imitation and adaptation resulted in a large variety of shiny and colorful houses, in which playful compositions of the latest industrial construction materials were combined with existing spatial functions. As soon as non-migrant families from lower-class ranks started copying and adapting elements from successful migrant homes, the new idiom became synonymous with a move out of poverty and stigmatization. House designs were the medium, and socio-economic success was the message.

Although specific characteristics of remittance architecture differ in each region, the spread of visibly outstanding houses had similar effects, as they usually contrasted with the models that local architects considered 'most appropriate' for the city. In Cuenca, for example, the elite created their own neo-vernacular style with local materials and craftsmanship which they call 'Arquitectura Cuencana' (Klaufus, 2012a). For the architects promoting that style it expressed local identity and 'refined taste'. For lower-class citizens it represented the luxurious stone villas of the privileged cultural elite. Remittance architecture challenged those models, and through that the designers' monopoly on the definitions of high culture and taste, by explicitly referencing international or global architecture. This solicited a response from authorities and professionals alike. An architect in Cuenca commented:

> This other recent architecture, which might relate to the migration – we should examine who the true owners are, but to me it seems to be a social sector that does not have the same roots in Cuenca ... They do not address the Cuencan identity theme, since they are far more interested in enhancing their profile in the city, as a powerful economic sector.
>
> They refuse to commit to a traditional social sector associated with family traditions and [Spanish] surnames. It is a new social sector that aims to stress its presence and to set itself apart from the rest, indicating a clear distinction: this is my architecture; this expresses who I am, and what my status is, like a new social status.
>
> (Adapted extract from interview, CDJ/21/11/02)

Visual distinction was an important asset for transnational families, who wanted to transcend their place in that local context. As a result, the transformation of peri-urban areas altered the symbolic value of the landscape, from land that used to belong to haciendas to modern suburban neighborhoods.

For individual families it remained difficult to decide which design to choose. Oftentimes, migrants would send home photographs, images from house magazines that are not available in Latin America's remote areas, or videotapes of a house they admired abroad. The 'original' sources were hard to locate. One successful transnational family living close to Huancayo built a house on the basis of an example from a house magazine obtained in Madrid. On a clipping the brother who had emigrated to Spain indicated to his family in Peru what he wanted the new house to look like; which parts to copy (interview MSO/010311). In Latin America, people are very conscious of the social ranking of construction materials and housing types, since most national governments include housing material and typology in their national censuses as indicators of poverty. Two implicit and intertwined rules of behavior could be discerned in this study. First, transnational families would not copy traditional elite house types. Second, they would not copy rural house types, as that signified their place in the old hierarchy. Instead, they searched for international models or symbols to stress the transnational status of their family. Local builders would adapt the examples to the available plots and construct them with the available materials and knowledge at hand, although not always in successful ways.

Of the three characteristics mentioned above – visibility, superfluousness and adaptability – the visibility factor was the easiest to achieve. Bright, shiny materials and contrasting color schemes as well as the relatively big size of the homes made them visibly distinct. Some owners put their names on the façade. This advertises the success of a specific family (see Figure 6.1) and may be a reference to elite customs, whereby monumental houses in the city center of Cuenca, for example, are known by the family name of the initial owners. A name on a new house in the urban periphery challenges the cultural codes of old elite groups. The inclusion of 'superfluous' elements to express a sense of luxury was encountered in different ways in different regions. In Cuenca, migrant houses were often associated with luxurious bathrooms and jacuzzis. Sometimes people mentioned that migrant homes have elevators (as in the myth described above), and electric doors (in Cuenca and Quetzaltenango). A resident from Cuenca explained how he used to recognize remittance architecture:

Author: How can you tell that a house belongs to a migrant?
'Francisco' [*smiles*]: By the garages and cars.
Author [*smiles*]: By the garages?
'Francisco': And the garage door opens automatically.
Author: Really?
'Francisco': Some have an alarm. We can't afford to live like that.
Author: Neither can I.
'Francisco' [*smiles*]: We bought a watchdog instead!

(Interview CRH/27/11/02)

In Huancayo, international communication facilities such as satellite dishes were the signs. The third factor, that of constant change, can be described only for Cuenca, where I did longitudinal research. The façades of migrant homes were often repainted in new color palettes. In 2001, the most successful houses were yellow. Several years later those same houses were repainted in blue/white combinations. In 2009 green seemed to be a popular color, whereas in 2011 some migrant homes had been repainted salmon pink.

The denial of the canonical architectural models propagated by culturally elite examples of 'good taste', such as the neo-vernacular Arquitectura Cuencana and imported French neo-classicism that represent the Republican era more generally, is apparent in all three cases. Primarily defined by what it is not, remittance architecture proves to be a flexible concept. Remittance architecture is a dynamically developing form of material culture that coincides with new construction technologies distributed in remote areas. The popular, colored polycarbonate sheets became available in Lima only after the turn of the century, but they are a booming manufacturing business in Huancayo. Taking the pace of cultural changes into account, non-conformity as a form of distinction is bound to weaken as the trend spreads because the majority of residents in the urban peripheries will soon copy those models. The intrinsic 'rules of the game' to establish a counter-hegemonic discourse remain, but with a territorial spread of remittance architecture the aesthetic outcomes will diversify and normalize.

The spread of popular house designs propagates a non-verbal message that resembles other case studies. Nickles's study (2002) illustrates that post-World War II consumer preferences of United States working-class families who had moved to middle-class suburbs did not copy the aesthetically sober middle-class taste as would have been expected, but employed a distinctive taste in their domestic material culture.

Their preference for shiny appliances and rosebud decorations, designs that were abhorred by the middle class, was about social identity, argues Nickles (2002: 582). Their 'more is better' attitude underlined their resistance toward assimilation into higher-class taste patterns. Unlike the efforts of migrants, they wanted to move up the social ladder without losing a shared working-class identity. The expression of social status through remittance architecture manifested in a new 'non-style norm' was not formally recognized, yet followed a re-occurring pattern. The sheer number of examples that were replicated and adapted, and the spread over different parts of the region, came to signify remittance architecture as a sense of social deviancy and an informal social movement. The architecture expresses that the owners do not consider themselves to be 'poor' or 'peasants' anymore. They escape old categorizations in order to claim self-determination and the right to an urban way of life; the 'right to the city'.

Unlike the people in Nickles' study, Latin American migrant families strategically use visually distinctive materials but they do not aim to construct a distinctive working-class identity. Whereas Nickles (2002: 609) argues that the 'style can be understood as a tool that women used to preserve class identity and reformulate social relations', the claims of migrant families are oriented towards obtaining respect as full-fledged middle-class citizens in urbanizing societies and to shake off the stigma of marginalization: 'For those successful in constructing a remittance house or for those who are still trying to build one, it is a matter of dignity' (Taracena Arriola 2010, translation by the author). The popularity of the new architectural idiom is an indicator of a social awareness that is spreading across the continent. It is a conscious mobilization of cultural resources by groups who make use of the extreme visibility of architecture, regardless of what the urban elite might think of their cultural taste (cf. Nickles 2002: 583).

CONCLUSION

Urban sprawl in Latin American metropolises has been replaced by rapid growth in the peri-urban areas of smaller cities. The densification of the built environment is characterized by a spread of new aesthetic preferences. Individual transnational migrants and their families with new economic possibilities and a sense of self-determinism were the initial agents of change. A process of demonstration, imitation and adaptation resulted in the contemporary architectural trend associated with transnational migration, remittances and the globalization of goods and ideas: remittance architecture.

The transformation of peripheral landscapes points to an increasing self-confidence of formerly marginalized groups to shake off the stigma of poverty. Individual architectural expressions are the medium and outcome of that process. The effect of that non-verbal yet highly visible demonstration is that the debate of professionals, authorities and academics has inadvertently stimulated the spread of those architectural representations through blogs and articles (Jaramillo 2002; Borrero 2002; Piedrasanta 2010). The phenomenon can be considered successful in its symbolic mobilization: spreading the message helps to de-marginalize the senders. Yet, the role of urban planning in Latin America to manage the rise in voluminous houses continues to be tested. Through cultural debates about appropriate architectural aesthetics that include participation by the new generation of individual house builders, effective planning models for sustainable urban growth can be developed.

ACKNOWLEDGEMENTS

An earlier version of this chapter was published in *Etnofoor* 23, 1: 10–28 (2011). The author received financial support from the EFL Foundation in The Hague. Many thanks go to the various organizations in Cuenca, Quetzaltenango and Huancayo that have contributed to this research.

REFERENCES

Arriola Quan, G. and Escobar, P. (2011) *Cifras para el desarrollo humano Quetzaltenango*, Guatemala: Programa de las Naciones Unidas para el Desarrollo.

Bendixen and Associates (2003) *Receptores de remesas en Ecuador: Una investigación del mercado*, Quito: Banco Inter-Americano de Desarrollo, Fondo Multilateral de Inversiones and Pew Hispanic Center, Online. http://www.iadb.org/mif/v2/files/BendixenEC.doc (accessed 25 January 2005).

Bendixen and Associates (2005) *Encuesta de opinion pública de receptores de remesas en Peru*, Online. www.bendixenandassociates.com/studies/IDB%20Peru%20Presentation%202005. pdf (accessed 2 March 2011).

Borrero Vega, A. L. (2002) 'La migración: estudio sobre las remesas de divisas que ingresan en el Ecuador', *Universitas* 1, 1: 79–87.

Carsten, J. and Hugh-Jones, S. (eds.) (1995) *About the House: Lévi-Strauss and Beyond*, Cambridge: Cambridge University Press.

Chambers, E. and Low, S. (eds.) (1989) *Housing, Culture, and Design: A Comparative Perspective*, Philadelphia: University of Pennsylvania Press.

Csikszentmihalyi, M. and Rochberg-Halton, E. (1981) *The Meaning of Things: Domestic Symbols and the Self*, Cambridge: Cambridge University Press.

Fernandez, J. (1974) 'The Mission of Metaphor in Expressive Culture', *Current Anthropology* 15, 2: 119–145.

Fernandez, J. (1992) 'Arquitectonic Inquiry', *Semiotic* 89, 1/3: 215–226.

Fisher, D. (2004) 'The Demonstration Effect Revisited', *Annuals of Tourism Research* 31, 2: 428–446.

Frampton, K. (2002) *Labour, Work and Architecture: Collected Essays on Architecture and Design*, London: Phaidon.

Georges, E. (1979) *The Making of a Transnational Community: Migration, Development, and Cultural Change in the Dominican Republic*, New York: Columbia University Press.

Glassie, H. (2000) *Vernacular Architecture*, Bloomington: Indiana University Press.

Goldstein, D. (2004) *The Spectacular City: Violence and Performance in Urban Bolivia*, Durham and London: Duke University Press.

Haller, A. and Borsdorf, A. (2013) 'Huancayo Metropolitano', *Cities* 31: 553–562.

Holston, J. (1991) 'Autoconstruction in Working-Class Brazil', *Cultural Anthropology* 6, 4: 447–465.

Horowitz, D. (1985) *Ethnic Groups in Conflict*, Berkeley: University of California Press.

Husock, H. (1996) 'Repairing the Ladder: Toward a New Housing Policy Paradigm', *Reason Foundation*, Online. http://reason.org/news/show/repairing-the-ladder (accessed 5 March 2011).

INE (Instituto Nacional de Estadística de Guatemala) (2008) 'XI Censo Nacional de Población y VI de Habitación (Censo 2002)', Online. www.ine.gob.gt (accessed 7 October 2007).

INEC (Instituto Nacional de Estadísticas y Censos del Ecuador) (2011) 'Resultados del Censo 2010 de Población y Vivienda en el Ecuador: Fascículo Provincial de Azuay', Online. http://www.ecuadorencifras.gob.ec/wp-content/descargas/Manu-lateral/Resultados-provinciales/azuay.pdf (accessed 8 September 2014).

INEI (Instituto National de Estadística e Información del Peru) (2008) 'Peru: Estadísticas de la migración internacional de peruanos, 1990–2007', Lima: International Organization for Migration.

Jacobs, J. (1961) *The Death and Life of Great American Cities*, New York: Random House.

James, J. (1987) 'Positional Goods, Conspicuous Consumption and the International Demonstration Effect Reconsidered', *World Development* 15, 4: 449–462.

Jaramillo, D. (2002) 'Globalización y cultura: del hogar a la casa fetiche en la arquitectura popular azuaya', *Universidad Verdad* 27: 185–195.

Jokisch, B. and Pribilsky, J. (2002) 'The Panic to Leave: Economic Crisis and the "New Emigration" from Ecuador', *International Migration* 40, 4: 75–101.

Klaufus, C. (2006) 'Globalization in Residential Architecture in Cuenca, Ecuador: Social and Cultural Diversification of Architects and their Clients', *Environment and Planning D Society and Space* 24, 1: 69–89.

Klaufus, C. (2010) 'Watching the City Grow: Remittances and Sprawl in Intermediate Central American Cities', *Environment and Urbanization* 22, 1: 125–137.

Klaufus, C. (2012a) *Urban Residence: Housing and Social Transformations in Globalizing Ecuador*, New York: Berghahn Books.

Klaufus, C. (2012b) 'The Symbolic Dimension of Mobility: Architecture and Social Status in Ecuadorian Informal Settlements', *International Journal of Urban and Regional Research* 36, 4: 689–705.

Kyle, D. (2000) *Transnational Peasants: Migrations, Networks, and Ethnicity in Andean Ecuador*, Baltimore: The Johns Hopkins University Press.

McBride, B. (2007) 'Building Capital: The Role of Migrant Remittances in Housing Improvement and Construction in El Salvador', Unpublished thesis, Rotterdam: Institute of Housing Studies.

Mancomunidad de Municipios Metrópoli de Los Altos (2007) 'Diagnóstico terriorial del valle de Quetzaltenango: proceso del plan estratégico territorial', Quetzaltenango: Equipo Técnico de la Unidad de Ordenamiento Territorial Mancomunidad de Municipios Metrópoli de Los Altos.

Miles, A. (1997) 'The High Cost of Leaving: Illegal Emigration from Cuenca, Ecuador and Family Separation', in A. Miles and H. Buechler (eds.) *Women and Economic Change: Andean Perspectives*, Arlington: American Anthropological Association.

MHP (Municipalidad Provincial de Huancayo) (2009) 'Mejoramiento y Actualización del Plan de Desarrollo Local Concertado Provincial 2007–2015', Huancayo: Municipalidad Provincial de Huancayo.

Moser, C. (2009) *Ordinary Families, Extraordinary Lives: Assets and Poverty Reduction in Guayaquil, 1978–2004*, Washington DC: Brookings Institution Press.

Nickles, S. (2002) 'More is Better: Mass Consumption, Gender, and Class Identity in Postwar America', *American Quarterly* 54, 4: 581–622.

Norberg-Schulz, C. (1980) *Meaning in Western Architecture*, New York: Rizzoli.

Oliver, P. (ed.) (1975) *Shelter, Sign and Symbol*, London: Barrie and Jenkins.

Oliver, P. (2003) *Dwellings: The Vernacular House World Wide*, London: Phaidon.

Parker Pearson, M. and Richards, C. (eds.) (1994) *Architecture and Order: Approaches to Social Space*, London: Routledge.

Perlman, J. (2010) *Favela: Four Decades of Living on the Edge in Rio de Janeiro*, Oxford and New York: Oxford University Press.

Pezo, D. (2009) 'Arquitectura chicha: lo cholo en la arquitectura', in S. Bedoya (ed.) *Coloquio lo cholo en el Peru: Tomo II. Migraciones y mixtura*, Lima: Biblioteca Nacional del Perú.

Piedrasanta, R. (ed.) (2010) *Arquitectura de la remesas*, Exhibition, book and blog, Guatemala City: AECID/CCE Guatemala/CCE El Salvador/CCE Honduras, http://arquitecturadelas-remesas.blogspot.com.

Pribilsky, J. (2007) *La Chulla Vida: Gender, Migration and the Family in Andean Ecuador and New York City*, Syracuse, NY: Syracuse University Press.

Rapoport, A. (1969) *House Form and Culture*, Englewood Cliffs, NJ: Prentice-Hall.

Rapoport, A. (1988) 'Spontaneous Settlements as Vernacular Design', in C. Patton (ed.) *Spontaneous Shelter: International Perspectives and Prospects*, Philadelphia, PA: Temple University Press.

Sheller, M. and Urry, J. (2006) 'The New Mobilities Paradigm', *Environment and Planning A* 38: 207–226.

Taracena Arriola, L. P. (2010) '"Conocer viendo" la arquitectura de remesas: Convergencia de miradas', Online. http://arquitecturadelasremesas.blogspot.com (accessed 17 April 2011).

Tamagno, C. (2003) '"Entre acá y allá": Vidas Transnacionales y Desarrollo. Peruanos entre Italia y Peru', PhD thesis, Wageningen University.

Turner, J. (1968) 'Housing Priorities, Settlement Patterns, and Urban Development in Modernizing Countries', *Journal of the American Planning Association* 34, 6: 354–363.

UN-Habitat (2012) *The State of Latin American and Caribbean Cities 2012: Towards a New Urban Transition*, Nairobi: United Nations Human Settlement Programme.

Veblen, T. (1953 [1899]) *The Theory of The Leisure Class: An Economic Study of Institutions*, New York: Mentor Books.

Walmsley, E. (2001) 'Transformando los pueblos: La migración internacional y el impacto social al nivel comunitario', *Ecuador Debate* 54: 155–174.

Chapter 7: Meanings of house materiality for Moroccan migrants in Israel

Iris Levin

THE ETHNO-ARCHITECTURE OF THE HOUSE AND MATERIAL CULTURE

Migrant ethno-architecture can be thought of through three scales of the urban environment that together situate ethno-architecture as focused on unprivileged migrants and on grass-roots processes of development, construction and design. First is the city-wide scale, where studies have shown how different policy programs have designed the distribution of immigrants in western cities (e.g. Tzfadia and Yacobi 2007). The second scale is the neighbourhood, where the urban landscape has mostly been influenced by the immigrants' presence in the construction of public 'ethnic' buildings, business signs in foreign languages, or housing, generating reactions from local residents to that change (e.g. Allon 2002; Mitchell 2004).

The third scale of ethno-architecture, and the centre of this chapter, is the house scale, where studies have focused on the physical and emotional relationships between past homes in the homeland and current houses in the host land (e.g. Jacobs 2004; King 1997; Thomas 1997), or on the relationship between migrants' housing and the dominant culture (e.g. Lozanovska 1997; 2008), which interpret the changes migrants make to their houses as manifestations against the dominant culture, diverting the gaze from the private to the public. The diverse approaches applied in the examination of ethno-architecture at the house scale demonstrate the importance and relevance of this inquiry. This chapter will further explore the ethno-architecture of the house by looking into the house and examining its materiality, utilising theories of material culture, in order to understand the meanings of house materiality for migrants from Morocco in Israel.

Studies of material culture are concerned with the concept of materiality and the conceptualization of things. One subject of inquiry within studies of material culture has been the home. Miller (2001) focuses on the inside realm of the house – the indoors, presenting ethnographic encounters that take place in the home. Miller discusses 'the processes by which a home and its inhabitants transform each other' (2001: 2–3), stating that the home is 'the single most important site for material studies', though this does not mean that it constitutes a simple dichotomy between the private and the public. Following Miller, discussions around the materiality of home – focused mostly on non-migrants – have looked into issues of consumption, home clutter, collection and display, the use of family photos and mementos, and the size of homes. For example, Noble (2002), studying possessions in working- and lower-middle-class households in Sydney, found that national icons and images of Australia pervaded the homes he studied, and yet this issue was rarely discussed in the interviews he conducted. Noble suggests that people are making themselves at home, 'at ease', not only in the specific, domestic context of their homes but also in a larger social space of the national imagery. From early in the new millennium, an emerging body of research emphasised aspects of materiality in the migrant house.

A prominent scholar of materiality in the migrant home, or housing ethno-architecture, is Tolia-Kelly (2004), who examines artefacts in the homes of Asian women in Britain. In particular, she looks at what she names 'precipitates of re-memories and narrated histories', namely souvenirs from the traversed landscapes of the journey, which are part of the diasporic community's re-memories. Re-memory is, according to Tolia-Kelly, an alternative social narrative to memory that is not an individual, linear, biographical narrative but is a conceptualization of encounters with memories, stimulated through scents, sounds and textures of the everyday (Tolia-Kelly 2004: 314). Tolia-Kelly traces religious and cultural artefacts in the women's homes, sees them as echoes of other textures of landscapes, narratives and social histories, and argues that they help to situate diasporic groups politically and socially in relation to their national identity (Tolia-Kelly 2004: 326–327). Likewise, Turan (2010: 43–44) explores the houses of Palestinian migrants in diaspora, illustrating how objects as symbols of a person's collective group help with the creation of a sheltering and nurturing environment. Turan highlights the materiality of objects and argues that their meaning and their capacity to prevent failing memory and sustain a collective identity are generated by their material characteristics, and not solely by their social value.

Not much has been written on the material aspects of the Moroccan migrant house that stands at the centre of this study (see Salih [2003] for a discussion of Moroccan sense of belonging and home). An exception is Dibbits' study (2009) which explores the meaning of the *sedari*, traditional-looking furniture in Moroccan homes in the Netherlands. The *sedari* are low banquettes running along the side of the room, found in many Muslim countries. Dibbits argues that the *sedari* are not only used as an ethnic symbol which connects Moroccan migrants to their homeland, but that they are also objects which mark wealth and fashion, and that by using them migrants create social experiences of community and conviviality in their homes.

For these groups of migrants – Asian women in Britain or Palestinians in the diaspora – the analysis of house materiality indicates that it means a collective sense of belonging and aesthetics. The study of Moroccan migrants in Israel provides interesting insights for the understanding of ethno-architecture because it embodies a long-standing conflict between the national story of the State and the individual migrant story. As will be soon revealed, these migrants had to defy the need to be assimilated in the Israeli melting pot and to confront strong stereotyping attitudes and stigmatisation in Israel as a result of their ethnic origin. Thus, ethno-architecture in this case needs to be understood through the lens of the national–individual tension. So what is the meaning of Moroccan-Israeli house materiality? This will be explored from the perspective of material culture.

MOROCCAN MIGRATION TO ISRAEL[1] – A DIFFICULT START

There were three main immigration waves from Morocco to Israel in the first two decades following the Second World War and the establishment of the Israeli state in 1948. In total, about 195,000 Moroccan Jews arrived in Israel between 1948 and 1964 (Mey-Ami 2005). Since the third wave ended, the population of Morocco-born Israelis has aged significantly. As many migrated in their old age, by 2013 there were only 148,400 persons living in Israel who were born in Morocco, representing 2 percent of Israel's Jewish population. Of these, 98.2 percent were over the age of 45. In contrast, there were 341,900 people of Moroccan heritage, representing 5 percent of Israel's Jewish population (CBS 2014). It is the second-largest ethnic group among Jews in Israel (after migrants from the former Soviet Union).

The first decades for Moroccan immigrants in Israel were characterised by adversity and hardship. Upon arriving in Israel, they were asked to assimilate and blend into the Israeli melting pot. They were expected to forgo their traditional values and symbols and to adopt Israeli western values. Coming from a Muslim country, they were seen by the western Jewish majority[2] as primitive and inferior to the western culture (Levy 1997). As discussed in the city-wide scale of ethno-architecture, the implementation of the assimilation policy led to an intensive interference in all areas of life, including settlement, employment and even personal hygiene. This attitude led to the breaking down of the traditional familial order and weakening of the patriarchal authority in Moroccan families (Mey-Ami 2005). In Morocco, Moroccan Jews lived in a multi-generational, patriarchal family formation and value was placed on having a large number of children. The receiving society in those years was essentially western-oriented, innovative and secular (Glassman and Eiskivoits 2006: 462). Moreover, Moroccan communities were separated from their spiritual leaders. For the most part these leaders stayed in Morocco, but even communities whose leaders migrated were spread around the country according to the arbitrary decisions of the settling institutions (Portugali 1993). Immigrants were forced to leave their belongings in Morocco and arrived in Israel with no financial means. Some of them were villagers, but many others were urbanites who had lived in large cities and were accustomed to urban life. But life in the pre-modern Moroccan city was very different to life in the new, modern state of Israel. Their trading skills and crafts were not appreciated and they were sent to live in new 'development towns'[3], facing either unemployment or labour-intensive work

(Levy 1997; Portugali 1993). Hundreds of thousands of immigrants were housed in the first decade (after 1948) in apartment blocks all around the country. This was the Modernity project of Israel – settling the people as a tool for the appropriation of the national space (Kallus and Law Yone 2002). Tsur (1997: 102) argues that Moroccan immigrants stood at the centre of what came to be known as an 'ethnic problem' from a very early stage after the establishment of the state of Israel. This happened due to tension between two conflicting societies (western and non-western Jews), caught between the generative orders of colonialism and nationalism.

In the 1960s, Moroccan Israelis were the lowest stratum of Israeli Jewish society and had high levels of unemployment and illiteracy. A group called 'Black Panthers' was established in 1971 by second-generation Oriental Jews[4] (many of Moroccan origin), demanding that their voices be heard by the establishment, which until then was comprised of only western Jews. This plea for social justice led to the gaining of political power by Oriental Jews for the first time in Israel. The Likud party[5] won the general election of 1977, representing a large number of Oriental Jews (Levy 1997; Mey-Ami 2005).

Some 60 years after migration, Moroccan-Israelis have largely integrated into Israeli society. Since the late 1980s, with a modest but systematic improvement in the socioeconomic status of many and the rise of some to positions of power in the socio-political structure, many of the adversities of the early days have been eased, though not entirely removed (Levy 1997: 28). As a study of Moroccan immigrants in Israel and the Netherlands reveals, Israeli-Moroccans experience little prejudice in Israel, as compared to their Dutch counterparts, whether they maintain their ethnic identity or not (Glassman and Eiskivoits 2006). Yet, Israelis of Moroccan origin are still overrepresented in the lower stratum of Israeli society (Levy 1997), and a large share of them still live in isolated, stigmatised and deprived urban areas, and are thus marginalised both geographically and socially (Yiftachel 2000: 434).

Meanings of 'Moroccan' ethno-architecture in Israel

The Moroccan-Israeli ethno-architecture of public buildings has been the focus of several studies (e.g. Alon-Mozes *et al.* 2009; Weingrod 1993). An example of such a 'Moroccan' building complex is the shrine and associated buildings around the grave of the Jewish Moroccan *zaddik* (saint) Baba-Sali in Netivot, a town in the southern periphery of Israel. Weingrod (1993) argues that the shrine and associated buildings have been designed to express a distinct Moroccan character. Although these buildings fit the surrounding landscape from a distance, inside they contain 'the Maghreb within' (Weingrod 1993: 370), using bold design and colours, and a fountain in the main courtyard. Weingrod argues that these buildings, the 'imagining of Morocco', can be best understood as a response to the long-standing Zionist Ashkenazi hegemony, signifying a deep break from the Zionist ideological system which has been the dominant discourse in Israel, and which has always contested the Moroccan-Jewish identity. Weingrod further states that the bold representation of Moroccan buildings transfers Morocco to Israel and renders it legitimate in the new land, and thus this ethnic group is raised up to the same level of significance as the ideology of Zionism.

Although Weingrod explains the meanings of 'Moroccan' public buildings, the meanings of 'Moroccan' housing and its materiality in Israel have yet to be studied. This will be explored through two homes of Moroccan immigrants which represent two different cases of material cultures reflecting – each in a different way – the tension between the Moroccan community and the national Zionist Israeli narrative.

EXPLORING MOROCCAN-ISRAELI HOUSE MATERIALITY

In order to reveal the meaning of the Moroccan house materiality, the paper draws on research undertaken between 2007 and 2008[6] in which twelve migrants from Morocco to Israel were interviewed in their homes in the Tel Aviv metropolitan region. The twelve migrants and their Moroccan and Israeli houses have been discussed elsewhere (Levin 2013), where it has been argued that these Moroccan-Israeli migrants tried to recreate feelings of community which were prevalent in their Moroccan homes, while simultaneously educating Israeli society about the rich Moroccan-Jewish culture and history.

This chapter is focused on two migrant households (of the twelve studied) which are located at the two extremes of an imagined housing modification scale. One house has hardly been changed and adapted by its owner, while the other has been heavily modified. Studying the two extreme cases and identifying diverse practices and representations of ethno-architecture may enable the exploration of the meaning of the house for Moroccan migrants in Israel and the ethno-architecture produced at the scale of the home. It is important to note that this is not a representative study of all Moroccan migrant houses in Israel. Rather, it is an exploratory study that may advance the understanding of the nature of Moroccan ethno-architecture in Israel, focusing on the house scale.

The interviews took place in the participants' homes that were both the locus and focus of conversation. Participants were asked to tell their stories of immigration and settlement in Tel Aviv, the construction of the houses, their feelings towards different spaces in it and the meanings behind objects in their homes. The interviews included tours of the houses, and photographs were taken. Participants were recruited through connections with family and friends as well as a cultural Moroccan organisation in Tel Aviv. Through examining material cultures in the homes of Moroccan migrants in Israel, the chapter seeks to situate everyday practices and representations of material cultures in the contextual narrative of this migration within the national Israeli story.

Alisa's house materiality[7]

Alisa's house was located in a disadvantaged town situated on the south-eastern outskirts of the Tel Aviv metropolitan region. She migrated in 1954 from Casablanca and moved into this house in 1974. The house in which the interview was conducted was a precast detached house built by the State just before Alisa moved in. From the outside, the house looked ordinary, without any marks signalling that it was different from any other house in the street. Like many neighbouring houses, it had been extended a number of times throughout the years but still did not reveal anything about the identity of its owners. Inside, however, the house told a different story.

Alisa's house was full of collections of objects, knick-knacks and souvenirs which filled every corner of the house. It seemed that each space had its own purpose for display – a nook where the collection of good-luck signs was displayed, a wall filled with decorated plates (Figure 7.1), a kitchen bench where a collection of serviette holders was placed, or another corner shelf with religious ornaments (Figure 7.2). There were many vases of flowers around the house, as well as pots of plants placed on shelves inside the house and on the front porch. Other walls were completely covered with family photographs and ornamented plates and every space was crammed with similar objects.

Following a tour of the house, the 'Moroccan' room was soon revealed. This was a small room covered from top to bottom with Moroccan objects from the past (Figure 7.3). In Morocco, Jews lived in one- or two-room apartments and shared kitchen and toilets with their neighbours. These modest apartments contained wooden furniture which served as both beds and couches and there was no place for displaying ornaments and decorating the walls. In Israel, Alisa's house was one of only two houses in the study (of twelve) which had a Moroccan room, but a few other women were familiar with it and told of other relatives in France or the US who had a Moroccan room in their house. Moroccan design is well known

Figure 7.1
A wall filled with decorated plates, souvenirs and good-luck charms, Alisa's house, Tel Aviv. Photograph by author.

Figure 7.2
A collection of Jewish religious ornaments, Alisa's house, Tel Aviv. Photograph by author.

for its recognisable character, readily lending itself to the creation of such a material 'ethnic' symbol.

Alisa's room did not have a door; instead it had a large opening in the wall, so one could see inside without entering it. In the room there was a *sedari* (although Alisa did not mention this word) built around the three walls and covered with red cloths and matching cushions. The *sedari* in Alisa's Moroccan room was not used in its everyday sense and it was not the focus of the living room as in the case of Moroccan-Dutch migrants (Dibbits 2009). It was used as an ethnic symbol that connected Alisa to her homeland, serving only on special occasions, and was there essentially for display.

On the side wall hung a wooden shelf that displayed copper utensils such as pots, trays and kettles or a colourful ceramic dish. There were a number of carpets hanging on the walls, all in dark red colours, matching the cushions. The floor was also covered with a red carpet, and in the middle of the room stood a small, round, copper table with a traditional set of ornamented glassware and a copper pot. Next to it was a Moroccan round cushion with the same colours. On the walls all around the room hung different objects that used to be part of Jewish everyday life and celebrations in Morocco. There were musical instruments such as the goblet drum, the cymbals and a number of tambourines, a few bellows and more copper trays and other ornaments. Alisa said:

> The cloths are from Israel but [designed] in a Moroccan style. You can take photos, I will tell you. All this is from Morocco, [things] which I bought and brought, this is also from Morocco, this basket. In this we put the bride and groom's presents. Wait, I will tell you, and in this, we put the *henna*, the bride and groom's *henna*; when my son got married I did for him exactly like this, exactly like this. Also this utensil, everything is from Morocco. This is an awl; these are the perfumes for the Sabbath evening, when we do the Havdalah,[8] this is for you to smell [sprinkling]. Do you see this utensil? It's authentic from Morocco … This is also Moroccan, you see? This bag is Moroccan, and all these are Moroccan. And this is Moroccan – they light the fire and make wind [a bellows] … This is *asli* [genuine] Moroccan, this primus [lamp] is also Moroccan, everything.

Alisa uttered the word Moroccan again and again while showing the room. It seems that by repeating the word Alisa bestowed an ethnic identity upon the

Figure 7.3
The Moroccan room serves as a mini-museum in Alisa's house, Tel Aviv. Photograph by author.

objects that filled the room, so they can physically connect her with her culture. For her, the objects were Moroccan in the same way the Moroccan-Jewish community was – with a story of rich, meaningful life in Morocco that ended with the move to Israel. Suddenly, in the new, modern country they became obsolete and outdated because they were not needed anymore and were not appreciated for their use value. But Alisa was determined to preserve them and give them a new meaning of display instead of use. Alisa created a space for display, and noted that she had designed the room: 'I did it all, according to my order, my wish and my fun. I love it so much and it's been almost 30 years, 30 years'. It was important to her to tell the story of these objects – where they came from (Morocco or Israel), to reassure that they were authentic and to explain how they were used in everyday life and holidays.

Alisa's room consisted of objects that generated sound, smells and visual stimulation in a similar way to Tolia-Kelly's concept of re-memory and the objects that invoke it (2004: 314). These objects helped Alisa to situate herself as part of a larger group, as being 'Moroccan' – whatever that may have meant to her – but her Moroccan room was constructed through a highly personal choice and agency, as a representation of previous life. While the outside of the *house* did not show Alisa's ethnic identity, the interiors of the *home* reflected it clearly. This is where the tension between the national story – the house – and the personal story – the home – was apparent. The Moroccan room, although personal, served the historical role of a museum in the house, displaying a collection of objects brought from another era and another place. Alisa had chosen to share her Moroccan identity with guests and family members through the construction of a mini-museum in her house which allowed her to tell the story of each object and her childhood memories from Morocco. She challenges the national story by telling her own story of life in Morocco, utilising the notion of re-memory through materiality in the room to include other people in her personal story of life in Morocco and migration to Israel.

Yehuda's house materiality

A very different house materiality was exposed in Yehuda's house, located in a wealthy inner-city suburb of the Tel Aviv metropolitan region. Yehuda migrated in 1948, also from Casablanca, at the age of 18, and went to live in the southern, unpopulated region of Israel. During the first years after migration he lived in a number of *kibbutzim*[9] in this region, and then became the mayor of a southern development town. After serving in this public role for 15 years, he retired and in 1992 moved to his current home, where the interview took place. He lived in an apartment tower of 20 floors with his wife, who was of Ashkenazi origin but was born in Israel, as Yehuda emphasised: 'She is a *tzabar*'.[10] Yehuda was recruited through a Moroccan cultural organisation which regarded him as a fine representation of Moroccan migration and integration in Israel. In his home he went straight to his study, where he worked on his lectures and computer presentations.

The rest of the apartment, which Yehuda was not interested in showing, was an ordinary middle-class apartment that did not display many ethnic or personal markers. He said:

> This is my home, this room where I spend most of the time, not most of the time but a large part of the time, I write, I make presentations, I document, as you can see I document the whole, not only the migration [but] the whole story from Morocco until today, with pictures, presentations and all sorts of things. This is for the children, the grandchildren and … all their friends, family and everybody, when they do a family tree they have material.

Yehuda has collected objects and materials from his previous life in Morocco with a conscious aim to preserve Moroccan history. He used this room as the centre for the conservation and dissemination of his memories and (hi)stories. Yehuda was telling his private story as it intermingled in the national story.

One wall of Yehuda's study room had a long desk along it which accommodated a computer, printer and a comfortable desk chair, where Yehuda prepared his computer presentations and spent most of his time in the room. On the opposite wall near the entrance door was a sofa, and by its side a wooden shelf unit placed on the floor which displayed copper utensils and tools that Yehuda's family had brought from Morocco. There were a mortar and pestle, a number of candle holders, and two copper trays. Yehuda turned on the computer and presented some of the digital presentations he had prepared for family celebrations. He then noted, talking about the object in the corner of the room:

> Yes, we brought [them] … This, on the *seder* night we do the *seder* plate with the *matza*,[11] these two, this is also from Morocco, all this … . This is from Morocco, and this is from Morocco, a mortar – do you know? So these are things that need to be given to a museum, if there is something like that.

Yehuda recognised that the objects in his study have a historical significance and need to be kept in a museum, much like Alisa's home-made museum. On the wall next to this display were photographs and framed documents (Figure 7.4), among them a framed picture made of combined photographs of Yehuda and his family, a map of Israel, and, as if to signify its importance, in the middle of that wall was a framed *ketubah*[12] of Yehuda's ancestors which was 'from 170 years ago'. Next to it was a framed prize awarded to Yehuda by the Centre of Local Government in 1976 for his contribution in making the development town successful, and near it were two framed letters written by David Ben-Gurion, the first Israeli Prime Minister. In 1953, while Yehuda was working in a *kibbutz* in the desert, Ben-Gurion praised him in these words:

> I was delighted to find a *kibbutz* manager, a young man from Morocco, who served the army and would not move from his place even if he were abandoned by others. I have not seen such an excellent man for a long time! Such a

grandiosity in a man, an excellent pioneer, and although I am certain that he had never read Goethe and had never heard his name, he is a person of culture of the first degree! This place has a bright future because it is managed by a person, Yehuda his name, who is worth a number of army divisions, and in his trusted hands we can rest the future of this *kibbutz*!

(Author's translation from the Hebrew)

Near the framed letters was a framed newspaper clipping from 1954. This newspaper article reported on an award which was meant to be given to Ben-Gurion, who had refused to accept it and instead recommended Yehuda as its worthy receiver (Figure 7.5). The display of these framed letters and newspaper article demonstrates Yehuda's desire to be accepted by the Ashkenazi establishment which Ben-Gurion represents in the public Israeli discourse. In contrast to the construction of the Baba-Sali grave estate, which can be understood as a reaction against the long-standing Zionist Ashkenazi hegemony (Weingrod 1993), here Yehuda embraced this same Zionist hegemony by adopting its values. Instead of resisting the establishment and its perceived superiority (expressed in Ben-Gurion's paternalistic words when he mentioned Yehuda's lack of knowledge of high culture, not reading Goethe!), he was proud of being accepted as 'one of them' as a public servant. But Yehuda did not abandon his ethnic origins either – he presented his ancestral *ketubah* in the middle of the wall, side by side with the letters from Ben-Gurion, to demonstrate that both are of the same importance in his life – where

Figure 7.4
The *Ketubah* displayed in the middle of the wall, Yehuda's house, Tel Aviv. Photograph by author.

Figure 7.5 Translated: 'This young Moroccan man deserves the award more than me'–said Ben Gurion, newspaper clipping, Yehuda's house, Tel Aviv. Photograph by author.

he had come from and what he had achieved. For him, Moroccan culture was not inferior to western culture and he was proud of it.

For Yehuda, the meaning of this room rested in its representation of his belonging to the national home. The objects in the room were signposts from Yehuda's life story, which included not only the private events that took place in it, but also the national story of building the State, populating the periphery (Kallus and Law Yone 2002), the recognition from the political founders and the instrumental role Moroccan migrants have had in this story. In a similar way to Tolia-Kelly (2004) and Turan (2010), who both emphasise the role material objects play in sustaining collective memory and national identity of migrants in their homes, Yehuda utilised his material objects in his study to locate him within the national story of the Israeli state and its building project. Although very different from Alisa's room in its purpose, as Yehuda's study was functional and practical, the tension between the *house* – the official, national story of the State – and the *home* – the personal interiors of the room – was similar to the tension reflected in Alisa's house.

MEANINGS OF MOROCCAN-ISRAELI HOUSE MATERIALITY

The homes of Alisa and Yehuda were different in their physical forms and uses of material culture, but both served the purpose of telling the story of Moroccan culture and history, invoking re-memory for those who did not come from Morocco and had not experienced it at first hand. Tolia-Kelly (2004: 322–323) refers to the concept of re-memory as a process 'engaged with the "interior-life" of post-colonial groups who are constantly negotiating between past landscapes and the present territories of citizenship'. In the case of Moroccans in Israel, the race politics are just as strong, even though citizenship was never an issue because, being Jewish migrants, they were granted automatic citizenship upon arriving in Israel (as all other Jewish immigrants in Israel). Yet, like South Asian women in Britain, Moroccan migrants felt they were denied recognition of their culture and were ruptured from their community and home. Alisa and Yehuda have gained back this sense of *home* through the textuality of the material culture in their *houses*. Both of them created, collected, framed and displayed objects that invoked discussion and reflection on their past memories and symbols of Moroccan culture in a very active way.

For Alisa, this was reflected in the reproduction of a room that artificially recreated everyday life in Morocco and was linked to her personal choice to display collections in the home. Alisa found joy in displaying objects that served no real purpose in her current life but allowed her to fully immerse her audience (guests and family members) in the experience of 'being in Morocco' through the texture of the objects, their visuality and their smells. For Yehuda, this was reflected in a more rational relationship between the objects he collected and the way he reflected upon them, linking together his personal story within the national story. Both of them, despite these major differences in their use of material culture, utilised the objects in their homes to tell the story of their cultural history to non-Moroccan Israelis or to their children. Alisa and Yehuda wished to communicate the richness of Moroccan Jewish culture, feeling that they have not been recognised adequately by Israeli authorities and have always been considered second-rate Israelis. As Weingrod (1993) notes, Moroccan immigrants have always felt that the prevailing Zionist ideology does not represent them well and hence they have sought to bring their values and traditions to the fore. They have done this in the construction of the grave estate of the Baba-Sali, and also, in a more subtle way, in the interiors of their homes. They have brought the national story into their domestic environment, making the private public. Thus the tension between the house and the home is the tension between the national story and the migrant story. The house represents the national-official agenda being part of the cityscape, while the home represents the individual-migrant story in its uniqueness and character.

The chapter has discussed two case studies which were chosen because they are very different from one another: one migrant house has a Moroccan room which is the epitome of Moroccan design, while the other has barely anything to indicate the ethnic identity of its owner. Yet, the migrants who live in these houses have created, each in their own way through the use of material cultures, the means to tell the story of Moroccan migration to Israel and gain the long-desired recognition of Moroccan culture in Israeli society. Through the understanding of these material cultures in the migrant house, it is possible to understand the ethno-architecture of the migrant experience at the scale of the house. The analysis of house materiality of these two Moroccan migrant homes in Israel has shown that, for them, there is a collective aesthetic and sense of belonging that situates them in a role of representing their culture and explaining it to others. Yet there is also the tension between the public and the private, the exterior and the interior, the house and the home, the national and the personal, that is reflected in these two stories. This exploration adds another layer to the ethno-architecture of the house: although looking into the interiors of the house, and thus different from other accounts of ethno-architecture of the house (e.g. Lozanovska 1997; Mitchell 2004), here too the relationship between the dominant society and the migrant community has been revealed.

NOTES

1 Throughout the chapter, the word Moroccan is used to denote the country of birth of those who participated in the research. This word may essentialise this diverse group of people, as all of them do not have unified qualities just because they happened to be born in the same country and migrate to another.

2 The founders of Israel, mostly Jewish immigrants who emigrated from Europe before 1948, Ashkenazi Jews.

3 'Development towns' were twenty eight settlements which were established in the periphery of Israel or on the outskirts of existing towns and cities during the 1950s, populated mostly by migrants.

4 Migrants of Middle Eastern or North African origin, *Mizrahim*.

5 Led by Menahem Begin (who was of western origin himself), the Likud was a right-wing party that came into power after almost thirty years of Labor leadership in Israel.

6 This was part of a larger research project which comprised data collection from 46 migrants from four origin countries and two destination countries.

7 All names used in this chapter are pseudonyms.

8 A Jewish ritual that marks the symbolic end of the Sabbath and Jewish holidays and ushers in the new week.

9 The plural form of *kibbutz*, which is a rural collective community in Israel.

10 Israel-born Jewish natives have been dubbed *tzabar*, which is also the Hebrew name of the prevalent common cactus (*Opuntia ficus-indica*).

11 The Passover dinner is called *seder*. *Matza* is unleavened bread eaten during the eight days of Passover.

12 A Jewish prenuptial agreement, signed by the fathers of the bride and groom.

REFERENCES

Allon, F. (2002) 'Translated Spaces/Translated Identities: The Production of Place, Culture and Memory in an Australian Suburb', *Journal of Australian Studies* 26, 72: 99–110.

Alon-Mozes, T., Shadar, H. and Vardi, L. (2009) 'The Poetics and the Politics of the Contemporary Sacred Place: Baba Sali's Grave Estate in Netivot, Israel', *Buildings & Landscapes* 16: 73–85.

CBS (2014) *Statistical Abstracts of Israel 2013*, Jerusalem: Central Bureau of Statistics.

Dibbits, H. (2009) 'Furnishing the Salon: Symbolic Ethnicity and Performative Practices in Moroccan-Dutch Domestic Interiors', *International Journal of Consumer Studies* 33: 550–557.

Glassman, I. and Eiskivoits, R. A. (2006) 'Intergenerational Transmission of Motherhood Patterns: Three Generations of Immigrant Mothers of Moroccan Descent in Israel', *Journal of Comparative Family Studies* 37: 461–477.

Jacobs, J. M. (2004) 'Too Many Houses for a Home: Narrating the House in the Chinese Diaspora', in S. Cairns (ed.) *Drifting: Architecture and Migrancy*, pp. 164–183, London and New York: Routledge.

Kallus, R. and Law Yone, H. (2002) 'National Home/Personal Home: Public Housing and the Shaping of National Space in Israel', *European Planning Studies* 10: 765–779.

King, A. D. (1997) 'Excavating the Multicultural Suburb: Hidden Histories of the Bungalow', in R. Silverstone (ed.) *Visions of Suburbia*, pp. 55–85, London: Routledge.

Levin, I. (2013) '"This is for the children, the grandchildren …": Houses of Moroccan Immigrants in Metropolitan Tel Aviv', *Housing, Theory and Society*, DOI: 10.1080/14036096.2013.782891.

Levy, A. (1997) 'To Morocco and Back: Tourism and Pilgrimage Among Morocco-born Israelis', in E. Ben-Ari and Y. Bilu (eds.) *Grasping Land: Space and Place in Contemporary Israeli Discourse and Experience*, pp. 25–46, New York: State University of New York Press.

Lozanovska, M. (1997) 'Abjection and Architecture: The Migrant House in Multicultural Australia', in G. B. Nalbontoglu and C. T. Wong (eds.) *Postcolonial Space(s)*, pp. 101–129, New York: Princeton Architectural Press.

Lozanovska, M. (2008) 'Resisting Assimilation: The Mild Aesthetics and Wild Perceptions of the Migrant House', Paper presented at the *XXXVth International Conference of the Society of Architectural Historians*, Australia and New Zealand, Geelong, Australia.

Mey-Ami, N. (2005) *The Jews of Morocco – Immigration and Absorption*, Jerusalem: The Knesset Research Centre [Hebrew].

Miller, D. (ed.) (2001) *Home Possessions: Material Culture Behind Closed Doors*, Oxford: Berg.

Mitchell, K. (2004) 'Conflicting Landscapes of Dwelling and Democracy in Canada', in S. Cairns (ed.) *Drifting: Architecture and Migrancy*, pp. 142–163, London: Routledge.

Noble, G. (2002) 'Comfortable and Relaxed: Furnishing the Home and Nation', *Continuum: Journal of Media & Cultural Studies* 16, 1: 53–66.

Portugali, M. (1993) *Roots in Morocco*, Bnei-Brak: Steimatzky [Hebrew].

Salih, R. (2003) *Gender in Transnationalism: Home, Longing and Belonging among Moroccan Migrant Women*, London: Routledge.

Thomas, M. (1997) 'Discordant Dwellings: Australian Houses and the Vietnamese Diaspora', in I. Ang and M. Symonds (eds.) *Home, Displacement, Belonging, Communal/Plural 5*, pp. 95–114, Sydney: Research Centre in Intercommunal Studies.

Tolia-Kelly, D. (2004) 'Locating Processes of Identification: Studying the Precipitates of Re-memory through Artefacts in the British Asian home', *Transactions of the Institute of British Geographers* 29: 314–329.

Tsur, Y. (1997) 'Carnival Fears: Moroccan Immigrants and the Ethnic Problem in the Young State of Israel', *Journal of Israeli History* 18, 1: 73–104.

Turan, Z. (2010) 'Material Objects as Facilitating Environments: The Palestinian Diaspora', *Home Cultures* 7: 43–56.

Tzfadia, E. and Yacobi, H. (2007) 'Identity, Migration, and the City: Russian Immigrants in Contested Urban Space in Israel', *Urban Geography* 28, 5: 436–455.

Weingrod, A. (1993) 'Changing Israeli Landscapes: Buildings and the Uses of the Past', *Cultural Anthropology* 8: 370–387.

Yiftachel, O. (2000) 'Social Control, Urban Planning and Ethno-class Relations: Mizrahi Jews in Israel's "Development Towns"', *International Journal of Urban and Regional Research 2000* 24, 2: 418–438.

Chapter 8: A comfortable home

Architecture, migration and old age in the Netherlands

Marcel Vellinga

LITTLE INDONESIA IN THE DUTCH *POLDER*

In 2005, reports appeared in the Dutch media about plans to build a so-called 'Indonesian village' in Almere (e.g. De Volkskrant 2005; Leidsch Dagblad 2005). Developed by the Foundation Rumah Senang (Indonesian for 'comfortable home'), the plans involved the construction of a distinct neighbourhood that, by means of its architecture and facilities, aimed to provide a setting where members of the Indisch community (descendants of mixed Indonesian and Dutch relationships) were reminded of 'the olden times' (Indonesian: tempo doeloe) as experienced in the former Dutch East Indies (the present-day Indonesia).[1] The proposals included the construction of 190 homes; a communal building in which social and recreational activities were to take place; and a restaurant and supermarket. A main building comprising of 46 apartments, four psycho-geriatric units, a communal kitchen and living room, and small enterprises including a hairdresser and pedicure, was meant to act as the focal point of the village. This main building was to be built in the style of a traditional Minangkabau house, as found in the Indonesian province of West Sumatra (see Vellinga 2004), complete with colourful woodcarvings and upsweeping roof spires. The other buildings were to be built in a 'more modest' Indonesian style, inspired by the architecture of the Karo Batak people in North Sumatra (Domenig 2003), adding to the Indonesian character of the village, whilst simultaneously meeting Dutch building requirements.[2]

Due to a lack of investment, the Rumah Senang village was never realised. In 2010, media reports announced the Foundation's reluctant decision to abandon the project (Almerevandaag 2010). By that time, however, a similar project had been proposed by the same initiators in the neighbouring city of Lelystad, this time entitled Desa Warande ('desa' meaning 'village' in Indonesian; 'warande' signifying 'park' in old Dutch) (De Telegraaf 2008). As in the case of Rumah Senang, this 'Indonesian village' project aimed to provide a setting that reminded its inhabitants of the Indonesian archipelago, comprising of a range of houses and communal facilities, including a restaurant and supermarket, built in an Indonesian style, this

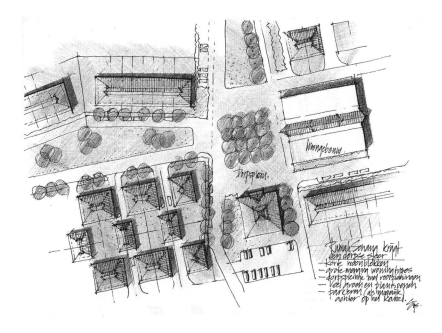

Figure 8.1
Rumah Senang, a
sketch plan, Almere.
Reproduction courtesy
Lex Burgersdijk.

Figure 8.2
Rumah Senang,
perspective sketch of a
family house, Almere.
Reproduction courtesy
of Lex Burgersdijk.

time on a small number of artificially created islands. The houses included so-called 'lifetime home' properties, as well as a significant number of psycho-geriatric apartments.[3] In contrast to Rumah Senang, all buildings in Desa Warande were to be built in an architectural style inspired by the Minangakabau vernacular, with exposed beams and spired gabled roofs. At the time of writing in 2014, this project had also been abandoned, due to a lack of financial means.

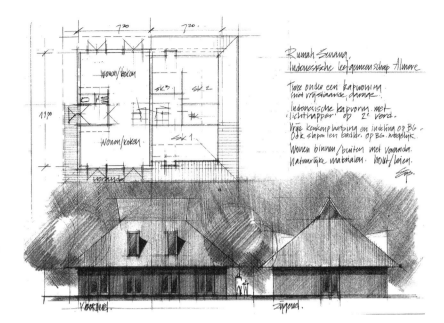

Figure 8.3
Rumah Senang, plan
and elevation sketch
of a family house,
Almere. Reproduction
courtesy of Lex
Burgersdijk.

Not surprisingly, the Rumah Senang and Desa Warande projects received a lot of attention in the Dutch media, featuring regularly in newspapers, radio broadcasts and online forums. The majority of this media coverage was sympathetic, outlining the motivations of the initiators and informing the public about the progress of the projects. Nonetheless, critical voices could be heard also (e.g. De Volkskrant 2005; De Gooi- en Eemlander 2005). Although distinctive in their intention to create Indisch villages in the Netherlands, neither project was unique in the context of Dutch housing in the early 2000s. At a time when the use of Dutch

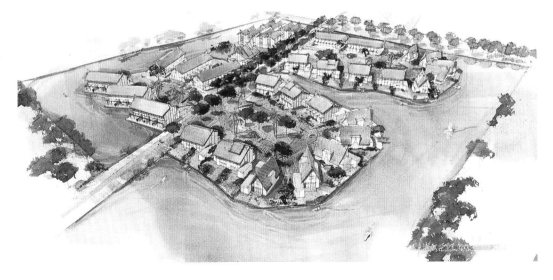

Figure 8.4 Desa Warande, an impression of the plan, Lelystad. Reproduction courtesy of Lex Burgersdijk.

Figure 8.5 Desa Warande, an impression of the family houses, Lelystad. Reproduction courtesy of Lex Burgersdijk.

vernacular precedents became a prominent force in Dutch architecture (Kersten 2007), other ethnically themed housing developments also began to appear, like Le Medi in Rotterdam, a housing complex inspired by Mediterranean architecture (Redactie ArchitectuurNL 2009). In a country wrestling with its secular and liberal traditions in the wake of extremist attacks and continued popular debates about the impacts of immigration (e.g. Scheffer 2000; Carle 2006), the emergence of housing developments identified by cultural association inevitably intensified discussions about multicultural integration. Subsequent debates about so-called 'halal houses' (a populist term referring to the design of houses that incorporate Islamic principles of spatial use) (De Telegraaf 2012), in reference to attempts to develop 'multi-cultural housing design' (e.g. VROM Raad 2002; Sohilait and Schmitz 2006), made ethnically inspired developments like Rumah Senang and Desa Warande politically charged projects.

In addition to the questions they raised about the impacts of immigration and multiculturalism in the Netherlands at the beginning of the twenty-first century, Rumah

Senang and Desa Warande also invited reflection on a range of architectural issues. Apart from calling attention to the role that architecture may play in the objectification of cultural identities, the projects raised questions about the appropriation of vernacular forms in contemporary design, the nature of lifetime homes, and the possibilities of so-called 'custom build' housing projects (Brown 2014). In this chapter, the focus will be restricted to the motivation behind the projects. It will be argued that the reason for their development is to be found in the way in which they responded to the needs of an ageing group of immigrants. Investigating the intentions and appeal of the projects on the basis of publicity materials, media reports and online forums, the argument is put forward that the projects represented a means by which the Indisch community in the Netherlands attempted to accommodate the wishes of its elderly 'first and second generation' members. In merging Indisch, Dutch and Indonesian traditions, the projects represented an 'Indonesian village' that never existed as such in the colonial Dutch Indies. Rather than attempts to create ethnic gated communities that defy or question the multicultural traditions of the Netherlands by holding on to strictly defined cultural traditions, they were projects that embraced the multicultural heritage of the Indisch community (and, indeed, the Netherlands) and tried to create a built environment that helps to constitute a contemporary sense of home, belonging and togetherness for its older members within an increasingly multicultural Dutch society.

MOTIVATIONS AND INTEREST

From the beginning, a nostalgic longing for the past appeared as a main motivation for both projects. Project documentation and publicity material emphatically announced the Foundation Rumah Senang as 'the Foundation that revives "*tempo doeloe*" ('the olden times')'. In the Foundation's newsletters and in media interviews, the initiators emphasised that the project would create an architectural and social environment that would help to invoke memories of the past and that would enable inhabitants to share those memories with each other. The same rationale lay behind the Desa Warande project. In the first Rumah Senang newsletter, a section entitled 'How it started' tells of the Foundation's chairman's dream: 'He dreamed that, in later life, he would grow old together with other people who love Indonesia, in a district built in an Indonesian style, where one will be reminded of the *tempo doeloe* of old' (Stichting Rumah Senang 2004: 2).[4] This dream, the chairman emphasised, was not just his own, but was shared by many other people of Indisch descent. 'During my career', he noted in an interview in De Gooi- en Eemlander (2005), 'I found that many others shared that dream. People have longed for this for years. They become homesick when they hear about our idea.' This nostalgic sentiment indeed seemed to be shared by those who expressed an interest in the projects, many of whom identified a strong desire to talk about their past and to share memories with other Indisch people (Leidsch Dagblad 2005; Indisch4ever.nu 2005). Nostalgia thus appeared to form a cornerstone of both projects.

Nonetheless, the projects were clearly as much, if not more, about the present as they were about the past. Alongside the desire to reminisce about the old times, the wish to be able to live together as an Indisch community, to eat together and chat and look after one another, here and now, appeared as a strong motivation. The project documentation and media reports consistently noted the importance of family and togetherness in the Indisch culture, and emphasised the projects' aim to create built environments in which these key elements of the Indisch identity could be enjoyed, and indeed reinforced, in unique and comfortable architectural surroundings (an ability not shared by other housing projects). In the words of the chairman: 'Our culture is one of eating and a lot of talking. Of course, those things are much cosier when one lives together as a group' (Leidsch Dagblad 2005). This longing for contemporary sociability was also noted among those interested in the project. One couple, for instance, noted that 'for us, it is mainly about the sociability (Dutch: *gezelligheid*) that we will find in the village. It must be lovely to live among all those Indisch people' (onzeplek.nl 2006). Although a need to talk about the past was regularly mentioned, it was the opportunity to enjoy those memories with those who share them, here and now, that appeared as a main motivation.

Notwithstanding the centrality of notions of togetherness and sociability in the conceptualisation and representation of both projects, the initiators, no doubt aware of the debates around multiculturalism, appeared inclusive rather than exclusive in their intentions. In all publicity it was expressly stated that 'all those with an affinity for Indonesia' were welcome in the villages. Although most interest was expected from people of Indisch descent, people of different cultural backgrounds, such as ethnic Dutch or Moluccans, were invited to register as well.[5] Some, indeed, appear to have done so, attracted by the perceived strong social cohesion of Indisch family life (Leidsch Dagblad 2005). A commitment to inclusivity was also apparent from the fact that people of all ages were welcome to register. The projects included lifetime homes and psycho-geriatric care units, which meant that the needs of young families, middle-aged couples and elderly people could all be accommodated. In the words of the secretary of the Foundation: 'Eating together and communally looking after one another are very important [in the Indisch culture]. This will be a village where you will not have to leave when you get old and needy' (pelita.nl 2006). In presenting the projects, the initiators thus took care to emphasise their commitment to inclusivity. Regardless of nationality, culture or age, people were welcome as long as they had an affinity with Indonesia.

Both projects appear to have been relatively popular. Although official figures are not available and the numbers used in the media vary, both projects were oversubscribed. Figures for Rumah Senang, range from 300 interested people in 2004 to 750 in 2006 and 900 in 2009 (pelita.nl 2006; Stadsradio Almere 2009), while Desa Warande attracted from 950 (lelystadnu.nl 2008) to 'nearly a 1,000' (Redactie ArchitectuurNL 2008) registrations.[6] Despite the inclusive intentions of the initiators, most of those interested appear to have been elderly people of Indisch descent, comprising members of the so-called first and second generation; that is, those Indisch people who were born in the former colonies, or who were born shortly after their parents migrated to the Netherlands (and who, by 2004, would have been at least in their mid-fifties). This demographic profile was no doubt anticipated by the initiators, who intended the projects to be retirement developments and had included a significant number of psycho-geriatric units (De Volkskrant 2005).[7] Indeed, they appear to have used the demographic profile of the registrants to speed up the development of the projects: 'We are in a hurry. A lot of people want to grow old in the village and I understand that one will already be unable to participate, as he passed away recently' (Leidsch Dagblad 2005). The popularity of the projects among elderly members of the Indisch community (and the limited interest among younger people) is perhaps not surprising. Interest in Indisch history, identity and culture is much stronger among members of the first and second generation than it is among the third and fourth generation. Indeed, it is so rapidly declining among the latter generations that it may no longer be possible to speak of an Indisch culture and community in the not-so-distant future (De Vries 2009: 358–363). To come together as members of the Indisch community, to feel a part of it, to maintain links with its past and to share memories of it; all of this is of great importance to elderly members of the community, but of limited appeal to younger generations.

REPATRIATION AND INTEGRATION

In one way, the almost exclusive interest in the project among the first or second generations is thus perfectly understandable. After all, they are the Indisch people who will have experienced life in the former Dutch Indies, albeit, in most cases, only as young children. The third and fourth generations would not have lived in Indonesia, and hence will not have the same affinity with it. However, from another perspective, the interest of the first and second generations also comes as a surprise. In 2004, most surviving members of the first and second generations would have lived in the Netherlands from a (very) young age. Although ethnically different, in terms of their economic and educational profile they will have been very similar to – if not indistinguishable – from other Dutch people. Studies of the Indisch community repeatedly emphasise the successful integration of its members into Dutch society (Van Amersfoort and Van Niekerk 2006). In order to do well, helped by their Dutch citizenship and their prior knowledge of Dutch culture, the Indisch community members generally blended in smoothly after their arrival in the 1940s and 1950s, adopting the customs of the Netherlands and developing only a few of the ethnically specific institutions (like clubs or newspapers) that are often set up by migrant groups to help maintain a group identity. The explicit emphasis, some 50 years later, on the Indisch past and identity that characterised both projects, and the apparent need of the initiators and registrants to distinguish them from other Dutch housing developments, was therefore unexpected.

To understand the reasons behind the appeal of the projects, an understanding of the history of the Indisch community and its migration to the Netherlands is required.[8] The term Indisch is used to identify people who are acknowledged descendants of mixed relations between Dutch colonials and native Indonesians (Van Amersfoort and Niekerk 2006). Numerous legalised relationships between, commonly, Dutch men and Indonesian women took place throughout the colonial period, resulting in a large Eurasian population in Indonesia who had Dutch citizenship. In terms of its social, economic and political status, this Indisch population had always been heterogeneous. Nonetheless, most of them occupied lower middle-class positions in the civil service or military, while the community as a whole occupied an intermediate position between the native Indonesians and Dutch colonial elite. Due to their mixed ethnic background, and despite their legal Dutch status, the Indisch community occupied a second-class position in colonial society in comparison to the European Dutch, and many of them suffered from discrimination (Van Amersfoort and Van Niekerk 2006). Notwithstanding this stigmatisation, the Indisch community commonly oriented itself toward Dutch culture, assuming Dutch lifestyles rather than native ones. In this way, the Indisch community became more and more entangled with the Dutch colonial rulers (De Vries 2009).

During the 1940s, when Indonesia was occupied by the Japanese and, after several years of bloody conflict, declared its independence from the Netherlands, the position of the Indisch community became increasingly difficult. Because of their close association with the Dutch colonial system due to their prominent role in the colonial military and civil service, Indisch people had been persecuted by both the Japanese occupiers and the nationalist native population. During the Second World War most were interned in Japanese camps, while many were used as forced labourers. An estimated 13–20% of the total Indisch population died (Bosma, Raben and Willems 2006). In response to the continuous violence directed at them during and after the war for Indonesian independence, the vast majority of Indisch people took the decision to migrate to the Netherlands. Although no exact figures exist, some 200,000 people (95% of the entire Indisch community) migrated to the Netherlands during the period 1945–65 (Van Amersfoort 1982). A significant number moved on to Australia, Canada and the US, but the majority stayed in the Netherlands. Together with the Dutch colonials, who were similarly repatriated after Indonesian independence, the Indisch people formed the most extensive category of international migrants ever to have settled in the Netherlands. Up until today, their descendants make up the largest group of immigrants in the country (De Vries 2009: 17).

The Dutch government and members of the Indisch community both understood that a return to Indonesia was unlikely and increasingly impossible. Van Amersfoort and Van Niekerk (2006) have detailed how the Dutch government put in place a top-down integration policy that aimed to quickly absorb the Indisch community into mainstream Dutch society. Despite the poverty, poor infrastructure and shortage of housing in the Netherlands in the 1950s (due to the fact that the country had itself been occupied by Germany during the Second World War), 5% of all new housing in the country was reserved for immigrants from Indonesia. A timely economic boom in the 1950s helped to alleviate the problem of unemployment that initially loomed large. The integration of the Indisch community into Dutch society was greatly helped by its members' determination to adapt to their new circumstances. Helped by their prior knowledge of Dutch culture, members of the Indisch community quickly managed to find employment and encouraged their children to benefit from the country's education system. By the 1970s, 'the problem of the absorption of immigrants from Indonesia had been solved insofar as participation in the labour and the housing markets and, for the younger generation, the educational system, was concerned' (Van Amersfoort and Van Niekerk 2006: 328). But with the successful integration into Dutch society, the interest among younger Indisch generations in life in the former colony had diminished. Although a revaluation of Indisch culture and a growing Indisch self-awareness among members of the second generation has been noted since the 1980s, possibly influenced by the growing multicultural demography of the Netherlands (De Vries 2009), the ethnic identification as Indisch seems no longer that important to young Indisch people.

TRAUMA AND GERIATRIC CARE

Although the integration process was generally speaking successful, it was not without its challenges. Many of the Indisch people felt insecure about their social status in the Netherlands. Although they had Dutch citizenship, they had always known that they occupied a second-class position in Indonesia, one located between the colonial elite and the native population. For most, their feelings of social inferiority were strengthened on arrival in the Netherlands, aware as they were that the Dutch government had not really wanted them to come. The vast majority of Indisch people had never been to the Netherlands before and knew the country and its people only from the media and geography lessons in school. They had not wanted to migrate and had no specific wish to stay, but realised they had no other choice. Having lived through a period of much uncertainty and hardship, their forced settlement in the Netherlands was a difficult process: 'They had to get to terms with a new country, a different climate, unfamiliar customs, different food and different people' (Engels 2010: 5). The reception by the Dutch was not always warm. Many Indisch people had the feeling that they were outsiders who, despite their citizenship, had to be thankful for being allowed to live in the Netherlands.

Undoubtedly influenced by their difficult experiences, a longing for the lifestyle associated with the colonial past remained strong among the migrants, especially the members of the first generation. Nonetheless, in their attempts to help their families integrate into Dutch society, this longing was often hidden from public view. To the outside world, they tried to be as Dutch as possible, commonly assuming a modest and resigned attitude in their relationship with their Dutch employers and neighbours. Their problems, fears and frustrations were not talked about, neither with Dutch people nor among members of the Indisch community themselves. Nor did they discuss their often traumatic experiences of the Second World War and subsequent struggle for Indonesian independence. As frequently noted (e.g. De Vries 2009; Engels 2010), this reticence about the Indisch past and identity was problematic for their children, the second generation, who found themselves caught between an Indisch and a Dutch world. On the one hand, they were taught by their parents to be modest in their relationships with the Dutch and to integrate as much as they could; on the other hand, they grew up as part of an

Indisch culture and sensed that their parents resented the Dutch for being rude, inhospitable and uninterested in their experiences. 'They were not allowed to be too *Indisch*, certainly not in public, but they could not be too Dutch either' (Engels n.d.). Only from the 1980s did the second generation start to become more explicit about its Indisch inheritance. Around the same time, an awareness of the hidden suffering of the first generation began to emerge.

Many of the first-generation Indisch had experienced violence, persecution, internment, forced labour and hunger during the Japanese occupation of Indonesia and the following struggle for independence. Once in the Netherlands, most had hidden the feelings of fear, guilt, anger and depression that often stay with people after such experiences (Stichting Centrum '45 2012), in public as well as within their own families. However, as the first generation became older, the traumas that had been suppressed for so long became more apparent, while the sense of their Indisch identity and the wish to reflect on it with people of a similar background grew stronger.[9] Increasingly also, with age, they became dependent on institutionalised elderly care (Engels 2010; Wallenburg 2011). Although geriatric care facilities were readily available in the Netherlands, ranging from hospitals and care homes to domestic help at home, it became apparent that the norms, values and behaviour of the Indisch community did not always accord with mainstream Dutch notions about ageing and elderly care. Many Indisch people found it difficult to articulate their wishes and needs, and their fears or worries (all of which they had hidden for so long) to their Dutch carers. This inability, coupled with a basic lack of understanding of the Indisch history and culture on the part of many carers, led to frustrations on both sides. Examples abound where Indisch people complained about the rude and inconsiderate behaviour of carers, while the staff complained about the cumbersomeness of the Indisch residents (e.g. Wallenburg 2011). Especially when traumatic experiences related to the past manifested themselves in confused, erratic or aggressive behaviour, carers were often unable to recognise the reasons for it or to formulate an appropriate response.

Although research into the influence of culture on the experience of the ageing process and elderly care is in its infancy, especially in the context of migration (Blakemore 1999; Torres 1999; Warnes *et al.* 2004), similar problems in care situations have been noted elsewhere (Chau and Yu 2000). In response to the growing awareness of the culturally specific nature of ageing and the need for appropriate elderly care provision, a number of geriatric-care housing projects that cater specifically for Indisch people were established during the 2000s. Care homes like Rumah Kita in Wageningen and Singel Senang in Den Haag aim to provide care that is in keeping with the Indisch lifestyle. They offer a combination of independent living apartments, communal facilities and activities, and psycho-geriatric units for people with dementia, and emphasise the Indisch heritage of the inhabitants. Carers speak Indonesian and Dutch, serve Indisch food, provide opportunities to talk about the Indisch past and take account of Indisch notions of privacy, personal hygiene and spirituality. Although all are housed in standard Dutch architecture, an Indisch atmosphere is created through the use of furniture, decorations and music. The care homes have proved very popular among members of the first and second generation and reflect the 'activist' model of ageing that is common in the Netherlands, where elderly people maintain control of their life in old age, stay independent as long as possible, engage in a variety of social activities and create living environments that suit their needs (Blakemore 1999).

CONTEMPORARY INDISCH ARCHITECTURE

When viewed in the wider context, the emphasis on the Indisch past and identity of both the Rumah Senang and Desa Warande projects no longer comes as a surprise. Both projects were very similar to care homes like Rumah Kita and Singel Senang, in that they also tried to provide settings where people could live together in a familiar Indisch atmosphere, sharing facilities, meals, reminiscences and activities. Nonetheless, there were differences too. One of the main ones is that both projects would have been open to people of all ages and cultural backgrounds and not just to ageing members of the Indisch community. Although both projects included psycho-geriatric units and proved particularly popular among elderly Indisch people, in principle they were available to everyone with an affinity for Indonesia. As well as reflecting an awareness of the sensitivity of ethnic developments in a country troubled by multiculturalism, this openness may be a result of an understanding on the initiators' part that if the projects were aimed at elderly Indisch people only, they would not have had much of a future. In line with the general declining interest in the Indisch culture among younger generations, studies of the Indisch care homes have shown that interest in them is almost absent among members of the third generation (Engels 2010; Wallenburg 2011). In view of the advanced age of the first and second generations, this means that the projects would probably have been of interest for about 15 years; a limited 'shelf life' indeed, and possibly one of the reasons why the initiators failed to raise the investment required.

Another difference between both projects and the Indisch care homes, one that is of particular interest here, is that the former attempted to go one step further in the creation of an environment that invoked an Indonesian atmosphere by using architectural forms that were inspired by buildings found traditionally in Indonesia. Most notable, in this respect, was the use of hipped roof forms and exposed beams, both distinctive characteristics of vernacular Indonesian building forms, to create a hint of 'Indonesia-ness'. This conscious strategy to express the affinity with Indonesia in architectural form indicates the potential of architecture to objectify and affirm cultural identities, as well as their suitability to draw attention to them. It also hints at the ability of traditions to create a sense of comfort, connection and trust (Bronner 2006). Perhaps not unexpectedly, however, this decision to use Indonesian architectural forms was critically received. Van Roosmalen (2006) questioned the initiators' decision to use Minangkabau and Karo Batak building traditions to create an Indisch what she called 'gated community'. The difference between Indonesian and Indisch, she noted, is a real one. The Indisch culture is a mixture of Dutch and Indonesian elements developed during the colonial period that in time produced its own form of architecture, distinct from vernacular Indonesian forms and more akin to European traditions.[10] It would have made more sense if the initiators and architect had used this Indisch architecture as inspiration: 'I am, *a priori*, no advocate for imitation "architecture"', she wrote. 'But if we have to choose imitation architecture, wouldn't it be most obvious to use *Indisch* architecture as an example for an *Indisch* village?' Not only did the use of vernacular Indonesian precedents show a lack of respect for the cultures concerned; their 'flat' and 'superficial' application did not, in Van Roosmalen's opinion, deserve the title of 'architecture'.

In reply, the architect of Rumah Senang, Eijsbouts (2006), noted that the choice of Indonesian traditions was a conscious one. Indisch, he noted, is a collective noun for various hybrid architectural styles. It consists of numerous European influences, 'from neo-classical to Dudok', mixed with various Indonesian vernacular traditions.[11] To attempt a contemporary interpretation of Indisch architecture would be to create 'a hybrid of a hybrid'. Instead of replicating a historical Indisch style, the initiators wanted to create a contemporary Indisch style, one that combined 'the here and now' with traditional Indonesian elements, so as to create 'a new Indisch' architecture that expressed the experience of being Indisch in the Netherlands at the beginning of the twenty-first century. Thus, traditional Indonesian architectural elements like the Minangkabau roof form have been combined with Dutch construction materials and building specifications to create contemporary versions of Indisch architecture that reflect the mixed Indonesian and Dutch heritage of the Indisch community. Eijsbouts emphasised that the use of Indonesian roof forms was not just 'for show'; in addition to providing an Indonesian feel, the characteristic eaves would serve as light wells that help to illuminate the central parts of the houses.

Whether this design approach was successful and resulted in 'architecture' or not will undoubtedly remain a matter of contention in architectural circles. Here, it is more interesting to note that the initiators were clearly not holding on to a static notion of what Indisch architecture is, but seemed more interested in creating a built environment that could be seen to objectify a contemporary sense of 'Indisch-ness'. Their approach recognised that being Indisch in the Netherlands in the early twenty-first century is a very different experience from what it was more than 60 years before in the Dutch East Indies. In the eyes of the initiators, this difference required an equally different architectural embodiment, one that drew on Indonesian and Dutch traditions but was able to meet the needs of Indisch people here and now. In this case, the main need was to create a comfortable home where elderly Indisch people might live together in familiar surroundings, in the company of family, friends and carers who understood their wishes and expectations. An architectural form that combined Dutch and Indonesian traditions was seen to be able to contribute to the creation of such familiarity.

Whether a desire among members of the younger generation to objectify their Indisch self-awareness also played a part, possibly in response to the increasingly multicultural demography of the Netherlands, remains a question.[12] The difference between the intention of the initiators to manifestly objectify their affinity with

Indonesia in architectural form and the earlier tendency of the Indisch community to be reticent about its Indonesian heritage is striking. As noted, the first generation was always cautious about showing its nostalgic longing for the past in public – a reticence that was problematic to later generations, who found themselves caught between two worlds. The Rumah Senang and Desa Warande projects reversed this attitude by openly declaring the importance of Indonesian heritage in meeting the current needs of the Indisch community. The use of architecture for the purpose of ethnic identification is of course nothing new and has regularly been observed around the world, in both the past and present. In this case, it gives rise to a range of questions that deserve further attention. To what extent, for instance, was the architectural objectification of the Indisch identity responsible for the more controversial reception of both projects, as compared to the other Indisch care homes? To what extent were the projects a conscious attempt on behalf of the Indisch community to affirm its position in the increasingly multicultural landscape of the contemporary Netherlands? And how did both projects relate and contribute to wider debates about migration and multiculturalism? The popularity of so-called 'retro-architecture' in the Netherlands during the same period is notable (Kersten 2007); as is the emergence of other ethnically themed housing developments (Redactie ArchitectuurNL 2009) and the official attempts to define so-called 'multicultural design' (VROM Raad 2002; Sohilait and Schmitz 2006).

All those developments seem to coincide with popular debates around the impacts of immigration. In what intricate way they all interrelate remains to be investigated. Whatever the case may be, the architectural designs for Rumah Senang and Desa Warande were certainly no unreflective 'imitations' of historic Indisch or vernacular Indonesian styles, as Van Roosmalen would have it (nor indeed, as shown before, were they 'gated communities'). In combining contemporary Dutch and traditional Indonesian styles, they tried to embrace the multicultural architectural heritage of the Indisch community, rather than attempt to be narrowly prescriptive about what are appropriate forms of Indisch architecture and what are not.

CONCLUSIONS

The motivation for Rumah Senang and Desa Warande appears to be found in the need of the Indisch community to provide comfortable surroundings for its elderly members. The first and second generation of Indisch migrants came to the Netherlands soon after the Second World War. Helped by their Dutch citizenship, their knowledge of the language and their work ethic, they quickly managed to settle into Dutch society. Nonetheless, a longing for the lifestyle associated with the colonial past remained strong among many, while the fears and frustrations that came with several years of hardship in Indonesia, followed by a process of forced displacement to the Netherlands, were commonly suppressed. As they grew older, a desire to reflect on their lives in the company of other Indisch people who shared their experiences became stronger, while traumas related to the past began to reveal themselves more clearly. With increased age, an awareness of the need for culturally appropriate geriatric care arose. A number of care institutions that cater for the Indisch community were established from the 2000s onwards. Both projects were clearly a part of this development, albeit that they were in principle also open to members of other age and cultural groups. What made them especially distinct from the other projects was the fact that they intended to create an architectural as well as social environment that reminded its inhabitants of Indonesia. It is this aspect, more than anything, that set them apart from other Indisch care homes and that resulted in the intense media attention and occasional raised eyebrow.

Despite what some commentators inferred, the initiators did not attempt to create ethnic 'gated communities'. Both projects were socially and culturally inclusive and refused to look backwards to a fixed and exclusive Indisch past in architectural terms. They attempted to create an environment that would meet the needs of elderly Indisch people, as ascertained in the Netherlands in the early 2000s. As such, they are examples of the 'custom-built' housing projects that were encouraged by the Dutch government at the time, as well as manifestations of an active ageing model that sees people take control of their life in old age (Blakemore 1999). As projects that have been instigated by migrant groups, they are also examples of the multicultural design projects promoted by the Dutch government (VROM Raad 2002; Sohilait and Schmitz 2006). Because the projects were never realised, possibly due to their brief 'shelf life', it is difficult to say if the Indonesian-styled architecture would have added something to the experience of the inhabitants, as opposed to the experience of residents in other Indisch care homes. Research into the relationship between architecture and elderly care (see for example Salmon 1994; Burton and Mitchell 2006), as well as into the efficacy of so-called historicist design (Harris and Dostrovsky 2008), suggests that this may well have been the case.

In the context of a discussion about architecture and migration, *Rumah Senang and Desa Warande* draw attention to an important area of research. Gerontological research into the impacts of (international) migration on the process of ageing has been slow to develop (Blakemore 1999; Torres 1999; Warnes *et al.* 2004). Those studies that exist have revealed very complex relationships between ageing and migration, due to the culturally diverse nature of notions of ageing and the manifold forms of migration (e.g. Keith *et al.* 1994; Featherstone and Wernick 1995; Daatland and Biggs 2006). Clearly, to understand the needs and expectations of migrants when they get older is of paramount importance in a rapidly ageing world in which international migration has reached an unprecedented scale (UN Population Division 2013; IOM 2013). Blakemore (1999) and others have identified the need to better understand the relationship between ageing, culture and migration. The case study of Rumah Senang and Desa Warande reveals that the way in which the built environment is implicated in this interrelationship (both in terms of how existing forms of architecture are affected by changing needs as well as how they could be employed to accommodate the latter) is an important factor to take into account. Architectural form has the potential to objectify, affirm and draw attention to cultural identities; a potential that would seem to be of much importance in an age that is increasingly characterised as one of migration, multiculturalism and an ageing population.

NOTES

1 Over the years, various terms have been used to identify the descendants of mixed Dutch and Indonesian relationships, including Indos, Indo-Europeans and Eurasians. The commonly used term today, in Dutch, is *Indische Nederlander* ('Indisch Dutch'). In everyday language, *Indische mensen* ('Indisch people') is often heard as well. The term Indisch is here used, as this means it can be used as an adjective (as in Indisch people, Indisch history, etc.). Indisch people tend to use the now obsolete writing system based on Dutch spelling that was common in the colonial period. In contemporary Indonesian, *tempo doeloe* is written as *tempo dulu*.

2 I would like to thank Lex Burgersdijk for allowing me to reproduce the images of both the Rumah Senang and Desa Warande projects.

3 'Lifetime homes' (Dutch: *levensloopbestendig wonen*) is a term that refers to houses that have been designed in such a way that their inhabitants can continue to live in them if their circumstances change due to ill-health, disability or age.

4 Translations from Dutch into English are all by the author.

5 The Netherlands is home to a substantial Moluccan community, whose first-generation members came to the Netherlands after Indonesian independence. For a short history of their integration into Dutch society, see Van Amersfoort and Van Niekerk (2006).

6 There is some lack of clarity about the number of homes in Rumah Senang. Official promotion material lists 190 homes (80 houses for sale, 40 houses to let, 46 apartments and 4 communal homes containing 6 rooms each). Media reports generally speak of 'around 200 homes', but some appear to exclude the apartments and communal homes from this figure. In 2007, when the Foundation was told by the city of Almere that it had to reduce the number of homes to 100, its secretary claimed that the original plans had included 250 homes.

7 One media report refers to plans by the initiators to build a so-called 'care hotel' (Dutch: *zorghotel*) in Spain. 'It will be a kind of annex of Almere,' the Chairman is quoted as saying. 'Inhabitants of the care apartments in *Rumah Senang* can spend the winter in Spain. The hotel will be built in the same Sumatran style as in Almere' (De Gooi- en Eemlander 2005).

8 The literature on the Indisch history is fairly extensive, but mainly in Dutch. Works include Beets *et al.* (2002); Bosma and Raben (2003) and Van Leeuwen (2008).

9 The manifestation of traumas in older age is often observed and appears related to the fact that physical ailments become more apparent and people are more frequently confronted with death, as members of the same generation begin to pass away (Stichting Centrum '45 2012: 8). Both occurrences tend to act as triggers. An increasing wish among elderly Indisch people to reminiscence about the past has been noted by Engels (2010) and Wallenburg (2011), among others.

10 Relatively little has been written about Indisch architecture. For a brief overview see Passchier (2007).

11 Dudok is the Dutch architect Willem Marinus Dudok (1884–1974).

12 Commenting on the potential political sensitivity of the Rumah Senang project, the secretary, Burgersdijk said: 'Don't forget: We are Dutch. We have a Dutch passport. The only difference is our coloured skin. With this village, we only want to give people more fun and joy in life. What is wrong with that?' (De Gooi- en Eemlander 2005).

REFERENCES

Almerevandaag.nl (2010) 'Stekker uit Rumah Senang na gebrek aan investeerders'. 21 April. Online. http://www.almerevandaag.nl/almere/article6016227.ece/Stekker-uit-Rumah-Senang-na-gebrek-aan-investeerders (accessed 28 September 2012).

Beets, G., Huisman, C., Van Imhoff, E., Koesoebjono, S. and Walhout, E. (2002) *De Demografische Geschiedenis van de Indische Nederlanders*, Den Haag: NIDI.

Blakemore, K. (1999) 'International Migration in Later Life: Social Care and Policy Implications', *Ageing and Society* 19, 6: 761–774.

Bosma, U. and Raben, R. (2003) *De Oude Indische Wereld 1500–1920*, Amsterdam: Bert Bakker.

Bosma, U., Raben, R. and Willems, W. (2006) *De Geschiedenis van Indische Nederlanders.* Amsterdam: Bert Bakker.

Bronner, S. (2006) 'Building tradition: Control and authority in vernacular architecture', in Asquith, L. and Vellinga, M. (eds.) *Vernacular Architecture in the Twenty-First Century: Theory, Education and Practice*, pp. 23–45, London: Taylor and Francis.

Brown, S. (2014) 'Successful Collective Custom Builds Will Depend On Who Does The Enabling', *RIBA Journal*, 1 May. Online. Available http://www.ribaj.com/culture/leading-questions (accessed 20 June 2014).

Burton, E. and Mitchell, L. (2006) *Inclusive Urban Design: Streets for Life*, Oxford: Architectural Press.

Carle, R. (2006) 'Demise of Dutch multiculturalism', *Society*, March/April: 68–74.

Chau, C. and Yu, W.K. (2000) 'Chinese Older People in Britain: Double Attachment to Double Detachment', in A.M. Warnes, L. Warren, and M. Nolan, (eds.) *Care Services for Later Life: Transformations and Critiques*, pp. 259–272, London: Jessica Kingsley.

Daatland, S.O. and Biggs, S. (2006) *Ageing and Diversity*, Bristol: The Policy Press.

De Gooi- en Eemlander (2005) 'Indische Nostalgie in Almeerse Nieuwbouwwijk', precise date unknown.

De Telegraaf (2008) 'Lelystad Krijgt Indisch Dorp', Online. http://www.telegraaf.nl/binnen-land/20761687/__Lelystad_krijgt_Indisch_dorp__.html (accessed 28 September 2012).

De Telegraaf (2012) 'Uitslag Stelling: Halal Huizen om te Huilen', 27 November. Online. http://www.telegraaf.nl/watuzegt/wuz_stelling/21112072/__Niets_mis_met_halal_won-ingen__.html (accessed 3 December 2012).

De Volkskrant (2005) 'We combineren Indische Vormen met Europese Materialen', 12 October.

De Vries, M. (2009) *'Indisch is een Gevoel': De Tweede en Derde Generatie Indische Nederlander*, Amsterdam: Amsterdam University Press.

Domenig, G. (2003) 'Consequences of Functional Change: Granaries, Granary-Dwellings and Houses of the Toba Batak', in R. Schefold, G. Domeig, and P.J.M. Nas (eds.) *Indonesian Houses: Tradition and Transformation in Vernacular Architecture*, pp. 61–98, Leiden: KITLV Press.

Eijsbouts, E. (2006) 'Rumah Senang, Indisch of Indonesisch?', Online. http://www.archined.nl/nieuws/indisch-dorp-in-de-polder/ (accessed 28 September 2012).

Engels, J. (n.d.) 'De bindende kracht van herinneringen', Online. http://www.indischhistorisch.nl/tweede/sociale-geschiedenis/sociale-geschiedenis-de-bindende-kracht-van-herinner-ingen-over-indische-ouderen-en-hun-specifieke-wensen-en-zorgbehoeften-deel-1/-2/-3 (accessed 20 June 2014).

Engels, J. (2010) 'Twee Culturen aan de Binnenkant: Een Onderzoek naar Sociale en Culturele Bindingen bij Indische Senioren en de Wenselijkheid van Categoriale Ouderenvoorzieningen', Unpublished Dissertation: University of Amsterdam.

Featherstone, M. and Wernick, A. (1995) *Images of Aging: Cultural Representations of Later Life*, London: Routledge.

Harris, R. and Dostrovsky, N. (2008) 'The Suburban Culture of Building and the Reassuring Revival of Historicist Architecture since 1970', *Home Cultures* 5, 2: 167–196.

Indisch4ever.nu (2005) 'Senang in Almere', Online. http://indisch4ever.nu/2005/01/22/sen-ang_in_almer/ (accessed 28 September 2012).

IOM (2013) *World Migration Report 2013: Migrant Well-Being and Development*, Geneva: International Organization for Migration.

Keith, J., Fry, C.L., Glascock, A.P., Ikels, C., Dickerson-Putman, J., Harpending, H.C., and Draper, P. (1994) *The Aging Experience: Diversity and Commonality across Cultures*, Thousand Oaks, CA: Sage.

Kersten, G. (2007) 'Retro-architectuur: Net echt of net nep', *TOPOS* 2: 50–53.

Leidsch Dagblad (2005) 'Klein Indonesië in de Polder', 11 October.

Lelystadnu.nl (2008) 'Indisch Dorp verrijst op "Indonesische Archipel', *Warande Lelystad*. Online. http://www.lelystadnu.nl/nieuws/3775-%26%2339%3BIndisch+Dorp%26%2339%3B+verrijst+op+%26%2339%3BIndonesische+Archipel%26%2339%3B+in+Warande+Lelystad.html (accessed 28 September 2012).

onzeplek.nl (2006) 'Indisch dorp in de polder'. Online. http://www.onzeplek.nl/forum/forum_posts.asp?TID=43 (accessed 28 September 2012).

Passchier, C. (2007) 'Colonial Architecture in Indonesia', in P.J.M. Nas (ed.) *The Past in the Present: Architecture in Indonesia*, Leiden: KITLV Press.

Pelita.nl (2006) 'Groen Licht Indisch Dorp', Online. http://www.pelita.nl/cms/publish/content/showpage.asp?pageid=865 (accessed 28 September 2012).

Redactie ArchitectuurNL (2008) 'Indisch Dorp op Schiereilandjes in Nieuwe Wijk'. Online. http://architectuur.nl/nieuws/indisch-dorp-op-schiereilandjes-in-nieuwe-wijk/ (accessed 28 September 2012).

Redactie ArchitectuurNL (2009) 'Le Medi Rotterdam', Online. http://www.architectuur.nl/project/le-medi-rotterdam/ (accessed 28 September 2012).

Salmon, G. (1994) *Caring Environments for Frail Elderly People*, London: Longman.

Scheffer, P. (2000) 'Het multi-culturele drama', *NRC Handelsblad*, 29 January.

Sohilait, R. and Schmitz, P. (2006) *Multicultureel Bouwen en Wonen: Het Actief Betrekken van Allochtone Bewoners bij Ontwerpopgaven*, Utrecht: FORUM Instituut voor Multiculturele Vraagstukken.

Stadsradio Almere 107.8 Fm (2009) *Politiek Nu*, 26 May, 21.00–22.00pm.

Stichting Centrum '45 (2012) *Ouderen met Traumatische Ervaringen: Zorg en Behandeling*, Oegstgeest: Stichting Centrum '45.

Stichting Rumah Senang (2004) *Nieuwsbrief*, nr: 1-2004.

Torres. S. (1999) 'A Culturally-Relevant Theoretical Framework for the Study of Successful Ageing', *Ageing and Society* 19, 1: 33–51.

UN Population Division (2013) *World Population Prospects: The 2012 Revision: Key Findings and Advance Table*, New York: United Nations.

Van Amersfoort, H. (1982) *Immigration and the Formation of Minority Groups: The Dutch Experience 1945–1975*, Cambridge: Cambridge University Press.

Van Amersfoort, H. and Van Niekerk, M. (2006) 'Immigration as a Colonial Inheritance: Post-Colonial Immigrants in the Netherlands, 1945–2002', *Journal of Ethnic and Migration Studies* 31, 3: 323–346.

Van Leeuwen, L. (2008) *Ons Indisch Erfgoed: Zestig Jaar Strijd om Cultuur en Identiteit*, Amsterdam: Bert Bakker.

Van Roosmalen, P. (2006) 'Indisch Dorp in de Polder', Online. http://www.archined.nl/nieuws/indisch-dorp-in-de-polder/ (accessed 28 September 2012).

Vellinga, M. (2004) *Constituting Unity and Difference: Vernacular Architecture in a Minangkabau Village*, Leiden: KITLV Press.

VROM Raad (2002) *Smaken Verschillen: Multicultureel Bouwen en Wonen*, Den Haag: VROM Raad.

Wallenburg, M. (2011) '"Oud Worden in een Vertrouwde Omgeving": Een Theoretische en Beleidsmatige Beschouwing over het Bestaansrecht van Cultuurspecifieke Zorg voor Ouderen', Unpublished dissertation: Universiteit voor Humanistiek.

Warnes, A.M., Friedrich, K., Kellaher, L. and Torres, S. (2004) 'The Diversity and Welfare of Older Migrants in Europe', *Ageing and Society* 24, 3: 307–326.

Temporality of migrant constructions

Chapter 9: Awe and order

Ethno-architecture in everyday life

Arijit Sen

Devon Avenue is a bustling retail street on the northern edge of the city of Chicago in the United States of America. A section of this street is known for its Indian, Pakistani and Bangladeshi ethnic stores (Figure 9.1). Chicago locals call it 'Little India'. Among the few original immigrant-owned businesses is Patel Brothers. The business patriarch, Mafatbhai Patel, recounts the difficult yet determined early days when the store opened at 2034 Devon Avenue in 1974, 'my brother was handling daytime [business], because we … [worked in] shifts. … My brother … and his wife, Aruna … were working from 10 [am]. … I was coming 4 o'clock after work and Tulasibhai [his brother] was going after 4 pm to job [his second job in addition to managing the store]' (Mafat Patel 2013).

Into the second decade of the new millennium, in addition to their many grocery store outlets, the Patels own a food packaging and distribution business, travel agencies, clothing and handicrafts stores, and cafes. The conglomeration of stores moved from the simple, two-roomed space to multiple storefronts in an entire block on Devon Avenue. Posters in the grocery store suggest that they 'recreate India' on Devon Avenue and 'bring the best ingredients from around the world, right to your doorstep'(Patel Brothers 2014).

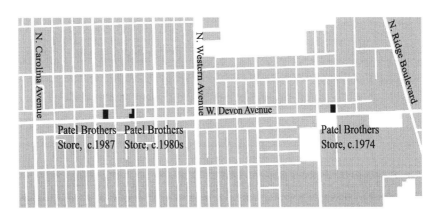

Figure 9.1
Map of Devon Avenue, Chicago showing various locations of Patel Brothers stores.
Copyright Arijit Sen.

Using the example of the Patel Brothers grocery store, this chapter examines how cultural, sensory, and symbolic cues, coded Indian, mark and claim territory on this street, and how the resultant ethno-architecture, in its turn, influences the way immigrants understand, perceive, and reproduce ethnicity. Ethno-architecture stages human behavior and interactions, promotes a sense of in-group belonging, cultivates distinction, and perpetuates cultural memory. In this, the smells of exotic food and sounds of foreign languages reproduce a unique sensorium. A complex visual culture made up of displays, signage, colors, advertisements, and imagery on the storefronts, contributes to a growing ethnic identity. All these together mark this street as ethnic and the store as an example of ethno-architecture.

Stereotypical descriptions of ethno-architecture are carefully reproduced in texts, images, and media forms. For example, in the *The Mistress of Spices*, Bay Area novelist Chitra Banerjee Divakaruni recreates an Indian spice store as exotic landscape and taste culture that is feminine and enticing (Banerjee 1998). Is this a form of 'self-commodification' or is it part of the narrative of poor-immigrant success stories, the heartwarming renditions of the possibilities of the American economic dream, the warm, fuzzy nostalgia of a world left behind, only to be dazzlingly recreated in a new metropolis (Mannur 2008: 56–71)? Such representations of the Indian grocery store are vivid in the American imagination, as is seen in the popular Indian spice tours along Devon Avenue (Singla 2014). One of the owners of the Patel Brothers stores, Swetal Patel, explains that the Indian grocery store has a unique image due to its visual and sensory ambience and the habitual daily activities inside the store. He invests in its sensorium: 'Your identity is still on bringing back the little touch of India with a modern effect. So, when you go into a Patel Brothers store, you know, as the owners are Hindu at 10 am you will have some sort of a *Ram Bhajan* [devotional songs] going until 10, 10:30, 11 o'clock, as there would be with an Indian shopkeeper in India' (Swetal Patel 2013). The social construction of an Indian store is sustained by persistent representations and practices.

Examining the store, media representations, interior ambience, and human activities in this grocery store gives a partial picture of the ethnic marketplace and how it is socially reproduced. The success of such places is built upon a carefully *ordered* world of enterprise and planning, and the sensuous and mysterious nature of the grocery store is not due to an unexplainable reproduction of cultural difference, or authentic Indianness seamlessly reproduced in America. The storeowners carefully curate these sensate landscapes and ambient atmospheres. Shoppers play a part too. Regular customers learn the internal layout and recognize where different kinds of merchandise are located, and thereby participate and perform in expected ways inside the stores. Therefore, while the ethnic store is a social construction, the store in turn reproduces and reiterates the cultural expectations, behavior, and identities of users.

Ethnic stores are also part of larger global flow of trade, migration, and representations. Hidden behind the hustle and bustle are carefully arranged processes where ethnic products are collected, distributed, organized, and reproduced using modern methods and economic considerations. A global marketplace sustained by the hard logic of economic enterprise coexists within these exotic spaces of cultural difference. Entrepreneurial success stories represent how immigrants skill-fully manipulate the marketplace by carefully calibrated, rearranged, and packaged items, producing the ethnic grocery store as a managed interior.

The goal of this chapter is to reexamine how the two ends of this complex world work in tandem. Understanding that the spaces of magical awe are sustained by invisible rules of economic order is central to understanding immigrant ethnic architecture in the United States. This reflexive relationship between place, representations, spatial practice, and structural forces is important to understanding how the very definitions of culture and tradition have changed over time.

READING ETHNO-ARCHITECTURE, METHODS AND THEORY

Contemporary immigrants in the United States do not build new buildings representative of their craft traditions as did the European immigrants who came to America during the eighteenth and nineteenth centuries (Palmqvist 1986, Hubka and Kenny 2000, Fitchen 2001). Nevertheless, this chapter argues that new immigrants make subtle changes—physical, symbolic, and sensory transformations—to their surrounding settings and buildings.

My primary approach towards the study of ethno-architecture uses a method called spatial ethnography. Spatial ethnography emerges from theoretical frameworks on embodied placemaking 'as a category of analysis—that is, foregrounding not only place but also the body's role within it as mutually constituent elements of the built environment' (Sen and Silverman 2014: 2). This method sees ethno-architecture as a form of verbal and non-verbal communication—engaging its users through grammar and syntax, experience, and emotions. Experiences and expressions of culture are held and learned by our body and expressed and repeated via habitual embodied practices in sites such as an ethnic grocery store. The act of shopping and engaging with a sensate environment in a store can be integral to the experience of what Pierre Bourdieu calls *habitus*, gathered via socially determined embodied practices and behavior (Bourdieu 2004). Bourdieu argues that social action and human agency emerge within a complex, overarching context—a system of discourse, practices, transactions, that are both overt and covert. For instance an analysis of the use, layout and material culture of the store indicates how different stakeholders and social groups maintain social and spatial boundaries. Store signs are visual symbols and texts that communicate cultural and economic messages to the customers. However, different social groups interpret the same sign in nuanced ways, depending on their interests as consumers. Display of merchandise produces consumer desire, but customer desire is inflected by individual tastes and contexts. On the one hand, cultural rules regulate human behavior and social action, while on the other hand, expressions of culture and cultural practices are inflected by individual backgrounds and idiosyncratic situations.

The experience of shopping in the grocery store produces embodied knowledge that may not be as overt and visible as the material culture but is nevertheless pertinent. The store interior generates a micro rhythm that engages individual bodies by the way merchandise sections are sequentially arranged and experienced. The sounds and smells of the store create a unique sensorium that reminds people of similar places elsewhere. Over time this experience of the ethnic grocery store becomes habitual, expected, and internalized as 'incorporating practices'—affective responses to the environment generated from embedded values, accepted maxims, and customs that are deeply cultural in nature (Connerton 1989: 88). Such practices may not be overt but nevertheless are powerful in a didactic sense, since they inform our kinesthetic and haptic engagement with our world. The way we situate ourselves is not merely a cognitive act described by speech and language but an embodied experience that depends on the nature of our engagement with the material world. Therefore the everyday and repeated act of shopping in a grocery store like Patel Brothers produces a personal as well as collective knowledge of ethno-architecture.

The second approach borrows from cultural landscape scholars and cultural anthropologists and seeks to situate ethno-architecture within larger systems of relationships, processes, and places (Jackson 1994, Upton 1997, Marcus and Clifford 1989, Falzon 2009). The second strategy emerges from the way a grocery store becomes a product of larger social, political, and economic forces. Such framings shift the perspective and scale of analysis from individual to collective bodies. In the past, ethnic stores, residential enclaves, and cultural spaces were seen as physically, culturally, and experientially different from the so-called mainstream (Gans 1962). Scholars have identified that ethnic spaces such as those along Devon Avenue are merely nodes within a territorially dispersed network of ethnic strip malls, residences, cultural institutions, and retail streets. Geographer Wilbur Zelinsky calls these networked spaces heterolocal geographies where propinquity is not the sole form of territoriality (Zelinsky and Lee 1998). Framing ethnicity solely within a single geographic context (urban, regional, or national) renders invisible connections and allegiances that transcend that geography (Li 1998, Wood 1997). In addition, transnationalism or transnational practices refer to networks and practices that extend beyond national boundaries (Gupta and Ferguson 1992, Sanjek 1978, Ashutosh 2008, Mankekar 2002, Blunt 2007, Glick Schiller *et al* 1992, Basch *et al* 1994). The logic of economic efficiency, market trends, and transnational movement of merchandise and capital regulate ethno-architecture when seen from this point of view. An invisible world of economic strategies and distribution flows props up the visible and experienced world of the grocery store.

These dual worlds—the local and the global, the tangible and the intangible, the material and the experiential—influence how identity, belonging, and ethnicity is enacted in everyday life. Practice and engagement within these spaces *produce ethnicity*—in the sense of embodied being interacting with and within the grocery store. Ethnic architecture is a somatic product of time and place as well as a node within a global system of flows of people, goods, money, media image, and ideas.

DEVON AVENUE ETHNIC RETAIL STRIP AND ITS URBAN CONTEXT

The historic built fabric, layout, and material culture of Devon Avenue is the first local actor in our story, shaping behavior and business practices. Immigrants operate within a preexisting cultural setting and larger history that frames the social construction of ethno-architecture. The physical setting of Devon Avenue is typical of ethnic retail strips found in immigrant-receiving urban centers across the United States. The street runs east to west, stretching from the edge of Lake Michigan into the suburban hinterland of Greater Chicago. This study includes a 15-block stretch between Ridge Avenue and California Avenue close to the eastern end of the street (see Figure 9.1). This gridded urban stretch grew as a retail street comprising rows of one- or two-storey commercial buildings in the 1920s when the City of Chicago grew northwards and new residential neighborhoods flourished. The commercial section is one urban block deep. Residential neighborhoods comprised of bungalows and apartments are neatly laid out north and south of this commercial strip.

A rich history of incremental growth and the resultant physical morphology of this street produce a feeling of visual density that urban planners call 'fine urban grain' (McNeill 2011). That term refers to the high ratio of built area in comparison to open unbuilt space. Visual density also refers to the overabundance of visual information and details such as signage, architectural ornaments, horizontal and vertical datum lines produced by cornices, walls, windows, sills, and parapets. In Devon Avenue, visual density promotes a sense of intimacy and contact. Rows of multistoried, mixed-use buildings are so designed that upper stories may be rented out to immigrants as residences, offices, and community services, while the ground-level spaces are used for retail businesses. Compact in scale, due to the long and thin lot sizes, the narrow side of the stores faces the sidewalk and party walls touch neighboring buildings. The deep interior allows for rear spaces for storage and service areas. Therefore the retail buildings provide formulaic front and back sections that the immigrant tenant reconfigures and adapts.

Immigrants with limited capital find it useful to rent these narrow stores. When a business grows and prospers, the storeowner tends to take over the next-door space, spreading out horizontally in the process. The turnover of businesses along this street is high—unsustainable projects going out of business only to be replaced by brash newcomers. It is also common for storeowners to move from one location to another as their business grows. Successful business owners such as Patel Brothers have made good use of the street infrastructure and morphology in order to consolidate their economic enterprise.

The historic buildings lining this street stand testimony to a diverse history of ethno-architecture predating the Indian immigrants. German and Irish immigrants built many of the buildings that host the stores, restaurants, and residences on this street (Archer and Santoro 2007, Jones 1995, Bennet *et al* 2006). Jewish families moved into the area after World War II, especially in the neighborhoods between Damen Avenue and Kedzie Avenue. By 1963 there were approximately 48,000 Jewish immigrants in the West Rogers Park area (Cutler 1996, Langer 2005). Since the late 1980s, the now-aging Jewish residents and their children began moving to suburban locations such as Skokie, Buffalo Grove, Highland Park, and Deerfield, and newer immigrants moved in (Loundy 2013, Turner 2010). [1]

Following preceding decades of Irish and German occupation (Archer and Santoro 2007, Jones 1995, Bennet *et al* 2006), Jewish refugees (Cutler 1996, Langer

2005), Indians, Pakistanis, and Bangladeshis, in addition to Russian Jewish émigrés (1990s) and Mexicans and Central Americans – evident by the many taqueria, laundromats, and the roving carts selling paletas from Paleteria La Monarca (Woodard 2013) – occupy this street. Stores selling halal food, businesses with prayer rooms, and mosques reflect the changing demographics of the street and arrival of Muslim immigrants.[2] Deep internal fissures that remain hidden to an outsider mark the ethnic community on Devon Avenue. Ethnic, religious, and language-based constituencies include Gujarati, Sri Lankan, Jain, Bengali, Indian, Pakistani, Baluchi, and Sindhi, and sectarian traditions such as Mahdavi, Tablighi, Deobandi, and Barelvi. Postcolonial national rivalry renders itself during national independence day parades or cricket matches between South Asian countries. Devon Avenue has a very complex and layered ecosystem in which diversity is contained within this dense streetscape. Ethnic stores cater to a variety of ethnic groups and operate as an intertwined transcultural context.

PATEL BROTHERS GROCERY STORE AS ETHNO-ARCHITECTURE

The managers at Patel Brothers Indian grocery store, located at 2612 West Devon Avenue, have carefully curated the architecture in order to successfully cater to the store's multiple constituencies. The store website declares that the business is more than a grocery store: 'At Patel Brothers, we're committed to sharing what we know best about our Indian heritage and culture: our food.' Food acts as a symbolic as well as a material marker of cultural heritage, and connects everyday family life (your dinner table) to community history (tradition and culture), nation-state (India), and global economic practices (store). On the one hand, this grocery store describes a unique sense of place, while on the other hand it is a mere node within a global economic landscape and a regional network of Patel Brothers stores (Figure 9.2) (Sen 2012, Zukin 1996).

The building grew in a modular, incremental fashion from a one-storey warehouse structure with high ceilings to an elaborate tiled entrance façade comprising

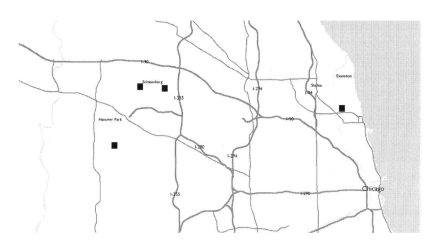

Figure 9.2
Map showing a chain of Patel Brothers grocery stores in the greater Chicago region. Copyright Arijit Sen.

three four-centered arched pediments. These pediments mark three separate front bays (Figure 9.3): two narrower bays flank the wide middle section, where the main entrance is located. The middle section has an oddly eclectic trefoil-cusped arch pattern (with the central arch shaped as an ogee arch) on the pediment, demarcated by black and white tiles. None of the arches is a perfect replica of eastern or Indian architecture. Rather, they are hybrid and symbolic, and their alien and hyper-visible forms set off the storefront of Patel Brothers against its context. The side bays demarcate adjoining stores and properties that the storeowners bought and incorporated into the grocery store as their business grew, including the Annapurna vegetarian restaurant, now united by the arched façade.

Mafat Patel emigrated from the small village of Bhandu in the district of Mehsana in the Indian state of Gujarat in early 1968. By 1971 his brother Tulasi and his wife joined him, and in 1974 the first Patel Brothers grocery store opened. Susan Patel, Tulasi's daughter, fondly remembers the old store: 'I remember that store, I remember that it was definitely dark and dingy and gray. Gray shelves! And it was so small— you know, we had one register, couple of rows and I remember, my dad being in the back packing spices and … and mom was a cashier.' This store was located at 2032 West Devon Avenue, on the eastern end of this retail strip, near the crossing of Devon and Ridge Avenues. The grocery store business flourished and soon the Patels moved to a bigger location at 2534 West Devon Avenue, on the crossing of Campbell Avenue, a minor residential cross street located centrally on this retail strip, and nine blocks west of their first store location. Susan remembers that this store was 'So much bigger. I remember playing tag in there and just running around in circles … It was a corner property so it was easy to run in and out and play on the sidewalk.' She remembers helping her father weigh groceries and grains, while her older cousins, Swetal and Rakesh (Mafat's sons), would help after school. It was indeed a typical immigrant-family business as described by scholars of ethnic enterprise in the United States (Gabaccia 1994: 56, Kaslow 1993, Light 1984).

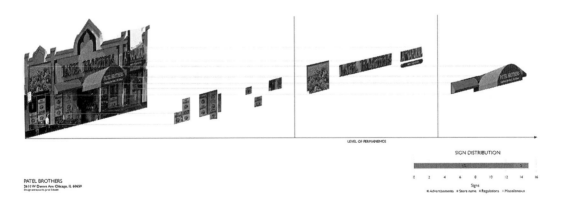

PATEL BROTHERS
2610 W Devon Ave Chicago, IL 60659
Design and layout by Jared Schmitt

Figure 9.3 Façade of a current Patel Brothers grocery store, showing signage. The awning and fixed signage are more permanent than the sales posters displayed on the storefront windows. Drawn by Jared Schmitz, copyright Arijit Sen.

Figure 9.4
Fresh produce
section inside a Patel
Brothers grocery store.
Photograph by Arijit
Sen.

In 1987 the Patels had bought the current location on 2610 West Devon Avenue, three blocks further west in a more upscale section of this strip, and in 1989 they purchased the corner building on the same block (2600 West Devon Avenue), and then the building opposite (2605–2609 West Devon Avenue). Much of their real-estate ownership may be invisible to a casual visitor but the Patel complex reflects the success of their enterprise and the incremental growth that is historically typical of this 'fine grained' street. Each of the stores located in the Patel complex belongs to a member of the extended Patel family. Mafat Patel handles Air Tours and Travels. Nirmala and Babu Patel and their son Bhavesh own Sahil, an upscale dress and clothing boutique catering to the high-end festival and marriage needs of the Indian-American community. Susan Patel owns Patel Brothers Handicrafts & Utensils on 2600 West Devon Avenue. Patel Café is the newest addition at the corner of this block.

Tulasi's daughter, Susan, compares the modern and slick new store to the older store: 'good fun memories are when Patel Brothers fliers went out … ten of us would sit on the floor and [it] would be like a chain … packing them with the rubber-band' (Susan Patel 2013). This description of communal family labor is like the ethnic enterprise described by immigrant scholars (Bonacich and Modell 1981), but her fond description of the family contribution and gathering is a reminder that a business strategy of family ownership has continued, even if efficiently run by employees and made efficient to respond to the current needs of globalized transnational trade

By the 1990s Patel Brothers had become the established Indian grocery store in Chicago, Mafat Patel recalls: 'people were coming to shop from Wisconsin, Minneapolis [Minnesota], Indiana, Michigan, Iowa, Kansas. Every weekend, they used to come to shop here' (2013). He remembered how a large parking lot on the cross street of Rockwell Avenue and Devon Avenue would fill up with cars with license plates from these states. This popularity led to the opening of grocery stores in major cities across the United States—New York, Houston, Atlanta, Detroit, extending across 52 locations. These are managed by members of five generations of the extended family and supplied by four distribution hubs located in Chicago, New York, Atlanta, and Houston. As an enterprise of an efficient and modern supply network and a distribution chain of multiple ethnic grocery stores has spread across the United States, Patel family members have kept the mega-business afloat.

In the 1990s Mafat Patel's sons gained degrees in Finance and Marketing and assisted in developing a nodal distribution network business model called Raja Foods Inc. One son, Swetal, remembers that 'it was time to shift away from bringing in 55 pound bags of chili power and selling 55 bags of chili powder. It's time to sell branded chili powder, branded whole chili, everything was in a brand at that time.' The packaging of food took place under the *Swad* label. With the organization of Raja Foods, spices, vegetables, and grains were packaged and sealed in the port city of Kandla in India, and then shipped off to New York and other ports and transported directly to the Patel Brothers warehouses. From two containers that shipped to each warehouse every month to two containers arriving every day! While someone has to service the front counter of Patel Brothers grocery store, according to Swetal Patel, the twenty-first-century ethnic grocery business is a virtual system of information management: 'all about forecasting. It's just forecast, after forecast, after forecast and … information into your computer and giving your numbers and saying that this is what your requirements are going to be.' An ethnic grocery store is no longer a brick-and-mortar family enterprise in a back alley, but a global network of securing good deals with your vendors so that the store and its architecture can be a stage for their display.

The process of stocking and staging merchandise has evolved since the 1980s, leading to a major change in the interior layout of the grocery store. With the introduction of forklifts and electric jacks the process of unloading merchandise into the back room has been mechanized. The Patel Brothers distribution center has nine forklifts and eleven electric jacks. While the back-store section on Devon Avenue has shrunk, an enormous Raja Foods warehouse, located at 8110 N St. Louis Avenue in the city of Skokie, 3.3 miles from the grocery store, is the primary storage. Unlike the grocery store with its Indian-looking façade, the warehouse is modern and unassuming: a brick-faced building with a modest vinyl banner nailed onto the façade, announcing 'Raja Food: Wholesalers of International Food'. The interior space is efficiently laid out into rows of merchandise, office spaces, refrigerated sections and loading ramps. The warehouse feeds regional Patel Brothers stores and supplies smaller local grocery stores (not owned by Patel Brothers) within the extended regional hinterland including cities across Michigan, Wisconsin, Indiana, and Minnesota.

The familiar grocery store—rows of plantains and mangos, unruly bins of rice, pulses, and spices—is the front end of this transnational economic enterprise.

Swetal Patel compares the new Patel Brothers to the old store, 'Back then, there was no pattern in the store ..., it was a square box ... and the perimeter had shelving. Then in the center of the store, you had rows of merchandise ... There was no system of setting things up. It just, sort of, worked themselves out ... canned goods here, packet of spices here, barrels of beans here, flour here. And that's how the categories were made.' The old store order was practical and tied to its immediate context as his father and other family members lugged those heavy sacks in and stacked them up in the store. The physical layout was not a predetermined, replicable template, but emerged incrementally, based on criteria and logic that existed at that time. Contemporary store layouts are predetermined, pre-planned, and dependent on complex considerations of schedule and trade practices beyond the parochial needs and organic production of the local store. Incremental changes that encourage efficient movement of people and to optimize shopping change the experience of 'India shopping' (Mankekar 2002). Aisles are wider and better organized. The grocery section is well lit and spacious. Specialty goods catering to subgroups are located in separate subsections and the frozen section is carefully rearranged to cater to new kinds of customers. Immigrants from East Africa, the Middle East, Southeast Asia, Nepal, and Sri Lanka patronize the store, as do Americans from a variety of persuasions who buy spices, fresh vegetables, newage medicine, and frozen dinners.

A customer explained that the redesigned aisles and shelves adjacent to the grocery bins influence her behavior. For instance, when confronted with the grocery aisle in Patel Brothers, she does not see discrete items—a gourd, a bundle of curry leaves, an eggplant, a pile of potatoes or a packet of nigella seeds—but a potential meal. A desire to recreate an ethnic meal is induced by the sight of individual ingredients: eggplants and greens become an image of *panch meshali*, an East Indian dish (Nirmal 2009), and a dining scene that is not yet realized. Reminded of a recipe, she proceeds to look for more ingredients in nearby shelves, illustrating how the layout of this section produces an affective reaction. The grocery interior space arouses her memory of a home-cooked meal and induces a certain shopping behavior such that the grocery store turns into *praesentia*, a presencing of something that is not really there (Hetherington 2003), and how food 'tends to generate a sense of home as a distant absent which becomes present in their present context' (Coakley 2003). As individuals step into the store, a sequence of encounters and sensory experiences unfold. These moments, despite their ephemerality and transience, define the grocery store as a place, a time, and an event/situation. Ethno-architecture becomes a stage—its atmosphere, sense of place, props, surrounding objects, other participating human bodies, boundaries delineating front and back zones, and other spatial ambiences. Reconceiving the interior of the store as a series of interrelated performance spaces brings out the social and architectural complexity of the grocery store and urges us to rethink the role of the architecture in maintaining cultural identity.

ETHNO-ARCHITECTURE AND IMMIGRANT WORLD MAKING
IN EVERYDAY LIFE

Ethnic place making is a dynamic production of culture and a process rather than a product. The ethnic store evoked via elaborate signage, interior ambience, and spatial qualities seems unique, local, and emplaced. Its careful management and business strategy is driven by global considerations. Occasionally a contradiction between the economic and organizational logic of ethnic enterprise and the evocation of collective memory erupts.

Recently, Patel Brothers took a major decision to sell frozen fish in their store on Devon Avenue. Since the owners are Gujarati Hindus, and refer to the Indian state of Gujarat where the term 'non-veg' is applied to those who eat meat, eggs or fish, this was a major decision. Non-veg is a linguistic act defining a social characteristic that locates persons as outsiders in caste Hindu Gujarati society. Given these social, cultural, and linguistic strictures against 'non-veg', the storeowners' decision to carry such products seems to be an act of apostasy. This decision reflects a certain pragmatism and business acumen, and acknowledgement of the growing diversity within the immigrant community, and the fish section was tucked away in the last aisle, behind the popular 'home-made' pickle jars, and many customers were not aware of it.

Immigrants shopping in stores along Devon Avenue have diversified. The Indian, Pakistani, and Bangladeshi community patronizing Devon Avenue is diverse by national origins, languages spoken, class and religious backgrounds, age and generational differences, and gender. Increasing numbers of first-generation Indian and mainstream Americans who shop at Patel Brothers have omnivorous food habits. The merchandise and layout of grocery stores reflect this diversity and the need to accommodate multiple group and individual needs even while recreating an overall ethnic identity. This is an intensely lived, everyday, and dynamic form of ethnic identity, transforming yet influenced by the exigencies of larger economic and social forces.

Within this context a complex and slippery diasporic identity emerges that is not defined by a single pre-existing category. The Indian ethnic identity in the context of Devon Avenue is a dynamic recombination of these categories. It undoubtedly results from trends in globalization but this identity is very local. It is articulated within the specific context of Devon Avenue and Chicago and reflects regional immigration trends, the demographic constitution of shoppers, and precise market conditions within this store. This identity is neither fixed nor autochthonous. Instead it incessantly redefines what it means to be Indian in the United States.

An analysis of ethno-architecture provides a unique glimpse into the social construction of ethnic identity in the United States. The very act of shopping in Patel Brothers reiterates communal cultural practices and solidifies collective memories. Entering such ethno-architecture reiterates a performance of 'being Indian' and also allows shoppers and storeowners to negotiate their place and presence within a global landscape of commerce and transactions. Indeed, these everyday, mundane, taken-for-granted embodied acts—opening a door, entering an aisle, smelling a mango, shifting one's gaze to scan a shelf full of spices, shunning stigmatized spaces–frame bodily and performative engagements and are central to a reading of contemporary ethno-architecture and Indian identity along Devon Avenue.

NOTES

1 In 1965, the passage of a new Immigration Act made it possible for highly skilled South Asians to enter the United States. Although the 1965 law lifted all geographical and racial quotas and let in only skilled immigrants it was only in the 1980s that the family reunification clauses brought in less-skilled South Asian immigrants' families to join their more educated and skilled compatriots. According to the 2000 Census, this area has 49.7% white residents, 6.78% black, 15.5% Hispanic, 22.3% Asians and 5.65% counted as 'others'.
2 This trend was reflected in the Greater Chicago region (Numrich 1997).

INTERVIEWS

Kalayil, A. (2009), interview by Arijit Sen, Devon Bank, Chicago.
Loundy, I. (2013), interview by Cynthia Anderson, Chicago.
Nirmal (2009), interview by Arijit Sen, Devon Avenue, Chicago.
Patel, M. (2013), interview by Arijit Sen, Devon Avenue, Chicago.
Patel, Susan (2013), interview by Arijit Sen, Devon Avenue, Chicago.
Patel, Swetal (2013), interview by Arijit Sen, Devon Avenue, Chicago.
Turner, T. (2010), interview by Arijit Sen, Skokie, Illinois.
Multiple (2009, 2013), Vox Populi surveys with shoppers on site.

REFERENCES

Archer, J. D. and Santoro, J. W. (2007) *Images of America: Roger's Park*, Chicago: Arcadia Publishing.
Ashutosh, I. (2008) 'Re-Creating the Community: South Asian Transnationalism on Chicago's Devon Avenue', *Urban Geography* 29, 3: 224–245.
Banerjee Divakaruni, C. (1998) *The Mistress of Spices*, New York: Anchor Books.
Basch, L., Glick Schiller, N. and Blanc-Szanton, C. (1994) *Nations Unbound: Transnational Projects, Postcolonial Predicaments, and Deterritorialized Nation-States*, New York: Gordon and Breach.
Bennet, L., Bennett, M. I. J., Demissie, F., Garner, R. and Kim, K. (eds.) (2006) *The New Chicago: A Social and Cultural Analysis*, Philadelphia, PA: Temple University Press.
Blunt, A. (2007) 'Cultural Geographies of Migration: Mobility, Transnationality and Diaspora', *Progress in Human Geography* 31: 684–694.
Bonacich, E. and Modell, J. (1981) *The Economic Basis of Ethnic Solidarity*, Berkeley and Los Angeles: University of California Press.
Bourdieu, P. (2004) 'Structures and the Habitus', in V. Buchli (ed.) *Material Culture: Critical Concepts in the Social Sciences*, vol. 1, part 1, London: Routledge.
Coakley, L. (2003) 'Exploring the Significance of Polish Shops within the Irish Foodscape', *Irish Geography* 43, 2:105–117.
Connerton, P. (1989) *How Societies Remember*, New York: Cambridge University Press.
Cutler, I. (1996) *The Jews of Chicago: From Shtetl to Suburb*, Chicago: University of Illinois Press.
Falzon, M. (2009) 'Introduction', *Multi-sited Ethnography: Theory, Praxis and Locality in Contemporary Research*, Aldershot: Ashgate.

Fitchen, J. (2001) *The New World Dutch Barn: The Evolution, Forms, and Structure of a Disappearing Icon*, edited by Greg Huber, Syracuse University Press.

Gabaccia, D. (1994) *From the Other Side: Women, Gender, and Immigrant Life in the U.S., 1820–1990*, Bloomington: Indiana University Press.

Gans, H. J. (1962) *The Urban Villagers: Group and Class in the Life of Italian-Americans*, New York: Free Press.

Glick Schiller, N., Basch, L. and Blanc-Szanton C. (1992) *Towards a Transnational Perspective on Migration: Race, Class, Ethnicity, and Nationalism Reconsidered*, New York: New York Academy of Sciences (second reprinting distributed by Johns Hopkins University Press).

Gupta, A. and Ferguson, J. (1992) 'Beyond "Culture": Space, Identity, and the Politics of Difference', *Cultural Anthropology* 7: 6–23.

Hetherington, K. (2003) 'Spatial Textures: Place, Touch, and Praesentia', *Environment and Planning A* 35, 11: 1933–1944.

Hubka, T. C. and Kenny, J. T. (2000) 'The Transformation of the Workers' Cottage in Milwaukee's Polish Community', *People, Power, Places: Perspectives in Vernacular Architecture* 8, Knoxville: University of Tennessee Press.

Jackson, J. B. (1994) *A Sense of Place, A Sense of Time*, New Haven, CT: Yale University Press.

Jones, P. (1995) *Ethnic Chicago: A Multicultural Portrait*, Grand Rapids, MI: Wm. B. Eerdmans Publishing Company.

Kaslow, F. (1993) 'The Lore and Lure of Family Business', *The American Journal of Family Therapy* 21, 1: 3–16.

Langer, A. (2005) *Crossing California*, New York: Riverbed Press.

Li, W. (1998) 'Anatomy of a New Ethnic Settlement: The Chinese Ethnoburb in Los Angeles', *Urban Studies* 35, 3: 479–501.

Light, I. (1984) 'Immigrant and Ethnic Enterprise in North America', *Ethnic and Racial Studies* 7, 2: 195–216.

Mankekar, M. (2002) '"India Shopping": Indian Grocery Stores and Transnational Configurations of Belonging', *Ethnos* 67, 1: 75- 98.

Mannur, A. (2008) 'Culinary Fictions: Immigrant Foodways and Race in Indian American Literature', in K. A. Ono (ed.) *Asian American Studies After Critical Mass*, New York: John Wiley and Sons.

Marcus, G. and Clifford, J. (1989) *Writing Culture: The Poetics and Politics of Ethnography*, Berkeley: University of California Press.

McNeill, D. (2011) 'Fine Grain, Global City: Jan Gehl, Public Space and Commercial Culture in Central Sydney', *Journal of Urban Design* 16, 2: 161–178.

Numrich, P. D. (1997) 'Recent Immigrant Religions in a Restructuring Metropolis: New Religious Landscapes in Chicago', *Journal of Cultural Geography* 17 (Fall/Winter): 55–77.

Palmqvist, L. (1986) *Swedes, America's Architectural Roots*, Washington DC: National Trust for Historic Preservation.

Patel Brothers (2014) 'Our Mission', *Patel Brothers*, Online. http://www.patelbros.com/about-us/our-mission.html (accessed 11 August 2015).

Sanjek, R. (1978) 'A Network Method and its Uses in Urban Ethnography', *Human Organization*, 37: 257–68.

Sen, A. (2012) 'From Curry Mahals to Chaat Cafes: Spatialities of the South Asian Culinary Landscape', in T. Srinivasan and K. Ray (ed.) *Curried Cultures*, Berkeley: University of California Press.

Sen, A. and Silverman, L. (2014) *Making Place: Space and Embodiment in the City*, Bloomington: Indiana University Press.

Singla, A. (2014) 'Spice/Bollywood Tours of Chicago's Little India', *Indian As Apple Pie*. Online. http://www.indianasapplepie.com/pages/indian-spice-tours-chicago-devon-avenue; http://spiceoflifetours.com/about-usblog.html (accessed 11 August 2014).

Spritzer, G. (2007) 'Immigration on Devon Avenue', *The Archives*, WBEZ 91.5, Chicago Public Library, 6 March. Online. http://www.wbez.org/episode-segments/immigration-devon-avenue (accessed 11 August 2014).

Stone, E. (2007) 'Chutney, Masala Paneer and More', *Crain's Chicago Business*, 26 November 2007. Online. http://www.chicagobusiness.com/article/20071124/ISSUE02/100028915/chutney-masala-paneer-and-more (accessed 11 August 2014).

Upton, D. (1997) 'Seen, Unseen, and Scene', in P. Groth and T.W. Bressi (eds.) *Understanding Ordinary Landscapes*, New Haven: Yale University Press.

Wood, J. (1997) 'Vietnamese American Place Making in Northern Virginia', *Geographical Review* 87: 58–72.

Woodard, B. (2013) 'Paleteria La Monarca's Ice Cream Carts Make Final Push of Season', *DNAinfo Chicago*, 11 September. Online. http://www.dnainfo.com/chicago/20130911/rogers-park/paleteria-la-monarcas-ice-cream-carts-make-final-push-of-season/slide-show/437185 (accessed 11 August 2014).

Zelinsky, W. and Lee, B. A. (1998) 'Heterolocalism: An Alternative Model of the Sociospatial Behaviour of Immigrant Ethnic Communities', *International Journal of Population Geography*, 4, 4: 281–98.

Zukin, S. (1996) *The Cultures of Cities*, New York: Blackwell.

Chapter 10: Doing everyday multiculturalism in Sydney Road, Melbourne

Ian Woodcock

INTRODUCTION

Australia is a highly urbanised nation, founded on a relatively recent legacy of colonial racism and dispossesion, now with one of the highest formal migrant intakes per capita globally. This makes Australian cities prime sites of the 'metropolitan paradox' (Back 2009: 5–6) for staging intercultural dialogue within an arena where enduring forms of prejudice co-exist. This chapter thus seeks to foreground how multiculturalism is 'done' in an ordinary street – Sydney Road in Melbourne, Australia's second-largest city inhabited by well over four million people. Recent studies in this area highlight a clear sense that not only is such everyday multiculturalism (Wise 2009) highly situated in place, but also it varies from place to place – especially with regard to the degree of mobility of the host culture. Further, it acknowledges the role agonism plays in the micro-publics of ordinary, everyday spaces (Amin 2002). For Mouffe, the concept of agonistic democracy accepts internal conflicts as an inevitable outcome of intersecting political traditions under the banner of 'liberal democracy' (Mouffe 2000: 2–3) that cannot be resolved through rational deliberation. Agonistic democracy re-frames conflictual interactions as between adversaries of equal value rather than contests in which one side must be defeated, or one set of values must be eclipsed. Agonism accepts conflicted co-existence without resorting to violence. Multiculturalism can thus be seen processually, with identities not fixed or finished, and like urban milieux where multiculture flourishes, in a constant state of becoming. This complicates concepts of conviviality and cohesion, by incorporating the negative and the difficult as essential to processes of becoming multicultural and forever in play (Modood 2007; Parekh 2002) in multiple ways and scales assembled through ordinary, everyday places (Wise and Velayutham 2009; Amin 2008; Amin and Graham 1997; Massey 1991). It reacts against previously prevailing ideas that the multiculutral project has failed (Lentin and Titley 2011; Alibhai-Brown *et al.* 2006; Vertovec and Wessendorf, 2009; Werbner 2009) and instead seeks to understand the capacities, morphologies, structures and practices that support a multicultural conviviality both in Australia (Fincher and Iveson 2008; Noble 2009, 2011; Pardy and Lee 2011; Wise and Velayutham 2014) and elsewhere (Hall 2011, 2013; Hall and Datta 2010; Wood and Landry 2008).

AUSTRALIA

Contemporary Australia has always been a migrant nation, though perhaps the idea that this applies to everyone here except the indigenous population has yet to become the dominant narrative. Up until the mid-1990s, mainstream history taught in Australian schools tended to mythologise the successes and failures of British settlers, bush pioneers and goldrush fortune-seekers (Ashton and Hamilton 2007:49). These frontier narratives of hardship and heroism were somewhat at odds with one of the most urbanised (and suburban) societies on the globe. Australia as a nation, born through an Act of the British Parliament, has been created by migrations and intermixings of ideas, ideologies and cultures as much as people. What had previously been a series of separate British colonies from 1788, with different modes of settlement, demographic origins and infra-structure standards, were hybridised into a federated composite nation in 1901. Many of the early pioneer migrants were of diverse origin: in addition to Britain and Ireland, migrants came from across Europe, the Americas and the Middle East, and particularly, Asia. However, Australia's first Act of Parliament was the notorious 'White Australia Policy' which, over the coming decades, served to whiten the national demographic palette. Four decades on, while Wirth pro-claimed from the United States that urbanism was defined by heterogeneity (Wirth 1938), and Gibbon's *Canadian Mosaic* (1938) promoted a national iden-tity founded in ethnic difference, Australia had become an almost entirely white nation, the remaining ethnic diversity subsumed under a hegemonic construct of 'whiteness' centred on Anglo-Celtic cultural capital that haunts contemporary multicultural discourse (Hage 1998). While there is now an increasingly popular narrative around Australian national identity forged through massive failure at Gallipoli in World War I, it was the post-World War II imperative to 'populate or perish' that re-opened migrant flows to increasingly off-white and 'third-world-looking people' (Hage 1998). Official multiculturalism replaced the White Australia Policy in the early 1970s and Australia now has one of the highest per capita formal migrant intakes in the OECD. By 2016, at just over 24 million, Australia's population will be three-and-a-half times what it was in 1945, primar-ily due to increasingly diverse migration.

Thus, the Australian experience inverts much of the discourse of migration and place with its focus on stories of strangers coming to town and their ways of becoming local: to be local in Australia is to have a sense of having roots elsewhere. Migration to Australia has always been highly differentiated, with many modes of arrival and points of departure. There is a proliferation of distinc-tions around selection criteria, visa classes and rights, creating sub-categories of tenure on citizenship and sense of belonging (Figure 10.2, top). Migrants are an ever-present background to public discourse, especially that associated with outbreaks of racialized social tension, the 'war on terror' and the politics of Australia's draconian treatment of asylum seekers. However, a defining aspect of Australian cities, in which almost 90% of the population live, is that they have been made entirely via processes of global migration – they are settler cities. Apart from the interim period between 1901 and 1945 (less than a quarter of contemporary Australian history), Australian urbanism has not been an autochthonous assemblage with claims to strong or continuous historical place-based foundations, mythical or otherwise.

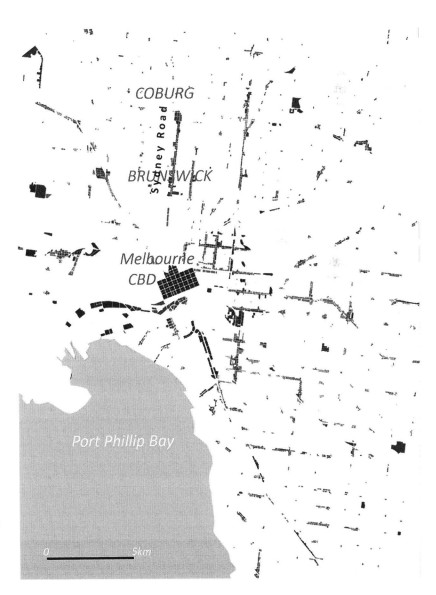

Figure 10.1
Map of Sydney Road and Melbourne's retail strips. Map by author.

All of the above is also to be understood within a dominant culture of 'Australianness' that is a local inflection of global western 'whiteness' with fantasies of supremacy that are increasingly shrill as much as under threat by everyday lived reality (Hage 1998; Woodcock 2005). Across Australian cities Anglo-Celts are the largest ethnic group and other ethnicities are rarely ever more than 10–20% of local populations; usually far less, with the main exceptions being the central cities of Melbourne and Sydney and some outer suburbs. Broadly speaking, there are suburbs that are predominantly white and white-migrant receiving, particularly on the urban fringes; large areas of middling multiculture where the statistical national average of 30% overseas-born applies, albeit with differing internal mixtures; and areas of above-average diversity where many non-western migrants have settled, where they may comprise between 50–70% of the population.

In terms of urban morphology, urban retail strips ('main' or 'high' streets) are primarily confined to the inner and middle suburbs developed between the 1830s and early 1960s, based on tram and rail transport (Figure 10.1). These strips, which are predominantly fine-grained, independently owned and accessible by walking, cycling and mass transit, make the economic and cultural presence of migrants publicly visible. The low-density, car-dependent outer suburbs are served by private shopping malls owned by global corporations. However, the public presence of non-white migrants in some outer suburbs is increasingly marked by large places of worship sited on the margins of industrial zones (Beynon 2002, 2005).

This introduction to Australia contextualises Sydney Road as a migrant place in a city in a nation of migrant places, rather than as a migrant place in an otherwise settled nation. Following the localist turn in urban scholarship focused on the 'ordinary' city (Amin and Graham 1997; Hall 2012), this chapter seeks to add to our understanding of how the micro-scale, place-based agonism of migrant societies (Amin 2002) 'hits the street' – streets that are, in the words of an interviewee, 'not overwhelming, not monocultural, not a set of monocultural bits, there's still things in-between there and I think that's the strength of the place' (Figures 10.2 and 10.3).

In what follows, historical insights and qualitative methods are applied to assemble socio-spatial relations underlying subjective experiences of the local: fieldwork surveys, street photography, participant observation and lengthy semi-structured interviews with about 40 people, men and women aged between 19 and 72 from diverse ethno-religious backgrounds who live, work, manage or shop in a place that for them is an everyday urban street. Rather than understanding the sense of multiculural place for a particular social or cultural group, the research sought a variety of takes on a single place from a multicultural sample. The interviews were conducted during the final term of the conservative national government led by John Howard, prior to the race riots at Cronulla Beach in Sydney in December 2005. In what follows, the street is described and the interview material is assembled around a series of themes that tell a variety of stories about engagement with the strip.

Figure 10.2 Sydney Road streetscape, Melbourne. Photographs by author.

SYDNEY ROAD

Jane Jacobs famously said that the recurrent image that comes to mind when people think of a city is its streets (1961: 29). Melbourne is often characterized as a city of streets and laneways, linear spaces rather than plazas and squares, organised in grids of varying degrees of formality. Sydney Road serves as the 'high

169 □

street' for Brunswick and Coburg: two of Melbourne's still gritty, but swiftly gen-
trifying inner-northern suburbs (Figure 10.1). As one of the city's most congested
and 'grungy' strips it is, in formal terms, the antithesis of an idealised 'good' public
space like the globally celebrated Federation Square (Dovey and Woodcock 2005).
Sydney Road is narrow in proportion to what flows through each day – a mere
20 metres separates the buildings on either side – yet it is a primary arterial route
between the central city and the northern suburbs, hosts one of the city's busi-
est tram lines and is crossed by bus routes every few hundred metres connecting
suburbs to the east and west. Melbourne's inner-north is a hot-spot for cycling,
making Sydney Road a major conflict zone over rights to public space for transport
(Figure 10.2, bottom; Figure 10.3, top).

Claimed in some tourist literature to be the longest retail strip in the southern
hemisphere, the main section of Sydney Road is a continuous mixed-use spine of
almost five kilometres comprising about a thousand different businesses, as well
as numerous health, community, sporting, religious and other service functions –
'there's one of everything'. It caters to a local population where almost every other
person is from a non-English-speaking background, a population of 47,000 people
with ancestry in 65 different countries in all six continents. The business proprietors in Sydney Road are for the most part representative of this local demography,
though many of them, like many customers, travel from much further away, connecting the place with many other places across Melbourne – as well as the world.

Slow-moving traffic gives rise to a culture of jay walking, exchanges of greet-
ings and snippets of gossip between people in vehicles and people on the street,
adding to the pulse of congestion. This theme of communication in the street via ges-
tures and words is seen by many interviewees as a marker of 'community' performed
through fleeting encounters between individuals often living and working many suburbs apart. One Sydney Road resident sees 'road rage, people doing freaky things
everywhere so, … there's just this whole bazaar atmosphere …' (Figure 10.3, top).

It would be possible to map the origins of proprietors and their staff in
premises along the strip and draw out their connections with and trajectories of
mobility from elsewhere (Hall and Datta 2010). It might be plausible to map the
shop signage and goods on sale, the practices of trading and arranging micro-
public spaces along the strip, and assign to these ethnic identifiers – just to check
how the officially diverse demographics correlate with expressions in public space.
And while this has been attempted, it will not be presented here. My reason-
ing is that this could encourage an essentialist reading of original or traditional
migrant identities. Comparisons might be made with traditions in places of origin,
within a framework that reifies ethnicity and culture with an agency that assem-
bles notions of race, culture and community (Bauman 1996, 1999), that then joins
them to notions of place and identity that are fixed, bounded and closed. Such an
approach would foreclose the processes of hybridisation and becoming 'together
in difference' (Ang 2003) in and through an 'open' or progessive 'global sense of
place' (Massey 1991) where places and identities are fluid, porous and iteratively
constituted by relations that are also in flux (Parekh 2002). Places of origin are in

Figure 10.3
Sydney Road
streetscape,
Melbourne.
Photographs by
author.

constant becoming as much as destinations are. Migrancy as a condition is more like a crowded thoroughfare with multiple flows, speeds and directions than a one-way street that takes people from an old country to a new one. As one of the interviewees said:

> we're in however many generations of transforming living with difference, everybody's, they're cool about having Asians in their Turkish shop [...] the thing that Sydney Rd always does for you is shake the apple cart, something is always coming and going ... the sense of flux and coexistence ... that we can rub shoulders with the public in very, very different ways ...

But Sydney Road has also been a place of conflict. From the late nineteenth and early twentieth centuries, sectarianism in Australia was endemic, and Sydney Road was a primary site for marches and clashes that enacted entrenched differences of ethnicity, theology, ideology and politics related to the three primary white ethnic groups: English, Scottish and Irish (Donati 2005: 73–75). During the Great Depression, Brunswick was a crucible for left-wing and anti-authoritarian political movements, notably being the site of free-speech campaigns by the Unemployed Workers Movement, with street protests in Sydney Road. In the post-World War II period, with the re-opening of Australia to non-whites, Sydney Road's industrial base and cheap residential catchment made it one of the main destinations for unskilled migrants from southern Europe, Turkey and later the Middle East, southern Asia and Africa. These conditions, combined with good public transport, proximity to the central city and two of Melbourne's main universities, made the area attractive to students and, since the late 1990s, to the burgeoning international student market hailing from South East Asia, the Indian sub-continent and the Middle East.

In the broader imagination of Melbourne (as presented by mainstream media), Sydney Road is frequently characterised as having a 'Middle Eastern character'. For the purposes of local cultural tourism, this means a combination of Turkish, Lebanese, Egyptian, Syrian, and Afghani restaurants, bakeries, grocery stores, Islamic clothing shops and specialist bookstores, halal butchers and shisha cafes. For many Melburnians of Turkish background there is a strong identification with Sydney Road, and occassionaly this connection has been enacted by literal occupation of the street with impromptu street parties and car-borne parades of flag-waving families when Turkey's national soccer team has won in global competitions. Such dominance by a single ethnicity is temporary in the case of the soccer fans. The 'Middle Eastern' image has been reinforced by self-conscious marketing of the food and retailing as a point of difference from, for example, the Italian 'flavour' of Lygon Street in nearby Carlton or the Vietnamese character of Victoria Street in Richmond, on the eastern margin of the central city. Neither is representative of the local demographics in its immediate hinterland and, like Sydney Road, they serve a much broader and diverse market across many suburbs.

A representative from the local council's communications department explained the decision to go with a 'middle-eastern' branding campaign. In this interviewee's comments we find some subtlety about how such perceptions work, how branding (and stereotyping) operates, while learning something about Sydney Road's version of diversity:

> Sydney Road's not 90% ethnic, though it is by impression. Might be an Italian-run café, but nothing 'Italian' on the window, so not an 'Italian' business. So the thought that all of these businesses cater to a specific ethnic market as distinct from multi-ethnic markets, is not true. There's more diversity there than that.

To measure and enumerate Sydney Road's diversity is, in practice, a task fraught with difficulty. This is partly because one of the things about Sydney Road that marks it most – its mixture and diversity – also causes many interviewees to question notions of identity. This works across a range of scales, starting with the street itself, as experienced by a shoptop resident:

> I think it's struggling for an identity, or it's trying, it's sort of new, a marriage of,
> I sometimes have this perception that there's this struggling to go forward, it
> can't go backwards … this slow state of struggle trying to decide where it wants
> to go, the road per se. (Figure 10.3, bottom, 10.4 and 10.5)

Most of the premises on Sydney Road are independent, and even those that are
not (such as banks) play a role in the everyday process of relating to and building
the social capital upon which business depends. This necessarily involves communicative competencies and an agonistic 'feel for the game' that constitutes a
multicultural *habitus* that for some may come at a price: 'it has a lot to offer
because there's that richness, people come over here for the same reasons that
they don't like it here'.

The primary attraction of Sydney Road is the diversity of uses, the multi-
scalar markets they serve and the relations of difference and indifference they
sustain (Tonkiss 2005). The intensity of local businesses that meet everyday needs
makes for a good place to assemble neighbourly relations and social capital, especially for those recently arrived, in this case, an interracial migrant couple from the
Philippines and Germany, who previously lived in Europe and South East Asia. The
Filipina interviewee reflects on the energy required to engage, and the fluidity of
relations in a street of changing proprietors:

> Sydney Road was a good starting point for me to start to live in Australia … it's
> a small street I live in, and it takes a day just to get to know the neighbours and
> there's a stability there … . Whereas if you step onto Sydney Road no one gives
> [a] damn. But if you want to, … [go] to certain restaurants all the time, establish a
> rapport [that] allows [you] to be recognised as a local, [get] involved in the local chit-
> chat … I do try, with the [Vietnamese] hairdresser I had before, with the bike shop,
> with the watchmaker, with … also the fish and chip shop, there were the Greek
> people in there when I came … [now] Chinese have moved in … (Figure 10.4, top)

Everyday multiculturalism's 'struggles with identity' operate at a number of scales.
Sydney Road is enmeshed in discourses of social positioning, enacted through
relations within a social field defined by an imagined community operating at metropolitan and national scales (Anderson 1983), with hierarchies of status and value
that articulate normatively stuctured relations (Hage 1998). Everyday multiculturalism in Sydney Road opens up questions about what an 'Australian' might be, and
where and how they behave, as the next three vignettes show. The first take on
this 'struggle for status' comes from the German partner of the Filipina interviewee
quoted earlier:

> there is such a mix of people and you don't really know who is who, status-
> wise, ethnic background-wise, you just don't know, its sometimes hard to tell.
> Yes, here, everybody's basically not Australian, here in Sydney Road, I'd say
> [that] true Aussies, [are] hard to find [here].

Figure 10.4
Sydney Road
streetscape,
Melbourne.
Photographs by
author.

There is a feeling that 'true Aussies' (however mythical they might be) bear a normative gaze. The effects of such panopticism are absent because Sydney Road's multiculture is sufficiently concrete to be a liberating force. The next interviewee is a post-graduate student from India, for whom the *habitus* of white Australia is experienced as a kind of double-bind that would foreclose all attempts at acculturation, so that migrants are 'damned if they do or damned if they don't':

> It just makes you less conscious of being an international student. If it was a completely white community you'd feel a little, you'd never know whether you're doing the right thing or is this the way to do it, or whatever, and here it doesn't matter, they're not Australians either, and there is no right or wrong … I think that the mixed culture is what's very comfortable and I kind of enjoy that. (Figure 10.4, bottom)

In this student's experience of the freedom afforded by Sydney Road, there is a recognition of the ways that formal boundaries of public and private, commerce and neighbourliness, are fluid; shop keepers are part of the social as well as the economic domain. This freedom to be and to become other is also a refrain raised by the next interviewee, a white professional who has lived in Brunswick all his adult life. He works as a social planner for the local council and has a particular and long-standing interest in the area's demographics. For him, Sydney Road has plenty of white Australians in the mix (after all, he knows the statistics as well as trusting his senses) and for him they might even be regarded as 'true Aussies', or at least, ordinary people:

> One of the other interesting things about Sydney Road is I think … the Anglo-Saxon Australians that end up going there … they're a little bit different too, … they're people who enjoy difference, you know. Some people would characterise them as bohemian … some of them are just regular people really, not terribly different to Australians anywhere else.

THE FORM OF MULTICULTURALISM

The built form of Sydney Road is relatively consistent in scale, being predominantly one or two storeys, with several church spires being the main high points. The twelve or so churches cover a range of denominations: Anglican, Uniting, Catholic, Baptist, Pentecostal, Latter Rain, Greek Orthodox, Spiritualist. While most are recognisable church buildings, a couple occupy converted warehouses, with one of the churches having been converted into a government-run community school in 1972. None of the three mosques is easily identifiable as such, being mixed with other functions: a school, a bookshop and an industrial building converted to offices and warehousing. The only signage designating a place of worship is a tiny notice in the bookshop window that says 'Prayer Room'. The mosques and churches sit cheek-by-jowl with shops, pubs, cafes and, in one part of the road, a very large strip and lap-dancing venue (Figure 10.5). This side-by-side co-location of the sacred and the profane produces mixtures of the formal and informal on the street, with shifts and encounters between obligations and desires. This particular confluence of form, space and function produces for some a kind everyday civility:

> the scale of the road, the shops facing it … here even the restaurants are very average you know, they're not like one of those fancy places where you have to dress up, and you can walk in the evening and still there'll be some shops that are open.

A very large proportion of Sydney Road's buildings are preserved by heritage controls that prevent removal and make redevelopment and renovation costly. This has particular effects in terms of the contributions that architectural surfaces make to the feeling of multiculture. In this instance, for the German interviewee quoted earlier, these unkempt and poorly maintained surfaces of the buildings have the most communicative power:

> I see decay, I see a lot of struggle in it ... there's an honesty in it, the façade is not done up like a showcase street ... You are closer to the people in that sense, the people who look as haggard as the buildings ...

This feeling of 'closeness to people', and a congruence between people and built form is here rendered as the authenticity of a place of constant flux and mobility. For the interviewee, this is evident at the micro scale of how signage is constructed on many premises in Sydney Road:

> So, we could call it a brutal honesty, so it has some charm, it has some positive touch to it, it can't afford to hide, it doesn't want to maybe to hide behind. I'll give you an example. Most of the time when the shop changes in other areas probably they would redo the whole outdoor décor but here they're using the same, almost the same signs, just tape it over with a different name.

A locally based artist sees the disjunctive combination of uses and built form as contributing to the urban assemblage (McFarlane 2011) of values, functions and buildings that produces an exploratory *habitus*:

> I think the people are in a more exploring mode, because they have to cope with the fact that [laughs] it's the Lebanese fascist bookshop ... it's coming from a different place, it shakes your knowns and your sense of comfort straight away. And in the disjunction of the architecture, it's rampant from the outset that this is going to be the case, and then the re-surfacing of it, so that the way it looks is an analogy for this, it's not homogeneous.

These external re-surfacings are a palimpsest that occurs within buildings too. For exmple, a 'pan-Asian' restaurant retains the classical columns from its previous life as an Italian food venue behind the glass-and-aluminium shopfront of a former jewellery store. The décor of many restaurants is part of their atmopsher that, for their customer,s can become associated with a migrant or ethnic asethetic. However, the next interviewee is the proprietor of one of Melbourne's oldest Turkish restaurants having, inherited the business from his Turkish migrant parents who established it in the late 1970s. For this restaurateur, the aesthetics of the premises derive from 'making do' with a found-object whose provenance is British migration and the tastes of its previous owners, rather than any conception of projecting a Turkish identity:

> it's just a whole heap of old Victorian buildings, you know, narrow and long, you know, that kind of terrace type thing which you know has been imported from over the UK ... I'm not sure it really suits Australian conditions but ... its here and we gotta do what we can with it, which is kind of rip holes between the walls and kind of make it one big thing ... but as for what it represents I think it just kind of grew out of what the founder of the shop loved and that's wood (laughs).

An aspect of the findings about multiculturalism's successes and failures that these quotes suggest is the way identities and sociality are constructed and produced, enabled and constrained, at the local and micro scales by the affordances of pre-existing built form. A proposition from Sydney Road is that the linearity of the strip combined with fine-grained property ownership can be major contributory factors, mediated by a combination of local planning controls and the spontaneous dynamics of everyday use. Significant here is the production of connections between tight budgets and bricolage due to heritage constraints: preservation of architecture by early British migrants provides a platform for later arrivals to inscribe new meanings without erasure of the past.

SYDNEY ROAD AS 'CULTURE C'

In conclusion, I introduce Professor Fuji (not his real name), who frequently visits Australia from Japan with his students. Professor Fuji's speciality is intercultural history and he sees the need for his students to learn how to live with difference for the good of Japan's future. He takes the long-term view that when Culture A interacts with Culture B, there are several possible outcomes. A may be subsumed by B or vice versa. Or A and B may create something new between them, Culture C, attended by variations of A and B in the form of A-dash and B-dash. Professor Fuji's question is, can we see Culture C? Professor Fuji was staying in Brunswick and stumbled upon Sydney Road one day when he decided to walk to the university rather than take the tram:

> I look around and I found so many types of shops! So this was my first experience or impression of [Sydney Road] and I thought it is very good idea to bring my students to this area, to this street, ... because they know only by books and articles and so on, but they can't have any feeling what it is like actually ... (Figure 10.5, bottom)

In Professor Fuji's view, Culture C takes a long time, a minimum of three generations, maybe even 100 years; but multiculturalism is supposedly only just over a generation old here. He found Culture C in Sydney Road's ordinariness, its multidimensional, everyday multiculturalism, and it became the starting point for his students' learning.

Out of curiosity, I attended one of the classes for his students at the university where he is a guest. At the workshop-seminar, Sydney Road's multiculture was performed for the young Japanese students with a video of the annual street party (a large, very popular, long-standing multicultural festival of food, dance and music) followed by a sound piece called 'The World in a Street'. The hosting lecturer then presented the students with statistics of the main ethnic groups in the area, figures that omitted any mention of white people. Ghassan Hage, an incisive critic of Australian multiculturalism as a 'white supremacist fantasy' was dutifully invoked with the line: 'some have criticised

Figure 10.5 Sydney Road streetscape, Melbourne. Interviewee: There's a prayer room which we call a mussala, that is just before Albion St. There's a really seedy sort of nightclub called Crystal T's or something, a few doors down from that, it looks like a bookshop but it's actually a prayer room at the back which is good because it's got wash facilities as well. Photographs by author.

multiculturalism as just being about white people and their enjoyment of diversity'. Then there was a show and tell: in broken English the students shared their experiences of Sydney Road. I wondered: When they think about all this in years to come, how will they remember their encounters with Sydney Road? As 'everyday multiculturalism' or just that place in Melbourne, Sydney Road? Or more poignantly, will they remember it as 'Australia, the home of Culture C'? Whatever they make of their lessons, there is always a place nearer home they can visit to find their own version of Culture C: Downtown Shinjuku in Tokyo, where the local population is more than 20% foreign, with its bars, cabarets, entertainment, prostitutes and danger. I ask the professor if it feels multicultural. His answer is a mirror of many of my interviewees about Sydney Road: 'Oh yes, yes, yes. You might feel that this is not Japan!' he laughs. But, unlike contemporary Australia, Japan is not linguistically or ethnically diverse, nor is it founded on migration – at least, not yet.

ACKNOWLEDGEMENTS

I am most grateful for the comments and insight of Dr Flavia Marcello, two anonymous referees, and the guidance of the editor, Dr Mirjana Lozanovska. All figures by the author.

REFERENCES

Alibhai-Brown, Y., Allen, C. et al. (2006) 'Multiculturalism: A Failed Experiment?', *Index on Censorship* 35, 2: 91–99.

Ashton, P. and Hamilton, H. (2007) 'Facing Facts? History Wars in Australian High Schools', *Journal of Australian Studies* 31, 91: 45–57.

Back, L. (2009) 'Researching Community and its Moral Projects', *21st Century Society: Journal of the Academy of Social Sciences* 4, 2: 201–214.

Amin, A. (2002) 'Ethnicity and the Multicultural City: Living with Diversity', *Environment and Planning A* 34, 1: 959–80.

Amin, A. (2008) 'Collective Culture and Urban Public Space', *City: Analysis of Urban Trends, Culture, Theory, Policy, Action* 12, 1: 5–14.

Amin, A. and Graham, S. (1997) 'The Ordinary City', *Transactions of the Institute of British Geographers* 22, 4: 411–429.

Anderson, B. (1983) *Imagined Communities: Reflections on the Origin and Spread of Nationalism*, London: Verso.

Ang, I. (2003) 'Together-in-Difference: Beyond Diaspora, into Hybridity', *Asian Studies Review* 27, 2: 141–154.

Bauman, Z. (1996) *Contesting Culture: Discourses of Identity in Multi-ethnic London*, Cambridge: Cambridge University Press.

Bauman, Z. (1999) *The Multicultural Riddle: Rethinking National, Ethnic, and Religious Identities*, New York: Routledge

Beynon, D. (2002) 'Cannibal Tastes: the Architecture of non-European Migrants in Australia', in S. Akkach (ed.) *Deplacing Difference: Architecture, Culture and Imaginative Geography*, pp. 217–228, Adelaide: Centre for Asian and Middle Eastern Architecture, University of Adelaide.

Beynon, D. (2005) 'Melbourne's "Third World-looking" Architecture', in C. Long, K. Shaw and C. Merlo (eds.) *Suburban fantasies: Melbourne unmasked*, pp. 68–83, Melbourne: Australian Scholarly Publishing.

Donati, L. (2005) *Almost Pretty: A History of Sydney Road*, Melbourne: Laura Donati.

Dovey, K. and Woodcock, I. (2005) 'Federation', in K. Dovey (ed.) *Fluid City: Transforming Melbourne's Urban Waterfront*, pp. 93–121, New York: Routledge.

Fincher, R. and Iveson, K. (2008) *The Social Logics of Urban Planning: Towards a Just Diversity in Cities*, London: Palgrave Macmillan.

Gibbon, J. (1938) *Canadian Mosaic: The Making of a Northern Nation*, Toronto: McClelland and Stewart.

Hage, G. (1998) *White Nation: Fantasies of White Supremacy in a Multicultural Society*, Sydney: Pluto Press.

Hall, S. (2011) 'High Street Adaptations: Ethnicity, Independent Retail Practices and Localism in London's Urban Margins', *Environment and Planning A* 43, 11: 2571–2588.

Hall, S. (2012) *City, Street and Citizen: The Measure of the Ordinary*, London: Routledge.

Hall, S. (2013) 'Super-Diverse Street: a "Trans-ethnography" Across Migrant Localities', *Ethnic and Racial Studies* 38, 1: 22–37.

Hall, S. and Datta, A. (2010) 'The "Translocal" Street: Shop Signs and Local Multi-Culture Along the Walworth Road, South London', *City, Culture and Society*, 1, 2: 69–77.

Jacobs, J. (1961) *The Death and Life of Great American Cities*, New York: Random House.

Lentin, A. and Titley, G. (2011) *The Crises of Multiculturalism: Racism in a Neoliberal Age*, London: Zed Books.

McFarlane, C. (2011) 'The City as Assemblage: Dwelling and Urban Space', *Environment and Planning D: Society and Space* 29: 649–671.

Massey, D. (1991) 'A Global Sense of Place', *Marxism Today* 38: 24–29.

Modood, T. (2007) *Multiculturalism: A Civic Idea*, Cambridge: Polity Press.

Mouffe, C. (2000) *The Democratic Paradox*, New York: Verso.

Noble, G. (2009) 'Everyday Cosmopolitanism and the Labour of Intercultural Community', in A. Wise and Velayutham (eds.) *Everyday Multiculturalism*, pp. 46–65, London: Palgrave.

Noble, G. (2011) 'Bumping into Alterity: Transacting Cultural Complexities', *Continuum: Journal of Media & Cultural Studies* 25, 6: 14.

Pardy, M. and Lee, C. (2011) 'Using Buzzwords of Belonging: Everyday Multiculturalism and Social Capital in Australia', *Journal of Australian Studies* 35, 3: 297–316.

Parekh, B. (2002) *Rethinking Multiculturalism*, Basingstoke: Palgrave Macmillan.

Tonkiss, F. (2005) *Space, the City and Social Theory: Social Relations and Urban Forms*, Cambridge: Polity Press.

Vertovec, S. and Wessendorf, S. (eds.) (2009) *The Multiculturalism Backlash: European Discourses, Policies and Practices*, London: Routledge.

Werbner, P. (2009) 'Revisiting the UK Muslim Diasporic Public Sphere at a Time of Terror: from Local (Benign) Invisible Spaces to Seditious Conspiratorial Spaces and the "Failure of Multiculturalism" Discourse', *South Asian Diaspora*, 1, 1: 19–45.

Wirth, L. (1938) 'Urbanism as a Way of Life', *The American Journal of Sociology* 44, 1: 1–24.

Wise, A. (2009) 'Everyday Multiculturalism: Transversal Crossings and Working Class Cosmopolitans', in A. Wise and S. Velayutham (eds.) *Everyday Multiculturalism*, pp. 21–45, Basingstoke: Palgrave Macmillan

Wise, A. and Velayutham, S. (2009) *Everyday Multiculturalism*, Basingstoke: Palgrave Macmillan.

Wise, A. and Velayutham, S. (2014) 'Conviviality in Everyday Multiculturalism: Some Brief Comparisons Between Singapore and Sydney', *European Journal of Cultural Studies* 17, 4: 406–430.

Wood, P. and Landry, C. (2008) *The Intercultural City: Planning for diversity Advantage*, London: Earthscan.

Woodcock, I. (2005) 'Multicultural Melbourne: Four Fantasies of Whitespace', in K. Shaw, C. Long and C. Merlo (eds.) *Suburban Fantasies: Melbourne Unmasked*, pp. 84–106, Melbourne: Australian Scholarly Publishing.

Chapter 11: Food, time and space

Mobile cuisine in New York and Portland

Karen A. Franck and Philip Speranza

In the twenty-first century one might expect that the age-old tradition of selling prepared foods in urban public space would have vanished. But in the US the custom flourishes, continuing to draw immigrants to its ranks. One may still encounter a lone Hispanic woman selling tamales, churros or sliced fruit from a grocery cart or Italian ices from a small cart she pushes by hand. But this is rare. Today nearly all vendors rely on trucks they drive or carts that are delivered to the chosen site. A recent change in food vending in the US, which accounts for the current flourishing of street food, is the emergence of the gourmet food truck. Their operators aspire not just to cook and sell food but to prepare food made with fresh, possibly local or exotic ingredients and of high enough quality to achieve the status of 'cuisine', but at affordable prices. The advent of Twitter, Facebook and Instagram allows such trucks to move from place to place without losing their customers. They now number 4,000 nationwide in cities with populations over 100,000 (redOrbit 2014).

To explore the topic of mobile cuisine we first take a brief look at the history of street food vending, primarily in New York. Then we consider four features of mobile cuisine: the food, the business, the vehicle and its use of space and time. Our data is drawn from interviews conducted in 2014 with 40 operators of mobile food trucks in New York and 42 operators of stationary carts and stationary trucks in Portland, Oregon, from observations of the sites where they are located and from online sources and previous academic research. In choosing a type of food, a type of vehicle, a business name and image and locations and times to operate, street food vendors create a kind of proto-architecture. The ethnicity of the vendors, the food and the identity of the business result in a frequently changing ethno-architecture in public space.

In both cities, as in other US cities, vendors make use of publicly accessible space to pursue a commercial activity, with or without official sanction from the property owner or the city government, and sometimes break explicit local regulations.

Vendors are determined and creative in determining what food to sell, in what manner, in what spaces and at what times and locations. They illustrate one of the many, increasingly varied ways that people are appropriating publicly accessible space in ways not originally intended in the design, planning and management of such space. Citizens' appropriation of public space has gained the attention of many researchers (Chase et al. 1999, 2008, Franck and Stevens 2007, Hou 2010, Bishop and Williams 2012). Food carts in particular are evidence of the 'the informal American city' (Mukhija and Loukaitou-Sideris 2014). In addition, temporary insertions into public space, some of which may last for a period of years, are now being encouraged and coordinated by designers and community activists under the banner of 'tactical urbanism' (Lydon and Garcia, 2015).

A BRIEF HISTORY

Selling food for immediate consumption in public space, without the benefit of a market or a permanent stall, has a long history in several US cities. In the nineteenth century, when oysters were still cheap and plentiful, vendors in New York sold them from wagons and wheelbarrows parked in the street. They shucked the oysters on the spot and offered customers standing on the sidewalk the added flavors of vinegar, salt and pepper (Ingersoll 1881). Other foods, such as boiled corn, were cooked elsewhere and brought to the street in baskets (Appleton 1850). With the subsequent influx of immigrants from Europe, other street foods appeared. In 1867 a German immigrant sold the first sausage in a white roll, which came to be known as a hot dog, from a pushcart on Coney Island (Wasserman 2009). An 1896 photograph shows a stout, smiling woman selling pretzels. She is dressed in dirndl, apron and kerchief as a German or Austrian immigrant might (http://digitalgallery.nypl.org/nypldigital/id?79779).

Jewish vendors from Eastern Europe sold knishes (baked or fried dumplings), sometimes from metal carts that contained a stove fueled with wood. A 1937 photograph shows a vendor selling roast potatoes from a similar cart with metal drawers above the flame in the stove for cooking the potatoes and keeping them warm (http://digitalgallery.nypl.org/nypldigital/id?732459f). Mexican immigrants sold tamales in nineteenth-century Los Angeles from horse-drawn wagons or from carts they pushed (Arellano 2013).

Selling food in public space offered an easily accessible means of earning income upon arrival in the US. It did not require much financial investment or much knowledge of English and one could sell food one knew well to fellow immigrants as well as to a larger market that eventually became familiar with the food. In all cases being able to move from place to place was key. And the initial step – a single pushcart or wagon – could eventually grow into a brick-and-mortar establishment. Yonah Schimmel, a Romanian immigrant, began selling knishes from a pushcart in New York in 1890. A few years later he opened a shop with a few tables. The business continues today, still at its 1919 location on Houston Street, still family owned (Berg 2009).

Another nineteenth-century precedent for today's food trucks is the night-lunch wagon. In New York in the 1890s temperance societies started operating them in order to serve hot food and coffee and tea to working people, from 7:30 pm to 4:30 am, after the 8 pm closing time of restaurants, to discourage them from seeking food in local taverns. The first enclosed lunch wagon, called the Owl, opened in Worcester, Massachusetts in 1887, taking food to local factories, and spawned a number of companies that specialized in the construction of such wagons (Schiller 2011).

In the twentieth century, engine-driven vehicles that incorporated kitchens made the cooking, moving and selling tasks easier and more efficient: operators could drive to various locations, be sheltered, and both cook and sell the food on site. Eventually known as lunch trucks, they often traveled to factories and construction sites. In the 1950s through the 1970s the owner of a Baltimore diner had a whole fleet of such trucks (Keiger 2008). In the 1970s immigrants from Mexico and other Latin American countries took advantage of the lunch-truck type, which came to be known as *lonceheras*, to start cooking and selling tacos and other Mexican dishes in the heavily Hispanic neighborhoods of East Los Angeles; they still do in various areas of Los Angeles (Hermosillo 2012). In the 1980s, lunch trucks, eventually known as 'grease trucks', started frequenting the Rutgers University campus in New Brunswick, New Jersey, becoming a permanent and continuing feature of campus life, well known for Fat Sandwiches (LaGorge 2012). Food trucks of all types now find customers on campuses throughout the country.

While the meals these food-truck operators continue to sell are often tasty and well received, their owners do not aim to prepare and sell high-end foods akin to meals more typical of restaurants. It was in the twenty-first century that owners of food trucks and carts began to pursue that goal. In 2007 Thomas DeGeest left a high-level job at IBM in New York to start Wafles and Dinges, a food-truck business specializing in waffles and toppings. Over the years he worked hard to achieve the crispy authenticity of the ones from his home country – Belgium (Wafels and Dinges). In 2013 DeGeest opened a café in the East Village serving the same but more diverse menu. In 2008 Roy Choi, the son of the owners of a Korean restaurant in Los Angeles, started what quickly became a widely recognized and inspirational food-truck business. Kogi BBQ combines Korean barbecue with Mexican-style tacos and burritos. Starting as it did during a recession, it demonstrated the possibilities of starting a successful street food business with a new, ethnically based cuisine in pressing economic circumstances. In 2010 *Zagat* began reviewing food trucks. That same year *Food and Wine Magazine* named Roy Choi its best new chef and a reality show, *The Great Food Truck Race*, aired on television. Mobile cuisine had arrived.

THE FOOD

It is the food that best distinguishes the newest generation of mobile cuisine from other historical and contemporary types of food vending in public space.

The operators seek to specialize, to serve distinctive dishes and to provide a particular eating experience, much as owners of restaurants do. They seek a niche in the market. The result is cuisine that varies by ethnic origin, kinds of ingredient, and savory or sweet, since some food trucks offer desserts and others serve savory meals and snacks. Earlier lunch wagons and those that now operate on or near college campuses do not show this degree of variation, serving instead generic kinds of food. Similarly, many food carts in New York adopt very similar menus, and *loncheras* in Los Angeles continue to specialize in tacos and burritos.

Serving a specific ethnic cuisine is one way vendors seek to offer a particular food experience. In New York, among the 40 trucks surveyed, the most common cuisines were Latin American (8 trucks) and Asian (5), with Lebanese, Indian, Italian and French or Belgian being less frequent (2 each) and one truck that serves Australian savory pies. Other trucks offer fusion cuisine such as Asian tacos. One of the most well-known New York trucks surveyed, Korilla, fuses Korean with Mexican, serving tacos and burritos stuffed with Korean fillings. Other foods are distinctive in other ways, drawing from particular locations or cultures such as Philadelphia cheese steak, Maine lobster, Jewish hot dogs and knishes or addressing dietary needs such as vegan and kosher. A lobster roll was the most expensive and possibly the most distinctive meal for street vending in New York ($18). The least expensive was a knish, probably not made on the truck ($3).

Among the 42 carts surveyed in Portland, the most common cuisines were Asian (7 carts) and Latin American (5),with Italian (3) being less frequent and one cart each serving the cuisines of Brazil, Romania, Scotland and Mauritius. The Italian cuisine varies between authentic northern Italian dishes (Burrasca) and locally adapted brick-oven pizza. Other foods in Portland originate from regions in the United States such as Kansas City barbecue, Southern and Alaskan reindeer sausage. Some cuisine came from a local, organic food movement: at Tastebud, food cooked in the cart's wood-burning oven comes from a nearby farm. The most expensive meal among the carts surveyed is a rib platter from Homegrown Smoker ($14); the least expensive include tacos for $1.50 each and seaweed salad for $2.50.

In both New York and Portland many operators of trucks and carts reported that their choice of cuisine came from their ethnic or family background (39 and 58 percent, respectively). Not surprisingly, then, family was often the source of recipes (50 percent and 63 percent, respectively). Choice of food was also based on market assessments: the food was not yet available (there was 'no Brazilian food in Portland') or that it would be popular (32 percent and 29 percent). Sometimes the reason was personal preference, eating food in other locations or an ideological position. In New York the choice of Canadian food came from travelling there; Philadelphia cheese steak from having a friend in Philadelphia; and fried chicken because 'I am very patriotic. I believe that American food needs to be served in New York City.' When asked why he chose the type of food his cart serves, one Romanian owner in Portland answered that he wanted to 'represent my [his] country'.

Some owners had learned recipes professionally, such as one longtime chef. The owner of Taste of Transylvania said 'I love to cook. My Romanian cookbook is ready to publish.' The owner of Burrasca, who immigrated from Italy to Portland specifically to open a food cart, changes his menu seasonally, serving meals he learned to cook from his grandmother in Tuscany such as sautéed squid, *zuppa lombarda* and *pasta e fagiol*. One customer wrote on Yelp: 'This cart is more like a bistro found in a winding Italian city than a cart' (Yelp). The bistro experience is enhanced by drinking wine purchased from another cart nearby. Since 2012, Portland food cart owners have this unusual advantage over their colleagues in many cities: they are legally able to sell beer and wine if it is consumed in designated areas with seating (Anderson 2014).

The foods described here increase the ethnic diversity of cuisine in a given neighborhood. In large cities like New York, that already have such diversity in some locations, it can bring that diversity to customers in other locations. The city government in Toronto tried out its own vending program to increase the ethnic diversity and healthiness of food sold from carts, particularly in neighborhoods that had few places to purchase food (Newman and Burnett 2013).

THE BUSINESS

Street food vending offers would-be entrepreneurs an affordable means of opening their own businesses. When asked why they started a food-vending business, a majority of Portland owners (82 percent) and over half of New York owners (59 percent) reported that they wanted to have their own business. A majority of operators are first- or second-generation Americans. Fifty-eight percent of the owners in Portland and 44 percent in New York are immigrants. In New York many others are first-generation US citizens (40 percent). This proportion is lower in Portland (10 percent). Most of the businesses are young: in Portland the average number of years a food cart has been in operation is two years; in New York it is four. In New York, however, three respondents have owned their businesses much longer: 12, 15 and 20 years.

Many owners turn to their countries of origin to choose what food to sell and, relatedly, for establishing the identity of the business. In other cases, owners choose a cuisine and a related identity based on their US cultural backgrounds. In almost all cases in Portland the identity of the business matches the owner's ethnic background as an immigrant or his or her cultural background in the US (92 percent). In New York a match between background and business identity is less frequent (46 percent), possibly because fewer owners there are immigrants. In Portland ethnicity of the cuisine is evident in 79 percent of the business names, including: Saaj Baghdad, The Flying Scotsman Fish and Chips, Delicious Taste of Transylvania, La Callejera and Burrasco. Regional US cultures are identified as well: Alaskan Reindeer Sausage and Kate's Southern Kitchen. In New York ethnicity or geographic origin is apparent in nearly half the names of the trucks surveyed, including: Taipan Express, Mausam Curry Bites,

La Belle Torte, Shorty's Philly Steaks and Sandwiches, Moo Shu Grill, Mamu Thai Noodle and Yankee Doodle Dandy. As in the early days of food vending in New York, mobile cuisine provides opportunities for small business owners to use their ethnic backgrounds as a resource. Our survey results suggest that in the twenty-first century the owners' backgrounds are valuable both for knowing how to prepare the foods and for creating a distinctive identity for the business. Entrepreneurship meets ethnicity.

The costs of opening and running a mobile cuisine business are relatively low. Among the respondents surveyed in Portland the average purchase price of a food cart or truck with kitchen equipment was $26,500. Owners can avoid that initial investment by leasing carts rather than owning them as 22 percent of those interviewed in Portland do. In New York the average purchase price for a truck is about $68,000 and nearly all the operators own their trucks (98 percent). Both trucks and carts can be re-sold to recoup at least part of the initial investment if the business does not succeed. The ease of entering the mobile cuisine business is also evident in its accessibility to those without previous experience in food-related fields. Over half of those interviewed held no previous position in food services (49 percent in Portland, 60 percent in New York). In Portland previous occupations included construction work, dance director, engineer, radio-show host and corporate manager. In New York owners had been teachers, actors, plumbers, business managers and film scouts. Adopting recipes from family members further enables the transition to mobile cuisine. Fifty-five percent of the owners in Portland and 47 percent in New York learned their recipes from family members. Recipes were often known prior to opening the business (69 percent in both cities). This prior knowledge of recipes from cultural and family origins also creates a personal connection between the owner's background and the identity of the business, one that connects the ethnicity of the owner to the ethnicity of the cuisine.

The difficulty of getting a license to vend in New York, the many, sometimes conflicting regulations along with harassment from police and local businesses, create a very difficult business environment for all types of vendors (Devlin 2011). Vendors in New York who use carts report experiencing more harassment than vendors using trucks (Dunn 2013). Certainly, the city government shows no interest in supporting mobile cuisine, limiting the number of licenses and making it illegal to park in the most attractive locations because those are metered parking spaces.

The survey findings from New York confirm the difficulties truck owners have. On a scale of one (easy) to five (difficult), 70 percent of the owners in New York rated the difficulty of city regulations as a four or higher, with the average rating being 4.0. Nearly 80 percent specifically cited the nearly daily parking violations that cost $65. One owner described New York as 'the most impossible city in the nation to do this'. Forty-one percent of owners have received health violations, receiving an average of two violations. One respondent reported that an inspector had said 'I have to give you something before I leave your truck.'

Portland city government has taken a more supportive approach, requiring that property owners who lease carts provide water and electricity services. Carts are required to have licenses and to comply with health and safety regulations but are allowed to have external additions, such as canopies, which actually violate the licensing restrictions (Newman and Burnett 2013). In general, authorities are not strict with code enforcement. Then city mayor Sam Adams commented in 2009, 'We have worked really hard to stay the hell out of the way' (Peat 2009). The food carts in Portland feature prominently in travel guides such as *Travel Portland*, which has a link on the city's official website: 'Portland's selection of 600+ food carts has drawn global acclaim.' Not surprisingly, few Portland owners expressed any difficulties with city regulations; the primary complaint was the city's requirement for grey water collection (16 percent).

THE VEHICLE

The New York vehicles surveyed are all trucks of different sizes and shapes. Most, manufactured to be food trucks with complete kitchens, can cost between $20,000 and $200,000. They can easily be moved under their own power. In Portland mobility is more theoretical. Most of the vehicles there are trailers modified in different ways: by installing kitchen equipment, making connections for utilities and creating openings and, sometimes, exterior counters. The price of carts ranges from $3,000 to $50,000. These carts can be moved if necessary, as required by Portland law, but they remain in place for years at a time. Operators often prop up the vehicle on cement blocks or jacks. Since they are stationary in Portland, food carts connect to electrical and water hookups provided by the owner of the site, as required by city regulations. Since they move each day in New York, food trucks must have their own generators for electricity, must carry their own fresh water and have sufficient storage for wastewater. In New York mobility is made possible with social media informing customers of location and cuisine: 72 percent of owners in New York display a way to access information online via Twitter, Facebook, Instagram and websites. Forty-five percent of owners in Portland do.

The New York trucks surveyed serve food from a window, located on one long side of the truck, which opens to the adjacent sidewalk or other pedestrian space. The window is usually a sliding one protected by a vertically hinged shutter. Orders are given at the window, food is received through the window and payment is made there, or sometimes to a person sitting in the front seat with the door open. The long side gives ample surface to post a menu, to advertise other locations the truck may frequent, to give contact information for hiring the truck as a caterer and to indicate the Facebook, Twitter, Instagram and website addresses. The entire surface of the truck serves as a moving billboard and is often covered by an all-encompassing vinyl wrap. Operators often hire a professional graphic designer to create a wrap that visually captures the character of the food offered, a useful branding technique that also makes the truck easily recognizable (Figure 11.1).

Figure 11.1
Moo Shu Grill food
truck, South Street
Seaport, New York.
Photograph by
Jonathan C. Jones,
2014.

The owner of Yankee Doodle Dandy, who is so keen to sell food that represents the US, has adorned his truck with images of the American flag and the Statue of Liberty. The food truck craze has led companies that design wraps to advertise their expertise online; many of those sites show images of trucks that have won recognition for their design. Online competitions, such as '1 designperday.com' sponsored by *Inspiration Product Design eMagazine*, invite customers to nominate candidates for best food truck designs. The site for that competition displays a Korilla BBQ truck from New York. Not all food trucks surveyed, however, take this high-style approach; some of them resemble more humble lunch wagons, displaying their stainless steel sides, with the main visual feature being color images of the food they offer. Such trucks are more likely to appear at one location, such as at a public park in Red Hook Brooklyn, so they have little need to be a traveling billboard as well as a food truck.

Most of the vehicles surveyed in Portland are former trailers that require a truck in order to be moved; a few are themselves trucks that remain in one place for extended periods of time. Both types of vehicles have a far more personal and hand-made appearance than trucks in New York. Many owners make their carts appear as established as possible, covering the empty space under the vehicle and around its wheels (Figure 11.2). Owners frequently decorate the exterior with wood or aluminum siding, shrubs in planters and even a picket fence. The overall effect is that of a small building with a foundation. In the majority of cases it appears that design professionals were not engaged, that the owners designed and fabricated the adaptations and decorations themselves, possibly with local crafts people. Some owners provide counter, stools, tables and chairs. Nearly all the carts have operating

Figure 11.2
La Jarochita food
cart, SW 5th Avenue
and SW Stark Street,
Portland, Oregon.
Photograph by Philip
Speranza, 2014.

canopies to protect customers at the window from rain. In parking lots the former trailers face head in – into the parking lot (see Figure 11.5). The window for serving customers is then at one short end, rather than on a long side, giving limited space for serving and limited surface area for advertising.

Relative to restaurants, the small size of vehicles minimizes overhead expenses for utilities, cleaning and the need to hire a large staff. In Portland 37 percent employ no staff at all; those that do employ on average two people. In New York, the likelihood of employing staff is much higher: 93 percent do and, on average, they employ four people. Even small restaurants employ far more staff. The Farm Café, a restaurant in Portland with only ten tables, depends on 25 employees to cover management, kitchen staff and wait staff.

Food trucks and carts offer opportunities not only for starting a business but also for growing and diversifying. Eighteen percent in New York and 10 percent in Portland currently own a brick-and-mortar restaurant in addition to their truck or cart with the same name, serving the same cuisine. Owners in New York diversify in another way: 18 percent also own a food cart or market stall. The desire among owners to open a restaurant in the future is notable, particularly in Portland, where a full 88 percent are keen to do so. In New York the figure was lower but still substantial: 35 percent. Owners in both cities would serve the same food as they do now. The owner of Sweet Chilli NYC explained: 'The truck is the first step toward opening a brick and mortar.' One of the reasons given in New York for establishing a food truck business was precisely to develop a brand: 'There is no better way to develop a product and a brand than by having a food truck in the city.'

Other owners saw restaurants as too much trouble and too competitive. One replied that it is 'easy to make a living with the truck'. Mobility works in the other direction as well: 11 percent in Portland and 10 percent in New York had owned a restaurant previously. While owners in Portland have plans to expand by opening a restaurant, it is more common in New York for owners to operate more than one truck: 30 percent of those interviewed do. Most own one or two additional trucks, but at least two owners have three or four other trucks. One owner expects to buy more trucks rather than opening a restaurant; others may own several trucks and still have plans for a restaurant. The business Korilla BBQ has three trucks and, since the survey was completed, has opened a restaurant as well. Other types of diversity are apparent. A banker in Japan owns the Minizo cart on the eastside of Portland that he uses to advertise his restaurant of the same name in downtown Portland. Tastebud, a food cart in downtown Portland, started out as a family farm that participated in the Community Supported Agriculture (CSA) program. In 2000 they brought a mobile wood-fired brick oven to the Portland Farmer's Market. In 2005, after selling their farm, they moved back to Portland. Now they have a cart, a truck and a restaurant.

SPACE AND TIME

Food vendors are able to seek out optimal locations and optimal times of the day, week and year for finding customers. In New York trucks move after a few hours. One truck in Portland varies location by season, as it travels to farmers markets in the spring, summer and fall and to locations near a park and a square during the winter. In Portland food carts stay in one location for a period of years but they can be moved, should conditions change.

According to the New York survey, the most frequented locations are along public sidewalks in Manhattan in the financial district, around Union Square and in midtown. The time spent at these locations is quite limited: a two- to three-hour period around lunch time on weekdays as they serve workers on their lunch break (11 am to about 2 pm). The routine is to park at a metered parking space and run the risk of paying a fine (since it is against New York City law to sell any goods from such spaces). Of those surveyed that park in such locations, 86 percent have received fines, the majority of them every single day they park in Manhattan. They consider the fine a cost of doing business.

The truck operators surveyed work an average of 5.5 hours on weekdays; most serve food only at lunchtime. A few trucks go to a section of the South Street Seaport where six trucks can share a pedestrian plaza on weekdays and weekends, all year, from 11 am to 7 pm. Three are accommodated at a privately owned parking lot in Brooklyn in the Dumbo neighborhood on weekdays at lunchtime. In these locations, the vendors pay the South Street Seaport management and the owner of the parking lot. During warmer months, options increase. From May to October, from 10 am to 6 pm on weekdays and until 7 pm on weekends, trucks can vend on Governors Island, paying a fee or a percentage of profit to the Trust for Governors Island.

Weekends in warmer months offer the widest choice of locations. The seven trucks around a park in Red Hook, Brooklyn go only to that location and only on weekends April through October, from 10 am to 8 pm. They pay no fee to use the public streets adjacent to the park. Other trucks go to the biweekly food rally held on Sunday afternoons in Grand Army Plaza next to Prospect Park in Brooklyn from

Figure 11.3 Food truck rally, Grand Army Plaza, Brooklyn, New York. Trucks open to the interior of the plaza. Photograph by Jonathan C. Jones, 2013.

June until October and pay the Prospect Park Alliance (Figure 11.3). A majority of trucks (85 percent) cater special events. Most of the others would like to cater but have not received requests.

When food trucks are located on streets and serve customers on the sidewalk, they use urban space much as the early vendors of oysters and roast potatoes did. Customers line up on the sidewalk, waiting to order or to receive an order. At some rallies, trucks line up facing each other across a linear pedestrian space, as on Governors Island. The arrangement is reminiscent of a street fair. Or they may form a circle facing inward, as at Grand Army Plaza, an arrangement resembling a food court. In both cases customers wait in line inside the collective, pedestrian space of the rally. At Red Hook, trucks are parked along two streets adjacent to the park, facing it. There, at South Street Seaport and at Governors Island customers can eat at adjacent picnic tables.

In New York only three sites where surveys were conducted are privately owned. The situation is dramatically different in Portland. All the carts and trucks surveyed rent space on a monthly basis from the owners either of parking lots or of vacant property not yet developed for other purposes. From 3 to 67 carts establish themselves on a single site forming what are locally called 'pods'. In four pods, in downtown Portland, the carts are always located on the outside edges of a parking lot (Figure 11.4). They serve customers on the adjacent public sidewalk who reach the pod on foot: tourists walking around the city, workers coming at lunchtime or late night revelers coming from clubs. On the more residential Eastside carts are more likely to occupy properties awaiting development; there they face inward toward a common space. The owner of the property may furnish this space with a canopy, protecting customers from the rain, and picnic tables and benches.

Figure 11.4
Food cart pod, SW 10th and Alder, Portland, Oregon. Photograph by Karen A. Franck, 2012.

The pod at Division and SE 50th even provides a fully enclosed, heated shed with tables and benches, a small children's library, a large-screen TV and free Wi-Fi. Given the low-density, residential nature of the area, customers are more likely to come to the pod by car and park on neighboring streets.

While trucks in New York travel to sites where they will find customers, often informing customers in advance where they will be, the fixed location of carts and trucks in Portland requires customers come to them, much as they might go to restaurants. Perhaps it follows, then, that in Portland, where the carts are in fixed locations, they tend to keep the hours of restaurants, being open for breakfast or lunch and into the evening. On the Westside of Portland, an area that tourists frequent and where clubs stay open late into the night, some are open until 5 am and one, Small Pharaoh's Egyptian and New Yorker Food, is open 24 hours. On the Eastside, which is more residential, carts stay open only into the late afternoon or early evening.

Food trucks and carts increase the color and visual complexity of what otherwise may well be more formal and less visually interesting urban settings. The sight and smell of food adds an additional sensual dimension. And when people line up to purchase items or find a place to eat nearby, the setting becomes even livelier. Customers may engage in conversation with each other and with the staff of the business. In all these respects, food vending enlivens urban public space as a street festival might, but everyday and also with an ethnic character that is generated by the ethnicities of the cuisine and the businesses One could well say that the trucks in New York and the carts in Portland create ethnoscapes in public space.

Food vending that brings liveliness to public space is particularly valuable in locations that would otherwise be deserted such as empty lots, the edges of parking lots or unused parcels, as in Portland. In that city food carts enliven urban space in different ways depending on their spatial arrangement. Carts in pods on the Westside of the city, at the edge of privately owned parking lots, face the publicly owned sidewalk. Consequently, they reinforce the interface between private property and the sidewalk public right-of-way, much as traditional storefronts do. Carts in pods on the Eastside transform privately owned lots, as yet undeveloped, into active public spaces, much like parks without the planting (Figure 11.5). Among the variations across the two cities, the pods on the Eastside stand out. With the support and additional amenities added by the owners of the empty lots, including seating and tents, the food vendors transform unused, privately owned space into places of eating and gathering. In New York when food trucks operate from individual parking spaces located at the curb of public streets, between a lane of traffic and the sidewalk, they bring lively commercial activity to that public sidewalk. Or, when a food truck rally is held at Grand Army Plaza in Brooklyn, it is temporarily transformed into an outdoor food court.

Food carts and trucks may increase the density of people in public space, bringing additional crowding to locations already congested, such as busy commercial sidewalks. As lines of people wait to place or receive an order, they may interrupt pedestrian flow, making it difficult for others to pass or to reach nearby shops and restaurants. This often raises the ire of local businesses and city government.

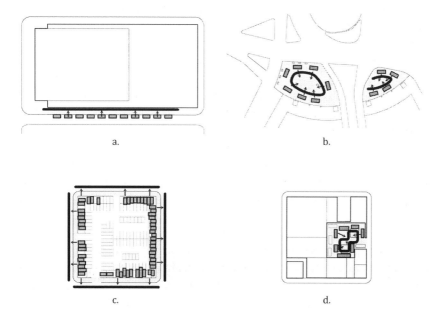

Figure 11.5
Spatial organization
of vehicles: a. Food
trucks at 47th Street
and Park Avenue,
Manhattan; b. Food
truck rally, Grand
Army Plaza, Brooklyn;
c. Food cart pod,
Alder and SW 10th
Street, Portland,
Oregon; d. Food cart
pod, Ankeny and SE
28th Street, Portland.
Graphics by Philip
Speranza.

It was such opposition to street vending that led to early regulations on the use of sidewalks (Loukaitou-Sideris and Ehrenfeucht 2009) and to the complete removal of pushcart markets from New York streets in the 1930s (Bluestone 1991). Opposition continues from businesses, and restaurant owners also hold that vending takes business away from them and, with the lower costs of operation, has unfair advantages. However, one market research survey of customers found that without the truck or cart, half the respondents would have obtained their meal from a fast food outlet and another 20 percent would have skipped the meal altogether (NPD 2013).

TEMPORARY AND ADAPTIVE

The temporary and highly adaptive features of mobile cuisine offer opportunities for owners, customers and cities. Owners can make an investment and commitment that is more delimited than what is required for a brick-and-mortar restaurant. This provides recent immigrants with invaluable opportunities to start a business. A recent documentary film, *Dog Days*, about hot dog carts in Washington DC, profiles a woman who emigrated from Eritrea. Over the 22 years she has been operating her cart, she has been able to send her children to college. The commitment can vary in duration. The vehicle can first be a test of the cuisine and the market as well as a way of building that market. In 1990, two immigrants from Egypt opened a single hot dog cart in New York. Noticing a possible market among cabdrivers, they changed to an Arab cuisine, including lamb, chicken and rice, drawing many customers from nearby offices. By 2014, the Halal Guys owned five carts and opened their first restaurant (Handschuh 2014) and are planning to open a nationwide franchise (Vadukul 2014). Mobile cuisine can serve as transition in the other direction: from a brick-and-mortar business to a cart or truck, allowing the owners to continue a food-related business but at less cost.

The mobility of a truck or a cart allows its operator to respond to an immediate market, to particular site conditions and to changes in both. It can stay in a given location for a short or longer period of time, depending upon the availability of customers, and move to preferred locations at preferred times as well as to catered events. When the vehicle remains in one location for an extended period of time, it still retains the potential for physical mobility. Consequently, should the site where it is located be slated for redevelopment, the owner can move the cart to a new location while still retaining the business. The same applies to trucks that may also be welcomed at privately owned, empty lots until they are redeveloped.

The temporary presence of the vehicle benefits those who own or manage publicly accessible spaces. The enlivening of space that occurs does not require long-term commitments from those who own the site or manage it, be they municipal agencies, the private market or civic organizations. As the needs and objectives of organizations and agencies change, so can their practices of leasing and managing the spaces where the trucks and carts park. Owners of parking lots and undeveloped property in Portland can derive income from renting space to carts but, should the opportunity for selling or developing the property arise, they can easily terminate that arrangement. Similarly in New York, corporate and civic organizations have the opportunity to invite food trucks to their properties during particular seasons of the year, on particular days or for just one event.

The temporary presence of mobile cuisine can benefit owners and hosts but the changing availability of sites and the changing content and enforcement of regulations also create a high degree of uncertainty for the business owners. That uncertainty can be exacerbated by unpredictable changes in the enforcement of regulations and by changes in the regulations themselves; both can work to the detriment or the benefit of food-vending businesses. It was a recent modification to state liquor laws in Oregon that allows them to serve beer and wine under prescribed circumstances (Anderson 2014). In many cities the regulations of food vending are being contested and modified (Gan 2014).

Despite the uncertainty of regulations and the severe constraints they can pose, mobile cuisine is proliferating throughout the country, inspiring other types of mobile commerce such as selling clothing (Best 2014). Both are cases of the larger phenomenon of temporary urbanism (Bishop and Williams 2012, Greco 2012) or tactical urbanism (Lydon and Garcia 2015). That is, the insertion of new, possibly short-term uses into publicly accessible spaces to transform them quickly without extensive planning or expense. Other examples include: pedestrian plazas incorporated into streets and alleys; parklets created in on-street parking spaces; community gardens and pop-up markets in empty lots; farmers' markets, flea markets and festivals wherever space can be found. Notably, many forms of temporary urbanism, like mobile cuisine, center on the production or consumption of food.

Food trucks and carts are not only temporary but, in their mobility, highly adaptive: they can move or be moved, intact, from one location to another as immediate or long-term needs and constraints change. As with other cases of temporary or tactical urbanism, food trucks and carts exemplify the responsiveness and flexibility of an *adaptive* urbanism where the vehicles themselves are changing and changeable urban design elements. Food trucks and carts are temporary material elements that locate themselves within the far more fixed framework of the urban infrastructure: streets, sidewalks, parking lots and other publicly owned as well as privately owned outdoor spaces.

Mobile cuisine and many other cases of temporary insertions demonstrate the continued burgeoning of grassroots appropriations of urban public space (Franck 2013). Governmental responses to these activities vary widely: in the case of food vending, from the enforcement of regulations that make it difficult to pursue policies that encourage and even promote it. It would be beneficial to vendors and to the public for more cities to allow and support food vending and to adopt ways of managing the 'unplanned' (Oswalt 2013). Food vending will continue, regardless. Citizens who invent and pursue this use of public space are creative and determined and a wider public, the many customers of mobile cuisine, welcomes them.

ACKNOWLEDGEMENTS

We appreciate the contributions of our graduate students in conducting surveys and analyzing the survey data: Stephen Maher at the University of Oregon and John Jones at the New Jersey Institute of Technology.

REFERENCES

Anderson, J. (2014) 'Food Cart Culture Digs In, Grows Up, Has a Few Drinks', *Portland Tribune*, 1 May. Online. http://portlandtribune.com/pt/9-news/218877–78013 (accessed 27 November 2014).

Appleton, G.S. (1850) *City Cries: A Peep at Scenes in America by an Observer*, New York: D. Appleton. Online. https://archive.org/details/citycriesorpeepa00croo (accessed 18 November 2014).

Arellano, G. (2013) 'Tamales, L.A.'s original street food', *Los Angeles Times*, 5 August. Online. http://articles.latimes.com/2011/sep/08/food/la-fo-tamales-20110908 (accessed 2 November 2014).

Berg, J. (2009) 'From the Big Bagel to the Big Roti? The Evolution of New York City's Food Icons', in A. Hauck-Lawson and J. Deutsch (eds.) *Gastropolis: Food and New York City*, New York: Columbia University Press.

Best, A. (2014) 'Shops on Wheels, But the Goods Aren't Sold From the Trunk', *New York Times*, 26 November. Online. http://www.nytimes.com/2014/11/27/business/smallbusiness/more-start-up-retailers-opt-for-the-freedom-and-lower-costs-of-selling-from-a-truck.html (accessed 26 November 2014).

Bishop, P. and Williams, L. (2012) *The Temporary City*, Abingdon: Routledge.

Bluestone, D.M. (1991) '"The pushcart evil": Peddlers, Merchants and New York City's Streets, 1890–1940', *Journal of Urban History* 18,10: 68–92.

Chase, J., Crawford, M. and Kaliski, J. (eds.) (1999) *Everyday Urbanism*, New York: Monacelli Press.

Chase, J., Crawford, M. and Kaliski, J. (eds.) (2008) *Everyday Urbanism*, new expanded edition, New York: Monacelli Press.

Devlin, R.T. (2011) '"An Area that Governs Itself": Informality, Uncertainty, and the Management of Street Vending in New York City', *Planning Theory* 10, 1: 53–65.

Dunn, K. (2013) 'Hucksters and Trucksters: Criminalization and Gentrification in New York City's Street Vending Industry', PhD dissertation, City University of New York.

Franck, K.A. (2013) 'Isn't All Public Space *Terrain Vague*?', in P. Barron and M. Marian (eds.) *Terrain Vague: Interstices at the Edge of the Pale*, New York: Routledge.

Franck, K.A. and Stevens, Q. (eds.) (2007) *Loose Space: Possibility and Diversity in Urban Life*, Abingdon: Routledge.

Gan, V. (2014) 'Cities Can't Ignore that Food Trucks Have Grown Up', *Next City*, 25 August, Online. http://nextcity.org/daily/entry/food-trucks-laws-zoning-regulations-dc-philadelphia-new-york-los-angeles (accessed 30 November 2014)

Greco, J. (2012) 'From Pop-up to Permanent', *Planning*, November, Online. http://ail.universitycity.org/sites/default/files/Popups%20Planning%20mag%20Nov%202012.pdf (accessed 15 September 2014).

Handschuh, D. (2014) 'The Halal Guys are Expanding from Food Carts to Restaurants', *New York Daily News*, 27 June, Online. http://www.nydailynews.com/life-style/halal-guys-expanding-food-carts-restaurants-article-1.1845910 (accessed 2 February 2015).

Hermosillo, J.A. (2012) 'Loncheras: A Look at Stationary Food Trucks in Los Angeles', Masters Thesis, University of California, Los Angeles. Online. http://ccaucla-laborcenter.electricembers.net/wp-content/uploads/downloads/2014/04/Loncheras.pdf (accessed 15 May 2013).

Hou, J. (ed.) (2010) *Insurgent Public Space: Guerilla Urbanism and the Remaking of Contemporary Cities*, Abingdon: Routledge.

Ingersoll, E. (1881) *A Report on the Oyster Industry of the United State*s, Washington DC: Government Printing Office. Online. https://archive.org/details/oysterindustry00inge (accessed 11 November 2014).

Keiger, D. (2008) 'Market Research', *Johns Hopkins Magazine* 80: 4. Online. http://pages.jh.edu/~jhumag/0908web/market.html (accessed 19 November 2014).

LaGorge, T (2012) 'For Fat Sandwiches, an Uncertain Future', *New York Times*, 28 September, Online. http://www.nytimes.com/2012/09/30/nyregion/rutgers-universitys-grease-trucks-face-uncertain-road.html (accessed 19 November 2014).

Loukaitou-Sideris, A. and Ehrenfeucht, R. (2009), *Sidewalks: Conflict and Negotiation over Public Space*, Cambridge, MA: MIT Press.

Lydon, M. and Garcia, A. (2015) *Tactical Urbanism: Long Term Action for Short Term Change*, Washington, DC: Island Press.

Mukhija, V. and Loukaitou-Sideris, A. (eds.) (2014) *The Informal American City: Beyond Taco Trucks and Day Labor*, Cambridge, MA: MIT Press.

Newman, L.L. and Burnett, K. (2013) 'Street Food and Vibrant Urban Spaces: Lessons from Portland, Oregon', *Local Environment* 18, 2: 233–248.

NPD Group (2013) 'Food Trucks Primarily Replace a Quick Service Restaurant', Online. https://www.npd.com/wps/portal/npd/us/news/press-releases/food-trucks-primarily-replace-a-quick-service-restaurant-visit-says-npd/ (accessed 19 November 2014).

Oswalt, P. (ed.) (2013) *Urban Catalyst: The Power of Temporary Use*, Berlin: DOM Publishers.

Peat, D. (2009) 'Food Carts Can Be Good Business', *Toronto Sun*, 31 August. http://www.torontosun.com/news/torontoandgta/2009/08/31/10683596-sun.html (accessed 2 February 2015).

redOrbit (2014) 'City Size, Rental Costs, Population Diversity among Factors Impacting Spread of Food Trucks', 19 August, Online. http://www.redorbit.com/news/science/1113215016/food-trucks-no-longer-considered-roach-coaches-081914/ (accessed 14 September 2014).

Schiller, J.K. (2011) 'Meals on Wheels – Night Lunch Wagons in NYC,' *Exploring Illustrations: Rockwell Center for American Visual Studies*. Online. Available HTTP: / http://www. rockwell-center.org/exploring-illustration/meals-on-wheels—night-lunch-wagons-in-nyc/ (accessed 15 November 2014).

Vadukul, A. (2014) 'The Halal Guys: Crashing in on Street Cred', *New York Times*, 13 June, Online. http://www.nytimes.com/2014/06/15/nyregion/the-halal-guys-cashing-in-on-street-cred.html (accessed 2 February 2015).

Wafels and Dinges. Online. http//www.wafelsanddinges.com/ (accessed 31 March 2015).

Wasserman, S. (2009) 'Hawkers and Gawkers: Peddling and Markets in New York City', in A. Hauck-Lawson and J. Deutsch (eds.) *Gastropolis: Food and New York City*, New York: Columbia University Press.

Yelp. 'Burrasca' Online. http://www.yelp.com/biz/burrasca-portland (accessed 31 March 2015).

Chapter 12: On the move

Temporalities in a Franco-German museum exhibition on representations of immigrants

Yannik Porsché

This chapter is concerned with different usages of the expression 'on the move': the physical move of how a temporary museum exhibition that was shown in several institutions 'migrates' in time across places, the pragmatics and politics of the continuous activity of meaning making and, lastly, attempts to advance public images through ideological change. This contribution draws on a study of an exhibition produced in French–German cooperation. It was first shown at the Cité Nationale de l'Histoire de l'Immigration (Cité)[1] in Paris with the title 'To Each Their Own Foreigners? France–Germany from 1871 until today'. Six months later a slightly modified version was presented at the Deutsches Historisches Museum (DHM) in Berlin. Here the exhibition was entitled 'Foreigners? Images of the Other in Germany and France since 1871'.[2] An exhibition that was relocated provides the opportunity to discuss different aspects of contextualisation and temporality at play in the institutional construction of knowledge.

Most exhibitions deal with the challenge of recontextualising something from outside the museum walls by selectively arranging and labelling exhibits within an exhibition space. This task becomes particularly difficult when curators search for exhibits that represent intangible notions such as collective images, emotions of strangeness or of feeling at home. In this case study, the exhibition, in its interaction with visitors, painted a picture of how the French and German publics perceive foreigners (and immigrants in particular). In doing so, the exhibition also constructed an image of the perceiving publics.

The exhibition's relocation highlights different moments, materialisations and contextualisations of the project across time. The analysis of the production process shows which particular actors were able to shape (or intervene in) the process of knowledge construction and when. This 'when' refers, firstly, to different moments of the making and presentation of the exhibition. Secondly, because the preparation of the exhibition temporally coincided with the creation of the French Cité, this exhibition also needs to be understood in relation to the institution's founding as one element of defining the museum institution in general. The case of the Cité is particularly interesting as the hosting architecture was the colonial Palais de la Porte Dorée, yet the declared aim of the new institution is to disrupt the colonial ideology that guided the museums previously housed there. Thirdly, the different ways in which actors shaped the exhibition entail different velocities. For instance, in the time frame of several months the exhibition's concept papers evolved with varying pace. The exhibition concept – in addition to, for instance, the setting in the museum buildings – can also be understood as part of the 'context' for the construction of knowledge that takes place through the museum. More rapidly changing 'contextualisation' (Gumperz 1982: 131) can be observed in 'talk-in-interaction' that occurred in 'events' (cf. Scheffer 2007 on events/processes) such as the guided tours that were given of the final exhibition.[3] Negotiations of the product intersect with processes of preparation when we take into account museum policies and the publications that guides drew on in their talks. Finally, time is at stake regarding what exhibits refer to: single events, longer periods of history or present-day society.

I start by outlining the relative importance of the museums' architectures as material and symbolic contexts for the exhibitions in Paris and Berlin. I then analyse the production process of the exhibition over time. When turning to the point in time in which the exhibition was presented to the public, the exhibits included reveal which ideas were put into practice. The analysis of the press and social interactions in guided tours sheds light on different temporalities of reception and on how a modification was discussed as an instance of political censorship.

THE MUSEUM BUILDINGS: SYMBOLIC ARCHITECTURE

The institutions' buildings not only constituted the material frames for the exhibition project in terms of hosting 'containers' but simultaneously served as sites of a considerable amount of symbolic and historical meaning. The Cité and DHM buildings both have very different (political) histories that frequently became relevant in the practices of producing and receiving the exhibition. In 1931 the French palace was part of a colonial exhibition before being turned into a museum of colonial art and history and then – with much controversy – reopening as the museum and network of French immigration history in 2007.[4] Former President Nicolas Sarkozy did not visit the institution, and only in December 2014 was the museum officially inaugurated by his successor, François Hollande. The inauguration of the DHM in Berlin as the German History Museum in 1987 also created concerns over the extent of its political neutrality. In addition, there was much discussion about how the museum format would guide its concept (e.g. with a permanent exhibition that teaches history, or rather a forum for debate and a laboratory of changing ideas).[5] The current permanent exhibition in the monumental Zeughaus opened to the public in 2006. The main building had previously served as an arsenal, a war museum for Nazi war propaganda and a German Democratic Republic (GDR) history museum. The temporary exhibition space is located in an annex named the Pei-Bau after its designer, the renowned architect Ieoh Ming Pei, who also created the Louvre's glass pyramid.

Figure 12.1
Façade, Palais de la
Porte Dorée, 1931,
Paris. Constructed
for the Colonial
Exhibition, the
bas-relief by Alfred
Auguste Janniot
depicts how France's
former colonies served
the French nation in
terms of resources and
how France in return
provided the colonies
with civilisation.
Image by author,
2015.

In particular in the Cité, the architecture and the decorations of the Palais de la Porte Dorée provide a powerful element of contextualisation for visitors and for staff. Albert Laprade constructed the palace in 1931 as the only permanent build-ing of the colonial world exhibition shown in Paris that year. In the view of many visitors, engravings on the outside walls and frescos inside recreate an atmosphere of the nation's colonial past. At the same time, contemporary art installations and present-day social practices in the museum refer to the building with the aim of criticising the ideology inscribed in the building.[6] Due to regulations that serve the purpose of conserving ancient monuments, the architects Patrick Bouchain and Loïc Julienne were very limited in the extent to which they could make changes to the colonial building. Social practices within the building thus are particularly important to reinterpreting the exterior. In addition to conceptual planning and renovation of the interior of the building at the time of the creation of the Cité, guided tours by museum staff of the construction site (and later in the exhibitions) were crucial for negotiating the meaning of the institution and its building. During my fieldwork at the time of renovation, the spatial separation between black peo-ple who were hired for the construction work and white staff in the offices was particularly noticeable. This racial distinction between kinds of work and the lim-ited interaction between these two groups (which also became apparent at festive events which were organised for all staff) should not, however, be read as neces-sarily more apparent in the Cité than elsewhere in France or other countries. It is remarkable, however, that in this case those who were more likely to have an immigrant background were renovating a building in which others, who less likely to have an immigrant background, worked conceptually and in interaction with visitors to construct images of immigrants.[7]

The question of whether having an immigrant background or academic competencies on the topic of immigration should constitute the main criteria for hiring staff is a point of debate in museum practice on migration (cf. Hampe 2005). For instance, the Dokumentationszentrum und Museum über die Migration in Deutschland (DOMiD, http://www.domid.org/) argues for the former and the Cité for the latter (Eryılmaz 2004: 319, Jamin 2005: 47). Nevertheless, 'mediators' in the Cité – who are not guides but in addition to their work as room attendants also provide information to visitors – had the impression that their ethnic origin was relevant in their employment. In the words of one informant, they were 'like the colours of Benetton', handpicked according to their skin colour (see Porsché 2014).

This illustrates the complexities of a 'front stage' and a 'back stage' (Goffman 1959) at work in the Cité. On the one hand, its concept appears very transparent, open to and involving the public. Early concepts of the institution, still in the planning stage, were made available on its website and the public had the chance to go on guided tours of the building during its renovation – this is remarkable, and certainly not standard procedure when planning (national) museum institutions. On the other hand, one might wonder whether mosaics with swastikas in the main hall (the *forum*) really had to be covered with wooden parquet for wheelchair-accessibility reasons and why original showcases from the colonial exhibition were not displayed in the permanent exhibition. To be fair, pictures of the swastikas can be found in a picture book by Murphy (2007) that is sold in the museum shop, a book that also shows the detention areas in the palace for unlicensed merchants (most of whom were Chinese). Moreover, members of staff were happy to take interested parties on special tours to see the 'back stage' showcases behind the offices. Although many argued that using the building for the Cité is ideal to signal a change of ideology, others noticed that contentious issues were avoided, or visible only to the interested and attentive visitor. In particular, some visitors criticised the marginalisation of dealing with the French colonial past. At the same time, some Cité historians were at pains to avoid equating immigration with colonialism, which is why they wished not to highlight it. They also argued that the French public were not ready to come to terms with their colonial history and that they did not want to fuel further political controversy surrounding the opening of the museum.

In terms of the relationship between the museums' architectures and the exhibition, it is notable that the DHM's architecture was rarely made relevant in discussion of or about the exhibition. Although the architecture by Pei might not be considered relevant for the topic of representations of foreigners, the spatial configuration of the building, and especially its prestigious status, were, however, consequential. The entrance fee, the impressive glass facade and its location in the centre of Berlin arguably encouraged certain visitor groups such as relatively wealthy tourists to visit, and discouraged less well-off visitors. In contrast, the Cité and the Kreuzbergmuseum are situated in the periphery of Paris and in a traditional working-class and immigrant district of Berlin, respectively. This can explain why more visitors with a working-class or immigrant background visited these two museums than the DHM. The size, shape, lighting and climate of the rooms in the museums further enabled certain exhibition designs and made others impossible. For example, certain arrangements of exhibits, and mitigation of risks that fragile exhibits would deteriorate due to temperature, humidity or exposure to light, were necessary.

The consequence of the exhibition layout for the construction of knowledge in social interactions in the exhibition space was that visitors were encouraged to question or discuss what they were presented with at certain points of the historical visit but not at others. For instance, in the present-day section of the exhibition especially, there was enough space for visitors and guides to have a conversation. In contrast, narrower sections of the exhibition in which visitors could not stand in a circle made discussion harder. The physical qualities of the exhibition space thus encouraged or discouraged shorter or longer social interactions. Moreover, the spatial layout organised the construction of knowledge about time in terms of 'time-as-history'[8]: since the exhibition presents a narrative of the nations' histories

Figure 12.2 An interior view of the French version of the exhibition 'À chacun ses étrangers?: France–Allemagne de 1871 à aujourd'hui' in the Cité Nationale de l'Histoire de l'Immigration, Palais de la Porte Dorée, Paris. Image courtesy of Deutsches Historisches Museum. Originally published in Beier-de Haan, R. and Werquet, J. (Eds.) (2009) *Fremde?: Bilder von den 'Anderen' in Deutschland und Frankreich seit 1871.* Dresden: Sandstein Verlag, p. 15.

until the present day, separations in space signal the elevated discursive importance of certain events or periods in time. For instance, in the DHM temporary walls
marked so-called 'zooms' in which a particular historical period was covered in
depth, or pillars set single exhibits apart from the other exhibits. Finally, in the Cité
and the DHM the chronological design of a uniform historical matrix constructed a
particular idea of time itself as linear and relatively continuous.

From the theoretical perspective that the meanings of a building's architecture are not fixed but are on-going negotiations of contextualisation practices,
how in the Cité the building was referred to in social interactions engendered
analysis of what relevance the building's architecture can have today. For instance,
interactions between a guide and students who visited the museum made clear
that the architectural design was neither irrelevant nor did it fully determine what
knowledge construction took place there. Moreover, the references were entangled in other discursive practices and in this situatedness served particular functions
in addition to establishing the meaning of the architecture. At the beginning of
one guided tour, for example, the engravings and frescoes of the Cité were used
to negotiate the social situation of interaction. The guide – in the museum's main
hall before taking the group to the room of the temporary exhibition – encouraged
the students to notice the propaganda on the walls, which suggested a certain
image of the foreigner (one which the Cité is now trying to change). Presumably

Figure 12.3 An interior of the German version of the Deutsches Historisches Museum exhibition 'Fremde?: Bilder von
den 'Anderen' in Deutschland und Frankreich seit 1871'. Image courtesy of Deutsches Historisches Museum. Originally
published in Vogel-Janotta, B. and Bresky, S. (Eds.) (2009) Fremde?: Bilder von den 'Anderen' in Deutschland und
Frankreich seit 1871. Berlin: Deutsches Historisches Museum, p. 10.

to the surprise of the guide, who introduced the topic as a serious one, a student attempted to turn the interaction into an entertaining one: he responded to the question of whether the students had noticed the museum's remarkable exterior with a simple 'there are a few engravings, we saw those' ['Il y a quelques gravures, on a vu']. It took the guide a moment to recognise the dry response as a joke, one that arose out of the stark contrast between the gravity attributed to the history of the depiction of France's former colonies and the non-significant contextualisation by the student. In this teaching situation the guide made explicit that the museum building was part of a forceful propaganda. Here, the question of time was relevant in terms of when an utterance was made in relation to the tour as a whole and in relation to the turns of talk preceding and following the utterance: a sequence of social interaction that occurred at the beginning of a tour set up the atmosphere for the tour as a whole. In addition, it was decisive in which particular context of talk colonial images were described as a mere engraving. An utterance that at the beginning of the tour was understood as a joke could later in the tour, for example in the context of atrocities committed against foreigners, be perceived as disrespectful or ignorant.

The museums' architectures preceded the exhibition in time and constituted its context not merely in terms of its physical properties, design or histories but also in terms of how these were oriented to in interactions in the media and among individuals in the exhibition spaces. In the following section, I will turn to the evolution of the exhibition concept, which significantly shaped processes of knowledge production. In the final section, I will examine examples of interaction in the exhibition space – this time in order to compare how a particular exhibit was talked about in the French and German versions of the finished exhibition.

VERSIONS OF THE EXHIBITION: POLITICS OF REPRESENTATION IN THE PRODUCTION PROCESS

The topic of the exhibition – public representations of foreigners – concerns the problem of representation in several ways. Representation can be defined as making something present that is absent, a cultural portrayal of something. Representation can also serve politically as a proxy for someone, a collective or an institution (cf. Pitkin 1967: 8 f., Spivak 1988: 275 ff.). In the two versions of the exhibition, first shown in Paris then in Berlin, representations of immigrants were discussed in order to reflect on collective publics in which these representations were said to circulate. This section will show that the construction of knowledge in the production process of the exhibition also involves politics of representation.

The exhibition's concept changed fundamentally during the two years of preparatory work between different institutions, disciplines and personalities. The Cité project manager formulated initial ideas for the exhibition. These built on her background in the German *Kulturwissenschaften* (similar to 'cultural studies') and philosophy. She planned thematic 'islands' to address the following topics: identities and images of immigrants coming to both France and Germany as well as national identities and representations of the hosting publics; processes of 'othering' (understood as exclusion and rejection by categorisations); how immigrants inscribe themselves in the cultural, political and social contexts of the respective nation; and how identity attributions that are performed by others or stereotypes that people hold are resisted or transformed. An art historian, proposed by the project manager, was then employed by the Cité. The art historian emphasised the function and consequences of the representation of immigrants in the public sphere. The initial concept focused on present-day representations. Historical explanations were meant to help the wider public to decode the representations, avoiding, however, a linear meta-narrative. The curators of the DHM, trained historians, grappled with how to narrow such a broad topic. As a result, they formulated a position paper in which they criticised the first Cité concept. The thematic islands based on cultural studies and cultural theory with limited historical contextualisation were not considered pertinent to maintaining the historical character and standard of quality of the DHM. The concept also remained unclear to museum practitioners in both institutions who were waiting for precise instructions as to what kind of objects they should be selecting. In addition to questions of how immigrants or the public are portrayed or spoken about, representations of the museum institutions and pragmatic questions of progressing the production of the exhibition were at stake.

As the pressure of time increased towards the planned opening date, the academic history committees of the DHM and the Cité agreed to take over control of the exhibition concept and fundamentally reformulated the exhibition draft. Free-floating theme islands or modules were replaced by a rigid chronological matrix dealing with the definition of the concept of the nation. The focus shifted to images of the Other, meaning anyone who was not considered part of the national public. This encompassed not only immigrants who were legally defined as foreign but also people who emotionally felt themselves to be, and in public practices were treated as, foreigners (for example Jews in Germany or colonial soldiers in France). The focus was no longer on issues of national identity or other understandings of the self, though these had been discussed in the early project titles. Ideas by the art curator for more creative ways of presenting objects, for example, by placing them in containers used on construction sites in order to illustrate the continuous building process of identities, were mostly discarded. In their place, traditional showcases were favoured. As well as conceptual and aesthetic issues, other factors affected the production process. Another reason for discarding the idea of containers was, for instance, that they would not fit through the room's doors in one piece. The curator, during the period of illness, was absent and unable to contribute. In some cases, problems in finding a suitable object meant that curators could not realise their ideas. For example, museum staff reported difficulty in finding exhibits in instances where some groups of immigrants tended not to leave material traces that could be displayed. At the same time, objects that the museum staff came across in their search also inspired them to include topics that had so far not been considered. In the process of materialisation, issues of academic disciplines intersect with institutional hierarchy and pragmatic concerns such as time or door frames.

Furthermore, some exhibits that were suggested by members of staff did not (or almost did not) find their way into the final presentation in the museums. Pieces of rap music which referred to France's colonial past or pictures of German detention centres for immigrants (*Abschiebelager*) were examples of (assumed) political and aesthetic concerns for the museum directors. In one case, the museum director of the DHM proposed bringing maps of global migration flows from the permanent Cité exhibition, but the curatorial team did not agree. Because the curators did not see the exhibition as primarily dealing with migration, yet wanted to avoid lengthy discussions with the director, a member of staff resorted to the following strategy: exhibiting the maps on migration flows at the end of the exhibition period – thus carrying out the directors orders while minimising the time that visitors would actually see the exhibit. This makes visible how the museum director's power to make executive decisions can be counteracted through subversive practices in the production process. Finally, the negotiation of a number of mp3 recordings from the immigrants' documentation initiative DOMiD was documented in the DHM's archive. The DHM director did not agree to DOMiD's offer to lend the recordings in return for a fee.[9] A member of staff attributed this to the DHM's not taking the DOMiD institution very seriously. In the end, a deal was made, however, after a curator explained to the director that not only would the exhibits enrich the exhibition but, for reasons of 'museum politics', it would be important to mention a loan from the immigrant initiative DOMiD in the exhibition catalogue.

The most consequential change for the exhibition's move from the Cité in France to the DHM in Germany concerned the different versions of text on one particular panel introducing the final section of the exhibition on present-day representations of foreigners. The text that was changed on the panel was discussed in the press as an instance of censorship. After being informed by an outraged member of the academic committee, journalists reported alleged pressure by the Bundeskulturministerium (German ministry of culture) and/or the museum director on museum staff to modify the label.

In the press coverage, most attention was given to the replacement of the final sentences on the panel. 'While in Europe boundaries disappear, the EU community increasingly shuts itself off from the outside. The "Fortress Europe" should be closed for refugees' was replaced by 'The federal Office for Migration and Refugees from this time on supports the integration of immigrants in Germany.'[10] This modification clearly changed the meaning from criticism of exclusionary European politics to the new label presenting the German government in a favourable light. The change of meaning was not least accomplished by subtle shifts in temporal descriptions. In the first version, increasing and permanent exclusion at the level of the EU coincided with the disappearance of borders within Europe. In the modified version, new laws were presented as the starting point of the government's support for the integration of foreigners in Germany (in an open-ended process). The temporal shift in the modified version paints a much more optimistic picture of the future. The press also pointed out the fact that the audio guide had not been modified. Interviews revealed that this has happened despite the fact that DHM staff called the director's attention in writing to the discrepancy between the audio guide and the new label. The audio guide was apparently perceived as less official or less consequential. Also, a caricature entitled 'Fortress Europe' in the final section of the exhibition was not removed – presumably because it represented the voice of a caricaturist and not a historical or governmental statement.

The fact that the ministry intervened makes apparent the symbolic importance attributed to museum exhibitions. Journalists and members of museum staff interpreted the modification as an effort to manage the government's positioning towards the exhibition, which is a way to articulate the government's voice. The interference occurred only a few days before the opening of the temporary exhibition – suggesting that politicians had a certain 'distance' from the exhibition's production process. The last-minute interference can also be read as an illustration of the status of temporary exhibitions in general. In contrast to permanent exhibitions, which tend to be scrutinised in more detail earlier in the production process because the installations are changed only infrequently, temporary exhibitions appear to constitute more experimental laboratories for debate (cf. discussions during the founding of the DHM about what kind of venue it should represent). In relation to the exhibition's production process, the point in time when suggestions for modifications were made – in addition to who made these suggestions – was important with respect to whether they were understood as an instance of political censorship. Moreover, the permanence or temporality of exhibitions appears to be decisive in determining whether knowledge is declared and taught or open to discussion.

The presentation of ethnographic observations, document analysis and interviews showed how the exhibition changed over time, both in the production process and in the presentation in two different institutional contexts. In the following, two examples of guides and visitors interacting with the final exhibition in the two museums, together with examples of politics in the production process, show how different actors at different times have different levers at their disposal to shape the construction of meaning.

EVENTS OF INTERACTION IN THE MUSEUM SPACES: WHITENESS AND THE OTHER

The construction of knowledge about history and the politics of representation is not settled once the exhibition is produced. The meaning of exhibits is only generated 'later' in processes of reception. The intersection of contextual features such as the museum buildings, the selection and arrangement of exhibits as well as *in situ* practices of contextualisation becomes visible when comparing interactions with a particular exhibit in the Cité and then in the DHM. In the following transcripts (cf. an explanation of the notation below) a guide and visitors in the Cité and the DHM, respectively, discussed three busts of ideal types of different human races exhibited in showcases in front of them.

Cité: busts in a colonial context

1 Guide: C'est des bustes qui auraient pu (être) exposés (.) dans ce bâtiment, et puisque ce
They are busts that could (have) been exposed (.) in this building, and since this

2 bâtiment il a été (construit) pour une exposition coloniale. Et il avait vocation
building it had been (built) for a colonial exhibition. And its purpose was

3 notamment >entre autre eh?< à (répartir) les différentes races
in particular >among other things eh?< to differentiate between the different races

4 présents dans les colonies françaises. On est vraiment dans ce discours-là dans tout
present in the French colonies. One is really in this discourse there of the very

5 le début du vingtième siècle (.) et avec l'idée du racialisme.
early twentieth century (.) and with the idea of racialism.

DHM: busts in an anthropological context

1 Guide: Ich fang an hier mit den drei anthropologischen (.) ehm Büsten, also es geht
I begin here with the three anthropological (.) ehm busts, so the overarching topic

2 insgesamt um das Thema ehm, ja, Rassetheorie, die sich im Laufe des siebzehnten
is, um yes, race theory, that was developed in the course of the seventeenth

3 Jahrhunderts entwickelt haben und ehm, bekannt ist, bekannt sind sicherlich die
century and um, known is, known are surely the

4 Einteilung in insgesamt vier Rassen, eh also in dem schwarzen Afrikaner, dem gelben
division into four races in total, eh so in the black African, the yellow

5 Asiaten, eh dem roten Indianer >also das soll der Mann mit den kurzen Haaren soll
Asian, the red Indian >so the man with the short hair is supposed to be an

6 Indianer sein< und natürlich ganz wichtig der weiße Europäer
Indian< and of course very important the white European

7 ((Guide holds up thumb)). Eh nicht=
((Guide holds up thumb)). Eh not=

8 Visitor: =wo ist der denn?
=where is he?

9 Guide: Der fehlt. ((laughs)) Dafür sind wir ((raises and shakes hands))
He is missing. ((laughs)) In his place we are ((raises and shakes hands))

10 sozusagen hier im Haus ((all laugh)) eh mit dieser Rasseneinteilung ging einher, ehm
so to speak here in the house ((all laugh)) eh with this division of races went, um

11 dass man der Meinung war, dass eh bestimmte Rassen eh höherwertig seien, in dem Fall
that one believed that eh certain races eh were superior, in the case

12 war es natürlich eh dann der weiße (.) Europäer.
it of course was eh then the white (.) European.

Processes of reception can have different velocities. The reception in interactions of staff and visitors with the exhibits happens from one turn of talk to another. Within the time frame of split seconds, irritations can be indicated by the hearer or (pre-emptively) hedged by the speaker (e.g. temporally marked by adding qualifications that are spoken more quickly than the surrounding talk or by hesitations when using the term 'race', cf. Cité transcript line 3 and DHM 2, 5–6). The temporal organization of speech also contributes to the characteristic style found in institutionalised guided tours (e.g. the micro-pauses in Cité, 5 or DHM, 12).

In contrast, the time of reception by an audience of the mass media coverage (and perhaps their responses in newspaper comments etc.) can occur much later in time. Moreover, processes involving longer stretches of time such as debates in the press can in talk be described in a figurative way. For instance, a guide described the relatively short period of time in which the allegation of political censorship was debated in the press as having only temporarily 'boiled up' in the press, i.e. having temporarily been made into a big deal. This was accompanied in a multimodal way by a rising and falling hand movement (see Porsché, forthcoming a).

Comparing the two transcripts presented here, it becomes apparent how the exhibits were discursively mobilised from a slightly different angle in the different institutions. In the Cité the busts were, sometimes with reference to the museum building (Cité, 1), part of a discourse on twentieth-century colonization (Cité, 4–5). In the DHM, they were instead presented in a section on seventeenth-century anthropology (DHM, 2–3). The different historical and thematic frames in which the busts were presented allowed the guides in the two museums to tie them into, and produce, different narratives.

It is not only the relevancies of the museum buildings that differ between the Cité and the DHM, but also the visiting publics play a different role. Echoing how the Cité was renovated mostly by black and ethnic minority workers whilst its exhibitions of representations of foreigners were curated by white staff, the racial context of the transcripts also reveals important differences. At the DHM, white staff and visitors observed representations of foreigners. At the Cité exhibition, participants were much more likely to be from different ethnic backgrounds. The guide in a DHM tour for teachers of the so-called 'integration classes' – obligatory classes for foreigners who do not speak German, to learn the language and about German culture – clearly talked *about* other ethnic groups. In this example, they did this by jokingly categorising present participants as members of the white race in contrast to the anthropological busts, which were understood to represent other races. Without assuming that the curators or the guide had any negative intentions (the joking modulation indicates a metapragmatic awareness that this perspective is not politically correct, DHM transcript, lines 9–10), the white race was nevertheless presented as the unquestioned norm and only the Other was objectified. This is particularly delicate in the case of a guided tour intended for foreigners participating in integration classes. It shows the ethnocentric orientation of the exhibition and highlights dimensions of time and audience; the guide suggested how she might conduct a future tour for integration classes. However, her presentation was clearly oriented to a white audience. At the time of such an 'advertising' tour the guide and visiting teachers thus both reproduce and problematise the category of absent racial Others.

CONCLUSION

The French–German museum exhibition on public representations of foreigners constituted a venue for teaching and self-reflection. In contrast to the exhibition's aim of portraying representations of foreigners (and immigrants in particular) that circulate in the French and German publics, the aim of this chapter was to provide some insight into *how* these representations were (re-) made in different institutional contexts. I focused on how questions of time and other institutional, material and political dimensions of context were relevant to this process of knowledge and memory construction. Analysis of the production process of the exhibition before it was shown and the modifications that were performed when it was moved from Paris to Berlin illustrated this framework. Particular events of social interaction in the exhibition spaces explored how the context is, however, always referred to – and in this sense only generated – at specific points in time, in a specific participatory framework and with specific functions.

With respect to the museum buildings and the exhibition's production process, different temporalities become important. These range from the buildings' and artifacts' persistence and decay over centuries, the continuous research of objects over months of exhibition planning, to abrupt changes in the direction of the research path due to disagreements within the production team or political influence. Other temporalities are also relevant in terms of how the exhibition was received, and it is important to understand its significance in the overall generation of meaning. I briefly noted the press coverage of one instance understood as political censorship. This points to two different temporal speeds. One is the relatively slow pace of interaction between museum staff presenting the exhibition and journalists taking up and responding to this presentation in publications; another is a much faster pace of interaction at work in face-to-face interactions in the exhibition space. In addition to the sequential temporality of talk-in-interaction and text production and reading, participants attribute different temporalities to processes and things. Historical exhibits can, for instance, be framed as referring to single events or longer stretches of time. Both of these can be characterised as closed and consensual matters that have been sufficiently dealt with by the nation, as controversial ones (of the past or the present) or as open-ended processes. In terms of contextual conditions and contextualising attribution, a myriad of temporalities are thus at play in processes and events of institutional and political negotiation of public representations of immigrants.

TRANSCRIPTION NOTATION – ADAPTED VERSION
OF GAIL JEFFERSON (2004)

underline	emphasis
(.)	micropause
(not sure)	there is doubt about accuracy of material in brackets
>faster<	speaking faster than surrounding talk
((laughing, taking a step back))	described phenomena/movement

ACKNOWLEDGEMENTS:

I would like to thank Adam Wood as well as the editor and an anonymous reviewer for very helpful comments on this chapter.

NOTES

1 In July 2013 the institution changed its name to Musée de l'Histoire de l'Immigration.

2 These are the literal translations of the French and German titles, respectively: À chacun ses étrangers? France-Allemagne de 1871 à aujourd'hui / Fremde? Bilder von den Anderen in Deutschland und Frankreich seit 1871. The exhibition was shown from 16 December 2008 until 19 April 2009 and from 15 October 2009 until 21 February 2010 in Paris and in Berlin, respectively. In Paris, the cultural association Goethe Institute organised accompanying events and a part of the exhibition shown on a different floor of the Cité was presented in the neighbourhood museum Friedrichshain-Kreuzberg in Berlin. This chapter focuses on examples of analysis that concern the Cité and the DHM. For the entire study see Porsché (2014).

3 In the case study notions of 'events' and 'processes' are used as well as 'contextualisation' and the 'context' in the methodology, which combines interaction analysis, discourse analysis and ethnography in a microsociological contextualisation analysis (Porsché 2012, 2013, 2014, 2015, forthcoming a, b, c).

4 Cf. Murphy (2007); Pippel (2013: 171–237); Stevens (2008)

5 Cf. Mälzer (2005); Stölzl (1988)

6 Stevens (2008: 254 f.) terms artists' commentaries on the building with reference to Edward Said and methods of identity politics as 'contrapuntal'. For instance, the temporary video installation 'Zon-mai' by the choreographer Sidi Larbi Cherkaoui and the visual artist Gilles Delmas consists of a house placed in the forum [main hall] of the Cité onto which choreographies were projected. Because it was set in the heart of the palace architecture it was seen as a critical comment on how France deals with its colonial past. Or the radio journalist Céline Develay-Mazurelle produced an audio tour guide to make visitors reflect on the difficult living conditions of the workers, many of which came from the former colonies, who built the grandiose architecture of the colonial palace.

7 See Stajić (23 November 2010) on protests by 'sans papiers', i.e. immigrants without French documents of citizenship, who were squatting the Cité. Here, people who come from French former colonies – and who are depicted on the walls of the colonial palace – are supported by the museum institution so as to raise awareness of their situation.

8 See Blommaert (2015) on the notions of 'chronotypes' and 'scales'. The former concept by Bakhtin denotes histories that connect time and space and that are discursively available as contextual frames. The latter concept builds on Braudel's 'levels of history' ranging from very slow geographical history (durée) to people's day-to-day history (événements) and refers to how accessible chronotypes are for participants' contextualisation practices.

9 Internal DHM communication (20 April 2009)
10 In German: Während innerhalb Europas die Grenzen verschwinden, schottet sich die
   Gemeinschaft der EU zunehmend nach außen ab. Die „Festung Europa" soll Flüchtlingen
   verschlossen bleiben. [Das Bundesamt für Migration und Flüchtlinge fördert seitdem
   staatlicherseits die Integration von Zuwanderern in Deutschland.]

REFERENCES

Blommaert, J. (2015) 'Chronotopes, scales and complexity in the study of language in society',
   Annual Review of Anthropology, 10: 1–24.

Eryılmaz, A. (2004) 'Deutschland braucht ein Migrationsmuseum. Plädoyer für einen
   Paradigmenwechsel in der Kulturpolitik', in J. Motte and R. Ohliger (eds.) *Geschichte
   und Gedächtnis in der Einwanderungsgesellschaft. Migration zwischen historischer
   Rekonstruktion und Erinnerungspolitik,* pp. 305–319, Essen: Klartext.

Goffman, E. (1959) *The Presentation of Self in Everyday Life*, Garden City: Doubleday.

Gumperz, J. J. (1982) *Discourse Strategies*, Cambridge: Cambridge University Press.

Hampe, H. (ed.) (2005) *Migration und Museum. Neue Ansätze in der Museumspraxis*,
   Münster: Lit Verlag.

Jamin, M. (2005) 'Deutschland braucht ein Migrationsmuseum. Erfahrungen und
   Schlussfolgerungen aus einem Ausstellungsprojekt', in H. Hampe (ed.) *Migration und
   Museum. Neue Ansätze in der Museumspraxis*, 43–50, Münster, Lit Verlag.

Jefferson, G. (2004) 'Glossary of transcript symbols with an introduction', in G. H. Lerner (ed.)
   Conversation Analysis: Studies from the first generation, 13–31, Amsterdam/Philadelphia:
   John Benjamins.

Mälzer, M. (2005) 'Ausstellungsstück Nation. Die Debatte um die Gründung des Deutschen
   Historischen Museums in Berlin', in D. Dowe (ed.) Gesprächskreis Geschichte, 1–144, Bonn:
   Friedrich-Ebert-Stiftung.

Murphy, M. (2007) *Un palais pour une cité. Du musée des Colonies à la Cité nationale de
   l'histoire de l'immigration*, Paris: Réunion des musées nationaux.

Pippel, N. (2013) *Museen kultureller Vielfalt. Diskussion und Repräsentation französischer
   Identität seit 1980*, Bielefeld: Transcript.

Pitkin, H. F. (1967) *The Concept of Representation*, Berkeley: University of California Press.

Porché, Y. (2012) 'Public Representations of Immigrants in Museums. Towards a
   Microsociological Contextualisation Analysis', *COLLeGIUM – Studies Across Disciplines in
   the Humanities and Social Sciences. Language, Space and Power: Urban Entanglements*
   13: 45–72.

Porché, Y. (2013) 'Multimodale Marker in Museen', in E. Bonn, C. Knöppler and M. Souza
   (eds.) *Was machen Marker? Logik, Materialität und Politik von Differenzierungsprozessen*,
   113–151, Bielefeld: Transcript.

Porché, Y. (2014) 'Re-presenting Foreigners – Representing the Public. A Microsociological
   Contextualisation Analysis of Franco-German Knowledge Construction in Museums',
   Unpublished PhD dissertation, Johannes Gutenberg University of Mainz/University of
   Burgundy.

Porché, Y. (2015) 'Kontextualisierung am Schnittpunkt von Museumsraum und Öffentlichkeit.
   Ethnomethodologische, poststrukturale und ethnographische Analyseheuristiken', in F.
   Schäfer, A. Daniel & F. Hillebrandt (eds.) *Methoden einer Soziologie der Praxis,* 239–265,
   Bielefeld, Transcript.

Porché, Y. (forthcoming a) 'Contextualising Culture – From Transcultural Theory to the
   Empirical Analysis of Participants' Practices', in J. Singh, A. Kantara, and D. Cserzö (eds.)
   Downscaling Culture: Revisiting Intercultural Communication. Newcastle, Cambridge
   Scholars.

Porsché, Y. (forthcoming b) 'Discursive Knowledge Construction or "There is only one thing worse than being talked about and that is not being talked about"', in P. Haslinger, A. Schweiger and J. A. Turkowska (eds.) *Wissen transnational. Funktionen – Praktiken – Repräsentationen.* Marburg, Herder Institut.

Porsché, Y. (forthcoming c) 'Politics of Public Representation: A Franco-German Museum Exhibition on Images of Immigrants', in A. Haynes, M. J. Power, E. Devereux, A. Dillane and J. Carr (eds.) *Public and Political Discourses of Migration: International Perspectives.*, London, Rowman and Littlefield.

Scheffer, T. (2007) 'Event and Process. An Exercise in Analytical Ethnography', *Human Studies* 30: 167–197.

Spivak, G. C. (1988) 'Can the Subaltern Speak?' in C. Nelson and L. Grossberg (eds.) *Marxism and the Interpretation of Culture*, London: Macmillan.

Stajić, O. (2010) *Ein Quantensprung in der Normalität Frankreichs*, daStandard.at-Interview, 23 November.

Stevens, M. (2008) 'Re-membering the Nation: The Project for the Cité nationale de l'histoire de l'immigration', Unpublished PhD dissertation, University College London.

Stölzl, C. (ed.) (1988) *Deutsches Historisches Museum. Ideen, Kontroversen, Perspektiven*, Berlin: Propyläen.

Conclusion

Chapter 13: Migration and ethno-architecture

Mirjana Lozanovska

Whereas academic studies within the humanities have addressed migration through frameworks of culture, belonging and mobility, in national, political and media discourse, migration is represented as problematic to the nation-state. Increased security of the geopolitical borders and the foreclosure of internal borders preserving the homogeneity of dominant cultures reinforce popular terms, such as 'alien' and 'foreigner', conveying the sense that migration is temporary and entails an invasion. Experts in migration studies note a discursive and theoretical gap between the developments in cultural studies and the blatant protests related to territory and rights in political discourse (Castles and Miller 2009). But neither focuses on the role of the architecture. The enduring and physical nature of architecture and building that has evolved from migrant individuals and communities, however, provides compelling evidence that these structures are neither temporary nor transient, nor that their migrant inhabitants, adaptors and makers lack belonging. The ethno-architecture of migrants defines and articulates a history of agency, making and expression that reframe the question of the politics of migration.

When people speak of 'ethnic' public buildings, 'ethnic' neighbourhoods or 'ethnic' housing they are using the adjective 'ethnic' to define migration in the context of architecture and the built environment. The word is deployed to characterise the environments produced by underprivileged migrant individuals and communities as they assimilate, adapt, remake, construct and express the architectural processes of resettlement. Stereotyping the visual manifestations of ethnicity in the built environments of migrant peoples entrenches a caricature that obscures their particular modes of production and affect. In addition to architecture and buildings, shop signage, temporary displays, atmospheres and activities all form environments that governments and tourism policies invoke to symbolise the plurality of their nation as multicultural society. At the same time migrants are targeted for the visual presentation of difference as an inappropriate 'ethnic' presence. Consequently, the architectural spaces, aesthetic styles and motif expressions of migrant cultures are extant in immigrant-receiving cities across the world, but are marginalised from aesthetic traditions persistently promoted as the norm, and from mainstream histories, disavowing decades of migrant settlement.

Migration has transformed urban cultures across the globe (Hannerz 1996). But what of the spatial and visual transformations activated through architecture? Alternative terms have opened the debate to the global delocalized and transnational textures of ethnicity. In geography, 'ethnoburbs' describe 'suburban ethnic clusters of residential areas and business districts in large American metropolitan areas. They are multi-ethnic communities in which one ethnic minority group has a significant concentration but does not necessarily comprise a majority' (Li 1998: 479). In sociology the term 'ethnopolis' refers to urban enclaves such as Chinatown or Little Italy, contemporary migrant environments integral to many world cities (Laguerre 2000: 11).[1] These popular contemporary urban sites were originally 'ethnic enclaves or ghettos' which evolved as protective concentrations of immigrants in a hostile context (Castles *et al.* 1988). In anthropology 'ethno-scape' has captured new modes of global flows, communications and economies that emerged over the late twentieth century and produced larger and more connected diasporic networks (Appadurai 1996).

In this set of terms, ethnicity is extracted from its historical rootedness in place, custom and language, and transported to the global arena through its rendition in the prefix 'ethno'. Like the other cognates of 'ethnic', ethno-architecture presents a way of thinking about globalisation and ethnicity, provoking critical questions about why and how ethnicity remains within the global, and how to rethink the global through situated, rather than abstract, mobility. This tension can be traced in the historic trajectories of 'ethnicity' braided throughout modernities in their contingent transnational crossings (Hall 1997b). The hybrid architecture and ad hoc urbanity of the border towns of U.S.–Mexico are obvious examples of this (King 2006: 69), but the effects are palpable in less publicly visible places as well. When diasporic subjects make return journeys to their homelands they disperse new imagery, technologies and architectural styles into the hinterlands of various national landscapes. Remittance constructions are transforming numerous traditional environments in the unknown villages and towns, and produce a very different interface of 'ethnicity' in relation to global flows.

The aim of this chapter is to build the meaning of ethno-architecture and to reflect on how it has been examined. It starts with problematising territoriality of dominant cultures, and develops a position on the nature of the migrating subject and her/his routes of migration that disrupts the cohesiveness of the dominant territoriality. Bringing the discourse to the discipline of architecture, the chapter outlines the failure of 'vernacular' to encompass the complexity of migrant physical (architectural) presence within dominant societies. This prepares the ground for the necessity of the term 'ethno-architecture' that has its own set of questions that the chapters in the book have engaged with.

SPACE AS TERRITORY

Theories that expose the links between the nation, space and culture elucidate why migrant architecture is not welcomed in the built environment. The first of these theories relates to the notion of 'whiteness' as a national cultural space, often termed 'white space'. 'Whiteness' is not necessarily about having white skin, as in the example of an eastern European immigrant with an accent; but about a stake in the claim to nationalistic belonging through the accumulation of cultural capital (Hage 1998). In the Australian context this can include various cultural alignments, from enjoying Australian football to identifying with Gallipoli. If whiteness is an identity that invests in remaining non-raced in a world of 'other' races, ethnicities and cultures (Dyer 1997), then the resort accommodation globally dispersed in contexts of the severe poverty of 'others' is an example of global white space, as is the erection of an Australian monument at the site of Gallipoli in Turkey.

Migration is undeniably political. The pressing question is how architectural and spatial production engages with the complex force field between whiteness and ethnicity. The idiom 'monster houses' captures an infamous confrontation between architecture and the politics of migration. The popular media coined it to describe the houses built by wealthy Hong Kong immigrants in the 1980s in Shaughnessy Heights, an upper middle-class suburb of Vancouver (Ley 1995; Mitchell 1998). A public debate initially erupted over the issue of architectural style: the Anglo-Celtic Canadian residents preferring English Cottage historicist-style dwellings in garden settings, and the Chinese immigrants preferring large contemporary forms that required the cutting down of old trees. Behind the emotional furore was another narrative related to the carefully defined borders that preserved the 'white' coding of this suburb and distinguished it from its ethnically mixed, east-side neighbourhoods. However, the debate between a vocal and wealthy resident community

Figure 13.1
Migrant house
in Melbourne
illustrating selection
of trees/landscape
and aesthetic
palette that is not a
reference to English
garden typologies
(Lozanovska 2012).

networked with planning authorities over zoning regulations and the preservation of the homogeneity of a neighbourhood developed into a bitter debate over competing narratives of citizenship and the nation. Explicitly waged as a fierce battle in the media, the fear of an 'Asian Invasion' was directly linked to the 'strangeness' of the new houses. Migrant houses became both the cause of, and the arena for, a heated public dispute over national territory and space.

In this framework, governments and the dominant majority identify ethnic 'others' as the passive objects of policies designed to benefit the majority. Individuals and communities assume the role of managing national and cultural space, and any person in the street can become a 'space manager' by pointing to the pervasive slogan 'go home' and managing the number of migrants entering (Hage 1998: 48). This role is especially activated as a protest against the buildings of migrants and migrant communities, including houses, worship temples of diverse denominations, ethnic clubs, retails strips, restaurants, and reception centres. Tensions have arisen in response to the identifiably 'non-European' built forms in suburban landscapes such as mosques or Hindu temples (Gleeson and Low 2001: 60), in addition to 'wog houses' or 'Mediterranean palaces' in Australia (Allon 2008) or the flamboyant apartments in Vienna (Şavas 2010). A persistent construction of 'host' and 'guest' in migration theory perpetuates a perception that migrants are not residents and yet are destroying local environments.

How are diverse cultures negotiated on the ground? The multicultural narrative can take two forms: first, government policies implemented to manage cultural diversity; and second, a cultural terrain resulting from the desires of various individuals and ethnic communities who feel excluded from the discourse and practices of nationalism (Gunew 1993: 2). Ethno-architecture defines the spaces for the practice of diverse traditions, languages and rituals, but the distribution of 'plurality' is not even as illustrated in how migrant houses have caused tension in

Figure 13.2
Migrant house in Melbourne illustrating flat roof and clean modernist lines in brick different to the weatherboard bungalow style house typology of the street context (Lozanovska 2012).

particular neighbourhoods and not others. If 'white' culture is the common ground between mainstream national citizens *whether or not* they agree with the policy of multiculturalism (Hage 1998: 17), the protest towards migrant construction can be explained as a fear of cultural change conceptualised as white cultural loss (Hage 1998: 179). While this is induced by globalisation, in much migration discourse the guest is constructed as an individual who is inserted into a context with pre-existing laws and rules. Architecture's non-temporary aspect points to the problem of the host–guest binary structure, even as it persists in discourse. The increasing social diversity whether in Melbourne, Australia or Queens, New York, causes an emotional reaction that fears multiculturalism will erode a foundational heritage – British or Irish/Italian/European cultures – respectively. Architecture and buildings that serve immigrant individuals and communities more concretely and evidently articulate and manifest difference, diversity and otherness, and thereby affront the white space of the national imaginary. The public debate over the migrant house, or over the mosques in Dandenong, Australia (Beynon, Chapter 2) and New York (Gillem and Pruitt, Chapter 4), illustrate that a society's laws determine not only criminal behaviour, but also cultural norms, aesthetic traditions and spatial appropriation. Lurking beneath anxieties over the appearance of architectural styles are anxieties about the proliferation of migrant buildings and their appropriation of the cultural space of a place, city or nation.

In highlighting the political and cultural dimensions of migration, this particular lens gives rise to an inherent territorial dimension of architecture. Often evaded in revisions of the canon, architecture's political and cultural territoriality is evident as the meta-narrative of colonial history (Scriver and Prakash, 2007; Crysler *et al.* 2012). Territoriality also operates through contemporary globalised flows of migration and its local and micro adaptation of buildings (Lozanovska 2004). Migratory trajectories call upon architecture as spatial and territorial practice in order to organise multiple and transnational environments and thereby to accommodate and mediate pre- and post-migratory social and cultural lives. And yet framing forms of settlement through invisibility (Gillem and Pruitt, Chapter 4) different to perceived visibility of ethnic communities (Frazier, Chapter 3) underscores the link to whiteness studies that have critically examined the racial underpinnings of institutional power (Dyer 1997).

Exclusionary landscapes and representations of national culture continue to be crucial in displacing those who cannot, or will not, identify with the national culture. Discourse on migration is separated from the postcolonial discourse of indigeneity; even so, many nations have histories of governance informed by racialised knowledge, and an inherited narrative of colonisation 'haunt[s] contemporary debates around the nation, citizenship and multiculturalism' (Gunew 2004: 10). This perspective shifts the scholarly tendency to address either indigenous *or* multicultural concerns. The interests of the First Nation peoples in the Vancouver 'monster house' debate were not merely ignored, but *a priori* elided in the colonialising structuring of space and territory. Most immigrant-receiving nations' practices of modernity and globalism are implicated in colonisation and, as such, they reproduce a foundational myth of the nation as a homogenous culture defined by opposition to both indigenous *and* multicultural others.

The names monster house, wog house or Mediterranean Palace belong to specific cultural and historical contexts, but such naming draws its authority from a transhistorical discourse of power. In these instances the act of naming redraws the divisive line between the host and the guest as individual member or communal group. The practice of identifying concentrated urban ethnic enclaves by a diminutive relationship to another place, as for example with Little Italy, Little Saigon or Little India, often authorised by municipalities, is historically actively resisted by the migrant inhabitants (Cairns 2004). The diminutive effectively belittles the migrant in relation to mainstream societal processes, systems and structures, producing precarious positions for the migrant subject (Sayad 2004; Berger and Mohr 1975). The operation of naming the boundary between belonging and not belonging through the term foreigner and its synonyms – alien, barbarian, monster, demon, non-western and 'other' – activates a territorial narrative. This narrative is integral to the history of civilisation, but the historical moment of colonial encounters is particularly important for the discipline of architecture and this book. Desire for the exotic and disgust of its difference in Banister Fletcher's foundational *History of Architecture* (Baydar 1998) pervades other canonical efforts to come to terms with the signs of architectural difference. In a counter move, authors have sought to shift the lines of division by employing irony as in 'Third World Looking Buildings' (Beynon 2005), 'Lion-taming territory' (Lozanovska 1997) and 'Too many houses for a home' (Jacobs 2004). These reiterate that migrant encounters are two-way, messy and complex processes that challenge assumptions and acknowledge the infiltration of 'otherness' within the mainstream (Abu-Lughod 1997). Chapters in this book have devised research methodologies that can capture migrants' views of the city and thereby promote new migrant agencies.

ETHNICITY, MOBILITY AND PRECARIOUS SUBJECTS

At one end of the spectrum migration is circumscribed by underprivileged migration conditions signified by the adjective 'ethnic', and at the other end by the more privileged international migratory trajectories of academic and diplomatic personnel and employees of transnational corporations. The 'international' urban enclave comprised of gated or privileged housing, and the accompanying infrastructure of services – work, education, house cleaning and leisure – promote an international and cosmopolitan urban taste culture that is distinct from the ethnically differentiated articulations of underprivileged migrant communities. Their different mode of mobility – departure, arrival, access, immigration and settlement – inscribes the limit to the 'free and speculative' exchange of commodities, economies and communication of globalisation (Castles and Miller 2009). Architectural discourse that passionately celebrates the privileged contracts of globalising economies – such as the iconic work for the Olympic Games, for example – while remaining silent about the substandard housing of migrants that constructed them spotlights that limit.

This distinction is the point of departure for this book. Historically, underprivileged migrants have been considered economic commodities, exploited by transnational or global economies and located within the consuming operations of nation-states. Short-term market interests and nation building, rather than a desire to create multi-ethnic or multicultural societies, have routinely generated large-scale labour migrations (Castles *et al.* 1988). However, the word migrant describes any person who is 'othered' by the process of migration, and this includes post-migration generations who experience the negative and disempowering effects of their differentiation from the norms of the community into which they resettle.

In this context, Butler's theory of sexuality (2004) as the practices through which normative human subjects are produced can be applied to culture, race and ethnicity (Butler 2009). Butler's notion of performativity refers to the reiterative everyday practices that enable or disenable normative subjectivity. While all subjects participate in normative identity, some have more precarious, marginalised, lawless positions from which to act and perform agency. Some subjects are eligible for recognition, while others are less so or not at all. Despite decades of critical investigations, ethnicity remains essentialised theoretically and conceptually in contemporary discursive arenas, including architecture. The notion of architectural value assumes an objective evaluation of 'authenticity', 'form' and 'style', veiling the fact that these qualities are derived from the particular histories that dominate the narrative of architecture. Exclusionary frameworks distinguish migrant from non-migrant housing and building practices. For example 'American' or 'Australian' houses are differentiated from migrant houses, even if both typologies are within non-architect-designed categories.

To construct the 'ethnic' subject as a 'collective' or 'group' disavows the individually differentiated pathways within migration, and assumes an authorial representation of the group. Ethnicity functions as a generalised term and limit to the non-ethnic, but this can be reconsidered by firstly thinking English – not as universal as is often assumed, but as an ethnicity – and secondly, dismantling what

Figure 13.3
Fragments of
otherness: house
fragments of
migrant adaptation
to existing
worker's cottage
in Melbourne
illustrating the
effort to transform
house to a
different aesthetic
and tradition
(Lozanovska 2001).

constitutes 'Englishness' and illustrating how 'others' and migration are integral to it (Hall 1997b). Work on migration and architecture tends to blur plural cultures of immigrant-receiving cities and disavow their particularity, or it produces case studies that examine isolated migrant communities producing 'ethno-architecture'. By contrast, the analysis of the local–global character of Walworth Road in South London combines globalism and particularity (Hall and Datta 2010). By tracing the origins and journeys of the migrants on a world map, and documenting the languages, style and investment in the shop signs, they effectively represent Warlworth Road as an ethnopolis. Such geo-migratory world maps are the surface plane of a potential visual counter-representation of ethnicity and architecture.

In contrast to the autonomous travel of twenty-first-century tourism, migrant mobility is characterised by multiple connectivities that are associated with networks of family and belonging (Glick Schiller and Çağlar, 2011). The mobility of under-privileged migration is related to resettlement. Displacement and place-memory are often linked to migrant identity, and yet this field's focus on place attachment and single place-identity is inadequate to describe migrant temporality. Migration discourse shifts the relationship between place and identity for two reasons: first, more places are involved; and second, places are not merely memorialised within a nostalgic past, but re-activated through travel (Massey and Jess 1995; Sandercock 2003). The migrant desire to construct houses in the original homeland, sometimes instead of building in the city of immigration, illustrates its situatedness in multiple sites and presents a more radical challenge to architecture discourse. In addition to houses, migrants have initiated the development of public or commercial buildings in 'homeland places'. This constitutes a dominating migrant agency and a more conscious role in the transformation of place (Lopez, Chapter 5).

Place, perceived through the matrix of underprivileged migration, is associated with routes and returns and embedded within fictionalised imaginary memories and possible future productions. Place is at once rooted within spatial boundaries and yet characterised by the dispersed network of accumulated itineraries, travels and absences of the migrant. This points to the many links and differences between place theory and migration discourse The desire and nostalgia of ageing migrants in Israel or in the Netherlands (Levin, Chapter 7 and Vellinga, Chapter 8) contest the premise of 'deep belonging' to place (Relph 1976) as it is framed in various interpretations of place-attachment theory (Low and Altman 1992). Does this yearning for architecture of belonging *after migration* present the discipline with the challenge of a different form of utopia, emerging parallel to the much-discussed global iconic architecture and global non-place? Dominant theoretical frameworks present the migrant's allegiances as split between two homelands. Yet migration can also connect two or more homelands, challenging both the exclusionary basis of the nation-state *and* the abstract notion of global mobility. Importantly, places assumed to be unrelated become connected, such that major world immigrant-receiving cities become routinely tied to unknown villages and towns of emigrant departures and exile.

Hotel lobbies, conference resorts, sparkling fast-train stations, cruise ships and air-conditioned luxury cars are not artefacts associated with the non-place of

underprivileged migration. The non-places of migrant travel might include detention centres, cargo containers, migrant construction-worker accommodation,
impromptu bus-car terminals, nation-state checkpoints, networks of illegal crossings, the Indian Ocean and airports. This is material for another book, however.
Here it is important to briefly distinguish between the transnational citizen who

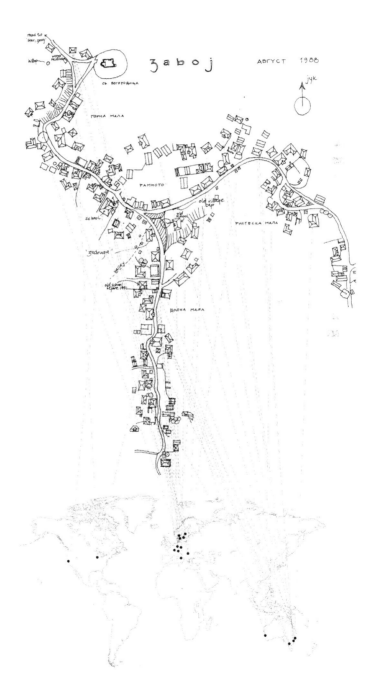

Figure 13.4
Village-cities network:
graphic representation
of emigrants' routes
from the village
Zavoj, Republic of
Macedonia to various
destinations in the
world (Lozanovska,
drawn by Leila
Mahmoudi Farhani).

travels light and yet gains access and whose privilege is visualised in Diller and Scofidio's 'tourist' (Diller and Scofidio 1994), and the underprivileged migrant who carries necessities and cultural baggage from one place to another in order to build a new life. The dominant discourse of non-place associated with abstraction, estrangement and individual autonomy cannot effectively describe mobility characterised by connectivity. Migrant mobility is configured as a thick layering of routes; each one induced by promise, nostalgia or escape and, sometimes, risk.

In contrast to the popular uptake of Deleuze and Guattari's utopian figure of the nomad in architecture, the mobility of the migrant, also discussed in *A Thousand Plateaus* (Deleuze and Guattari 1987) and differentiated from both the sedentary human figure and the nomad, produces materialities of attachment. Mobility is differentiated and is not always a generic global mobility: 'It matters who moves and how you move. Nomadism is also the mantra of the neoliberal: financial capital is constantly circulating; the factory may be "fly-by-night". (And what of the rights of migration?)' (Massey 2003: 117). Numerous stories of the to-and-fro journeys of migration exemplify the opportunities afforded by the blinks in the temporal and spatial surveillance of cities, like the temporary appropriation of city space by food trucks in New York or Portland (Franck and Speranza, Chapter 11). The migrant is not a passive recipient, but must remain active and organised in order to 'turn' away from surveillance and embark on, plan and execute departures and returns (de Certeau, 1984).

Narratives of globalisation often overlook the actual physicality of place that manifests, indeed articulates, global cities, especially those spaces and structures inhabited and transformed by labour migrants (Sassen 2007). Focussing on the information economy, telecommunications, global transmission and transnational global corporate culture, such narratives mask a hidden form of globalisation that is empirical, physical and located. This includes built infrastructure, service and manufacturing labour, the (immigrant) workers, and the multiplicity of cultural environments. To consider globalisation from the lens of underprivileged migration involves taking a parallax view of globalisation and the global economies which produce architecture. Further from the dominant matrix is the architectural productivity of 'rural' sites. Radical mixings of urban, rural, ethnically cultural and contemporary produce what might better be defined as a global diasporic architecture erupting beyond the boundaries of nation-states, cities and villages, and undermining the very static framework that the global aesthetic is 'urban'. The distinction between the urban and rural as twenty-first-century sites of exchange is blurred, as is the distinction between 'generic (international universal, modern) and cultural (ethnic, exotic, differentiating)' (Cairns 2004: 19).

COUNTER-NARRATIVES OF TWENTY-FIRST-CENTURY VERNACULAR

What can be learnt from the architecture, building and environments associated with migration and migrant communities if the material productions are simultaneously read as the results of global flows, routes and mobilities, and inherently 'ethnologised' interpretations and representations of either particular ethnic groups or ethnicity per se? If migration brings into confrontation the assumed global and a perceived ethnic limit, can more inventive theoretical approaches to place, the vernacular, critical regionalism and architecture evolve?

Due to their focus on culture, ordinary people and non-architect-designed architecture, both ethno- and ethnic architecture are linked to theories of vernacular architecture. In the twenty-first century, vernacular architecture is a problematic field and its redefinition provides a way of accounting for globalised exchanges as well as the varied traditions of popular, kitsch and 'everyday' architecture (after the profound influence of the theories of Michel de Certeau 1984 and Henri Lefebvre 1991). Considering the established critique of the western gaze towards sites of otherness, a study of these structures requires 'an entirely reimagined terrain' of vernacular architecture studies (King 2006: 70). Are the processes of migration accommodated within the new scope and terrain of vernacular architecture? In architectural history, the vernacular is constituted as the non-architectural component of a mainstream narrative of architecture, frequently presented ahistorically, and at best through a problematic historiography that charts the structural biases of a dominant western history (Baydar 2004). Old-fashioned definitions of vernacular architecture as authentic, fixed and static are challenged by a new scope of the vernacular that encompasses many spatial, architectural and constructional building typologies, that is, everything *except* architect-designed architecture (Brown and Maudlin 2012). Yet such comprehensive theoretical appraisals of vernacular architecture do not always discuss migration as a significant force altering the theoretical terrain of vernacular architecture. While *The Sage Handbook of Theory* (which includes Brown and Maudlin's chapter) has tried to shift the canonical position towards a more cultural and postcolonial perspective, it omits migration and its various renditions – migrancy, migrant – in its contents and index (Crysler *et al.* 2012). This is surprising because key authors, including Paul Oliver (2003) and Amos Rapoport (1969), and theorisation of vernacular architecture in *Vernacular Architecture in the Twenty-first Century* (Asquith and Vellinga, 2006) bring exchange and migration into the framing of vernacular architecture.

One problem with this omission is highlighted by the constructions and interventions built by emigrants in the hometowns to which they regularly return. Both remittance and vernacular architecture are linked to cultural theoretical frameworks related to ordinary people. But local debates illustrate that remittance architecture is opposed to the vernacular or traditional architecture (Lopez, Chapter 5 and Klaufus, Chapter 6 in this volume; Van der Horst 2010). The vernacular haunts the nostalgic architecture revisions of elderly immigrants, as with the Indisch in the Netherlands (Vellinga, Chapter 8) or Moroccan Jews in Israel (Levin, Chapter 7). If not originating from the local context, how do architectural ideas, aspirations and the imagery of returning migrant architecture evolve? What is the origin, and does it resemble vernacular architecture traditions? How can the production of ethno-architecture be characterised? What do descriptions as kitsch or pop mean in relation to transnational contemporaneity, and are they adequate to define a distinction from the local and vernacular? Migrant stories of return trips illustrate that vernacular culture has never been rooted and static but has evolved through imprints and transformations realised through travel, in addition to dwelling in place (Clifford 1997: 251). But twenty-first-century migrant architecture involves a flux of visual imagery gathered through various media, providing the articulation of an imaginary landscape of itineraries, multiple places and aspirations. The temporal dimension and internet are folded in the spatial processes of culture and dwelling.

Colonial encounters in the eighteenth century engendered the work of documenting non-Western temples and palaces, and produced a body of work that challenged the canonical distinction between what is architecture and what is not architecture. While the vernacular 'entailed, not the discovery of vernacular buildings, but the *revernacularisation* of classicism with which to substantiate a myth of origins' (Colquhoun 1989: 30), unlike housing, temples and palaces could not easily be relegated to this role of nourishing dominant narratives. The eighteenth century marked a decisive historical moment when the discipline had to rethink its epistemological terrain because cultural particularity entered the scene of architecture and contested a single Eurocentric origin (Baydar 2004). From a postcolonial perspective it can be argued that the vernacular is deployed in the same way as the concepts of 'oriental' or 'other' have been in the servicing of the European subject, as its defining limit, the negative against which it defines itself as subject. Yet neither the canon nor the discipline of architecture is a fixed and autonomous entity with clear, stable and secure boundaries, and the current investment in what might be called 'minor historiography' further highlights permeability and exchange between architecture and the vernacular.

Theorisation of the impact of globalisation, mobility and the information era in relation to architecture in the twenty-first century includes the interest and critique of large-scale transnational projects, the phenomena of the star-chitect, and

Figure 13.5 House-states: developing research methodologies to capture complex conditions of architecture. Construction of the house in sites of origin is a process rather than a product that occurs in piecemeal ways depending on capacity for funding and travel. House in Zavoj village, Republic of Macedonia (Lozanovska field work 2007–2013).

the homogenising of the most remote sites through the same global architecture imagery. Does this mark a current moment when the discipline is rethinking its epistemological terrain, and what is the impact of migration in this field? Multiple situatedness – being grounded, in place and marked by ethnicity while simultaneously networked globally – illuminates how architecture mediates the dominant local–global framework. Thinking about the local is dominated by spatial boundary or scale in architecture and geography, but a reconceptualisation of the neighbourhood through temporality, relationality and contexts, and as a *property of social life*, gives emphasis to 'the production of locality' (Appadurai 1996: 182 his italics). Locality cannot be taken as a given because even in the most traditional of societies 'locality is ephemeral unless hard and regular work is undertaken to produce and maintain its materiality' (Appadurai 1996: 180). Temporality reconfigures architectural thinking as its elements stage particular social practices and reiterate cultural inscriptions through practice. The various temporal narratives of the Indian grocery store (Sen, Chapter 9) interact with the spatial scales of local site and trans-regional ethnic contexts (Indian/Asian and American), in addition to the micro-affects on the human body. How architecture relates to 'social life' provides access to temporal processes and diverse palettes of global imagery that influence the visual and spatial articulation of locality.

Architectural discourse privileges the object as stylistic artefact rather than considering the social role of architectural spaces and envelopes in the ways people organise their lives. The early work of anthropologist Mary Douglas (1970) and sociologist Pierre Bourdieu (1973) reminds us that space is produced through ritual and ceremony. Attention is given to a hierarchy of time as seasons, as ceremonial calendar and as everyday activities evident in the material and spatial inscription: the plan of the settlement, the division of inside and outside, internal hierarchy and system of openings, as well as the pattern of ornamentation. Interaction and sensory affect with this ritually inscribed space produce an embodied and lived narrative of meaning and value, such that human subjects are expanded and limited by the cultural laws inherent in the architecture. The eventful temporality of food trucks and its impact on public space illustrates the role of food at this anthropological-architectural intersection (Franck and Speranza, Chapter 11). The architectural world is not only spatial, physical, scaled and ordered as a rational system, but a system within which magic, fiction and fantasy as well as fear, emotions and protection operate. If architecture is interactive, the altered environments produced through migration engender new heterogeneous or heterolocal cultures.

Migration and its modernities and mobilities challenge theories that depend on the secure boundaries of places, histories, artefacts and cultures. This challenge can occur from underneath canonical narratives and the precedents that architectural discourse privileges, as outlined in the chapters in this book. Architecture takes on different meanings according to location, how it operates in relation to social hierarchies, how it is theorised and by whom. The perceived difference between 'ethno' and 'ethnicity' is produced by discursive structures of the political and cultural context. Migration also takes on different meanings according to location and perspective, as illustrated in the production of a major exhibition on migration in Paris and Berlin (Porsche, Chapter 12). 'Ethnicity' crossed with migration shifts the focus from 'locatedness' to the new global contexts of 'ethno'. By combining 'ethno' and 'architecture', this collection aims to refunction architectural theory through the concepts of mobility and migration. The scope of architecture is related both to a politics of identity and to architecture as an incomplete term whose value and meaning must be negotiated through narration.

ETHNO-ARCHITECTURE AND CRITICAL OTHERNESS

Much of the twenty-first-century built environment evolves through the mobility, settlement and itineraries of migrants. Numerous studies are carried out on particular migrant communities and particular sites, but very few as collective phenomenon, its impact on built environments and its challenge to architectural thinking. Framing migration and its resultant ethno-architecture as problematic to immigrant-receiving societies elides the discussion of heterogeneous locality inhabited by culturally diverse communities. Conversely, framing ethno-architecture through the celebratory tone of diverse and rich cultures avoids developing resilient positions relating architecture to critical otherness. Additionally, omitting critical studies of remittance architecture in the homeland sites continues a perspective focussed on western cities, raising the question 'what places matter?' when we speak of the global environment.

Theoretical positions that critique the interests of the nation-state and its spatial boundaries have challenged a persistent negative attitude to the strange and the stranger. The most radical and innovative of these is the theorisation of 'diasporic cosmopolitanism'. In joining diaspora, signified through the vernacular, rooted and ghetto, and cosmopolitanism, signified through urbane, worldly and open, it offers a critique of the universalising theorisation of cosmopolitanism and its rootless, abstract and transhistoric modes of mobility (Glick Schiller and Çağlar, 2011; Sandercock 2003). Recognition of migrants' investment and contribution to the social and urban cultures that have made many cities liveable requires rethinking about who engages with the other. Ethno-architecture extends this urban and cultural theory towards the on-site spatial and physical manifestations and the political and cultural negotiations made through architecture.

Theorising the cosmopolitan and global through the figure of the migrant requires negotiating frameworks of routes and roots, of diaspora as a necessary heterogeneity and diversity (Hall 1997a). However, one's 'entry point' into the migration discourse determines the tension of identity and difference. A positivist and constructional agenda drives architectural practices. The construction and extent of ethno-architecture in many parts of the world represent the efforts of migrants to build and adapt their lives in a new local context. Many disciplines assume migrants are bound by homesickness and nostalgia (Hage 1997), but ethno-architecture, and its global distribution and volume, shifts the identity of the migrant from stranger and guest to local and resident, respectively.

The transformation of neighbourhoods, commercial and retail strips, public architecture and urban space provides the empirical landscape and evidence that ethno-architecture is as temporary or permanent as any other architecture defining the culture of place (Beynon, Chapter 2; Woodcock, Chapter 10). The buildings of migrants have had to negotiate laws, norms, authorities and public opinion in order to be erected, and then to be accommodated and tolerated within their local contexts.

However, ethno-architecture incites debate and raises more questions about the stranger and guest, and the local and resident. Home building is not a unified process occurring in one place. The migrant is often compelled to articulate and manifest connection to two or several sites through architecture. To look critically at various sites, including the homeland sites, means to account for a dominating migrant agency and capacity to build. The interface between migrant construction and vernacular architecture gives rise to more pressing questions relating to the local and the stranger. Effects on places of emigration, resulting in blurred rural–urban developments, contest generalised theories of ethno-scapes (Appadurai 1996) and diasporic cosmopolitanism (Glick Schiller and Çağlar, 2011) from perspectives of minor historiography. Thus migration is not one way, and must be reframed in order to identify how it contributes to the production of heterogeneous or indeed homogenising global locality. Migration promotes redistribution of globalising economies through remittance and the construction of fictive and embodied connectivity to multiple places. But do these migrant trajectories offer an alternative position towards place, through diversity and the stranger, rather than territorial frontiers? The emphasis of architecture mediated through migration is to dismantle the bounded concepts of ethnic community and urban neighbourhood that service the hierarchies of nationalist paradigms. Architecture's appropriation of space and material definition of place make it critical to this discussion, and through visual presentation, architecture speaks to the larger public of the nation and global economy. It speaks not only about territory but also about a cultural existentiality that has symbolic intent.

NOTE

1 Is the Chinatown in New York the same as the Chinatown in Melbourne; is Little India in Singapore the same as or different from the one in Toronto? It would be interesting to examine the similarities and differences of the 'ethnopolis' from on city to another.

REFERENCES

Abu-Lughod, J. (1997) 'Going Beyond Global Babble', in A. King (ed.) *Culture, Globalization and the World-System: Contemporary Conditions for the Representation of Identity*, Minnesota: University of Minnesota Press.

Allon, F. (2008) *Renovation Nation: Our Obsession with Home*, Sydney: University of New South Wales Press.

Appadurai, A. (1996) *Modernity at Large: Cultural Dimensions of Globalization*, Minneapolis: University of Minnesota Press.

Asquith, L., and Vellinga, M (eds.) (2006) *Vernacular architecture in the twenty-first century: theory, education and practice*, London and New York: Taylor and Francis Group.

Baydar, G. (1998) 'Towards Postcolonial Openings: Rereading Sir Banister Fletcher's *History of Architecture*', *Assemblage* 35: 6–17.

Baydar, G. (2004) 'The Cultural Burden of Architecture', *Journal of Architectural Education* 57, 4: 19–27.

Berger, J. and Mohr, J. (1975) *A Seventh Man: The Story of Migrant Worker in Europe*, Cambridge: Granta Books.

Beynon, D. (2005) 'Melbourne's Third World-Looking' Architecture' in C. Long, K. Shaw and C. Merlo (eds.) *Suburban Fantasies: Melbourne Unmasked*, Melbourne: Australian Scholarly Publishing.

Bourdieu, P. (1973) 'The Berber House', in M. Douglas (ed.) *Rules and Meanings: The Anthropology of Everyday Knowledge*, London: Penguin Books Ltd.

Brown, R. and Maudlin, D. (2012) 'Concepts of Vernacular Architecture', in G. Crysler, S. Cairns and H. Heynen (eds.) *The Sage Handbook of Architectural Theory*, pp. 340–368, London: Sage Publications.

Butler, J. (2004) *Undoing Gender*, New York: Routledge.

Butler, J. (2009) 'Performative Preclarity and Sexual Politics', *AIBR: Revista de Antropologia Iberoamericana*, 4, 3: 321–336 Online. http://www.aibr.org/antropologia/04v03/criticos/040301b.pdf (accessed 28 September 2012).

Cairns, S. (ed.) (2004) *Drifting: Architecture and Migrancy*, New York: Routledge.

Castles, S. and Miller, M. (2009) *The Age of Migration: International Population Movements in the Modern World*, Hampshire and London: Macmillan.

Castles, S., Kalantzis, M., Cope, B. and Morrissey, M. (1988) *Mistaken Identity: Multiculturalism and the Demise of Nationalism in Australia*, 2nd edn, Sydney: Pluto Press.

Clifford, J. (1997) *Routes: Travel and Translation in the Late Twentieth Century*, Cambridge, MA: Harvard University Press.

Colquhoun, A. (1989) *Modernity and the Classical Tradition: Architecture Essays 1980–1987*, Cambridge, MA: MIT Press.

Crysler, C., Cairns, S. and Heynen, H. (eds.) (2012) *The SAGE Handbook of Architectural Theory*, London: Sage Publications.

de Certeau, M. (1984) *The Practice of Everyday Life*, Berkeley: University of California Press.

Deleuze, G. and Guattari, F. (1987) *A Thousand Plateaus: Capitalism and Schizophrenia*, trans. B. Massimi, Minneapolis: University of Minneapolis Press.

Diller, E. and Scofidio, R. (eds.) (1994), *Back to the Front: Tourisms of War*, F.R.A.C. Basse-Normandie.

Douglas, M. (1970) *Purity and Danger: An Analysis of Concepts of Pollution and Taboo*, London: Pelican (Penguin).

Dyer, R. (1997) *White*, London: Routledge

Gleeson, B. and Low, N. (2001) *Australian Urban Planning: New Challenges, New Agendas*, St Leonards: Allen and Unwin.

Glick Schiller, N. and Çağlar, A. (eds.) (2011) *Locating Migration: Rescaling Cities and Migrants*, Ithaca, NY: Cornell University Press.

Gunew, S. (1993) 'Feminism and the Politics of Irreducible Differences: Multi-Culturalism/Ethnicity/Race', in S. Gunew and A. Yeatman (eds.) *Feminism and the Politics of Difference*, pp. 1–19, Sydney: Allen & Unwin.

Gunew, S. (2004) *Haunted Nations: The Colonial Dimensions of Multiculturalisms*, London: Routledge.

Hage, G. (1997) 'At Home in the Entrails of the West: Multiculturalism, "Ethnic Food" and Migrant Home-Building', in H. Grace, G. Hage, L. Johnson, J. Langsworth and M. Symonds (eds.) *Home/World: Space, Community and Marginality in Sydney's West*, pp. 99–153, Annandale, NSW: Pluto Press.

Hage, G. (1998) *White Nation: Fantasies of White Supremacy in a Multicultural Society*, Annandale: Pluto Press.

Hall, S. (1997a) 'The Local and the Global: Globalization and Ethnicity', in A. King (ed.) *Culture, Globalization and the World-System: Contemporary Conditions for the Representation of Identity*, pp. 19–40, Minnesota: University of Minnesota Press.

Hall, S. (1997b) 'Old and New Identities, Old and New Ethnicities', in A. King (ed.) *Culture, Globalization and the World-System: Contemporary Conditions for the Representation of Identity*, pp. 41–68, Minnesota: University of Minnesota Press.

Hall, S. and Datta, A. (2010) 'The Translocal Street: Shop Signs and Local Multi-Culture Along the Walworth Road, South London', *City, Culture and Society* 1: 69–77.

Hannerz, U. (1996) *Transnational Connections: Culture, People, Places*, London: Routledge.

Jacobs, J. (2004) 'Too Many Houses for a Home: Narrating the House in the Chinese Diaspora', in S. Cairns (ed.) *Drifting: Architecture and Migrancy*, pp. 184 – 202, London: Routledge.

King, A. (2006/2007) 'Internationalism, Imperialism, Postcolonialism, Globalisation: Frameworks for Vernacular Architecture', *Perspectives in Vernacular Architecture*, Special 25th Anniversary Issue, 13, 2: 64–75.

Laguerre, M. (2000) *The Global Ethnopolis: Chinatown, Japantown, and Manilatown in American Society*, New York: St. Martin's Press.

Lefebvre, H. (1991) *The Production of Space*, trans. D. Nicholson-Smith, Oxford: Blackwell.

Li, W. (1998) 'Anatomy of a New Ethnic Settlement: The Chinese Ethnoburb in Los Angeles', *Urban Studies* 35, 3: 479–501.

Ley, D. (1995) 'Between Europe and Asia: The Case of the Missing Sequoias', *Ecumene: A Journal of Environment/Culture/Meaning* 2, 2: 185–210.

Low, S. and Altman, I. (1992) 'Place Attachment: A Conceptual Inquiry', *Human Behavior and Environment: Advances in Theory and Research* 12: 1–12.

Lozanovska, M. (1997) 'Abjection and Architecture: The Migrant House in Multicultural Australia', in G.B. Nalbantoglou and C.T. Wong (eds.) *Postcolonial Spaces*, pp. 101–130, New York: Princeton Architectural Press.

Lozanovska, M. (2004) 'Emigration/Immigration: Maps Myths Origins', in S. Cairns (ed.) *Drifting: Architecture and Migrancy*, pp. 184–202, London: Routledge.

Massey, D. (2003) 'Some Times of Space', in S. May (ed.) *Olafur Eliasson: The Weather Project*, Exhibition catalogue, pp. 107–118, London: Tate Publishing.

Massey, D. and Jess, P. (1995) *A Place in the World?: Places, Cultures and Globalization*, London: Oxford University Press in association with Open University.

Mitchell, K. (1998) 'Fast Capital, Race, Modernity, and the Monster House', in R. Marangoly George (ed.) *Burning Down the House: Recycling Domesticity*, pp. 187–211, Boulder, CO: Westview Press.

Oliver, P. (2003) *Dwellings: The Vernacular House Across the World*, London: Phaidon.

Rapoport, A. (1969) *House, Form and Culture*, Englewood Cliffs, NJ: Prentice-Hall.

Relph, E. (1976) *Place and Placelessness*, London: Pion.

Sandercock, L. (2003) *Cosmopolis II: Mongrel Cities in the 21st Century*, London: Continuum.

Sassen, S. (2007) *Elements for a Sociology of Globalization*, New York: W.W. Norton.

Şavas, Ö. (2010) 'The Collective Turkish Home in Vienna: Aesthetic Narratives of Migration and Belonging', *Home Cultures* 7, 3: 313–340.

Sayad, A. (2004) *The Suffering of the Immigrant*, Cambridge: Polity.

Scriver, P. and Prakash, V. (eds.) (2007) *Colonial Modernities: Building, Dwelling and Architecture in British India and Ceylon*, London: Routledge.

Van der Horst, H. (2010) 'Dwellings in Transnational Lives: A Biographical Perspective on "Turkish-Dutch" Houses in Turkey', *Journal of Ethnic and Migration Studies* 36, 7: 1175–1192.

Index